STUDIES IN WELSH HISTORY

Editors

RALPH A. GRIFFITHS   KENNETH O. MORGAN
GLANMOR WILLIAMS

———————

6

'ORGANISE! ORGANISE! ORGANISE!'

A STUDY OF REFORM AGITATIONS IN
WALES, 1840–1886

The counties of Wales (to 1973)

(Reproduced from *Rebirth of a Nation: Wales 1880–1980* by K. O. Morgan, by permission of Oxford University Press.)

ORGANISE! ORGANISE! ORGANISE!'

A STUDY OF REFORM AGITATIONS
IN WALES, 1840–1886

by

RYLAND WALLACE

Published on behalf of the
History and Law Committee
of the Board of Celtic Studies

CARDIFF
UNIVERSITY OF WALES PRESS
1991

© University of Wales, 1991

British Library Cataloguing in Publication Data

Wallace, Ryland *1951–*
  Organise! Organise! Organise!: a study of reform
  agitations in Wales, 1840–1886.
  1. Wales. Social movements. History
  I. Title   II. Series
  322.4409429

  ISBN 0–7083–1078–8

Typeset by BP Integraphics, Bath
Printed in Great Britain by Bookcraft, Avon

EDITORS' FOREWORD

Since the Second World War, Welsh history has attracted considerable scholarly attention and enjoyed a vigorous popularity. Not only have the approaches, both traditional and new, to the study of history in general been successfully applied to Wales's past, but the number of scholars engaged in this enterprise has multiplied during these years. These advances have been especially marked in the University of Wales.

In order to make more widely available the conclusions of recent research, much of it of limited accessibility in post-graduate dissertations and theses, in 1977 the History and Law Committee of the Board of Celtic Studies inaugurated this new series of monographs, *Studies in Welsh History*. It was anticipated that many of the volumes would originate in research conducted in the University of Wales or under the auspices of the Board of Celtic Studies. But the series does not exclude significant contributions made by researchers in other universities and elsewhere. Its primary aim is to serve historical scholarship and to encourage the study of Welsh history. Each volume so far published has fulfilled that aim in ample measure, and it is a pleasure to welcome the most recent addition to the list.

PREFACE

This book is a substantially revised version of my Ph.D. thesis originally submitted to the University of Wales. Accordingly, I am greatly indebted to my supervisor at Aberystwyth, Emeritus Professor Ieuan Gwynedd Jones, for his stimulus, guidance and support both during my studentship and in subsequent years. The editors of the 'Studies in Welsh History Series', Emeritus Professor Glanmor Williams, Professor Ralph Griffiths and Professor Kenneth O. Morgan, also read the manuscript and I have benefited considerably from their knowledge, advice and encouragement. The shortcomings and errors which remain are, of course, my own responsibility.

During the course of my researches I have had cause to be grateful to a great many librarians and archivists in Wales and England. In particular, I wish to thank the staffs of the British Newspaper Library, the Bishopsgate Institute, the Fawcett Library and, above all, the National Library of Wales.

Versions of Chapters II and VII were published as articles in the *Welsh History Review*, in June 1986 and December 1983 respectively, and I acknowledge the permission granted by the editor to reproduce much of that material here.

Mrs Ceinwen Jones of the University of Wales Press guided the volume through the various stages of publication with expertise and thoroughness.

My wife cheerfully undertook the burden of typing the manuscript, while my two children, Laura and Mark, uncomplainingly tolerated a sometimes reclusive father. My final debt is to my mother and late father and it is to them that this book is dedicated.

CONTENTS

ABBREVIATIONS

A.A.M.	Amalgamated Association of Miners
A.B.T.C.	Anti-Bread Tax Circular
A.C.L.L.	Anti-Corn Law League
A.C.L.C.	Anti-Corn Law Circular
A.L.	Anti-League
A.R.A.	Administrative Reform Association
A.S.C.A.	British Anti-State-Church Association
BC	Henry Broadhurst Collection, British Library of Political and Economic Science
C.D.I.	Church Defence Institution
C.S.U.	National Complete Suffrage Union
F.L.S.	National Freehold Land Society
HC	George Howell Collection, Bishopsgate Institute, London
HO	Home Office Letters and Papers, Public Record Office
JBC	Josephine Butler Collection, Fawcett Library, City of London Polytechnic
L.B.	Letter Book(s)
L.N.A.	Ladies' National Association for the Repeal of the Contagious Diseases Acts
L.R.L.	Labour Representation League
M.C.A.	Magna Charta Association
N.A.	National Association for the Repeal of the Contagious Diseases Acts
N.A.L.U.	National Agricultural Labourers' Union
N.C.A.	National Charter Association
N.E.L.	National Education League
N.L.F.	National Liberal Federation
NLW	National Library of Wales, Aberystwyth
N.P.U.	National Political Union for the Obtainment of the People's Charter
N.R.A.	National Parliamentary and Financial Reform Association
N.R.U.	National Reform Union
N.S.W.S.	National Society for Women's Suffrage
N.W.Q.U.	North Wales Quarrymen's Union
PP	Parliamentary Papers
P.R.L.	Political Reform League
R.L.	Reform League
S.D.F.	Social Democratic Federation
T.U.C.	Trades Union Congress
W.E.A.	Welsh Educational Alliance
WHR	*Welsh History Review*
WSRO	West Sussex Record Office, Chichester

INTRODUCTION

'The current revolution in the fate of nations', observed one Welsh periodical in 1846, 'has forced those governing this country, and every other country, to give careful consideration to the voice of the people.'[1] Indeed, legislative reform throughout Victorian Britain was rarely a simple illustration of the enterprise and zeal of the government of the day. Public opinion and pressure often played significant roles.

Defenders of this development emphasized that agitation was essential for progress in an age when government was unrepresentative and invariably slow-moving. 'Let us not imagine', insisted the *Merthyr Star*, 'that the House of Commons is so full of justice and fair play as to carry any substantial measure of reform without a good deal of pressure from without.'[2] The *Cardiff and Merthyr Guardian* was equally assertive: 'Give peace in our time is the natural aspiration of every Cabinet, and unless they are kept up to the mark by "pressure from without", there is a greater tendency in every Ministry to go to sleep and do as little as they can.'[3] The *Carnarvon and Denbigh Herald* took the argument a step further: 'Wholesome agitation is the sole precursor of improvement in a constitution like ours: for why should a government help those who do not declare their need for help, or institute reforms which are not demanded by the public will?'[4]

Others, however, saw agitation as undesirable, even menacing. Inevitably, the Anti-Corn Law League, as the archetype and exemplar of the nineteenth-century pressure organization, was singled out for condemnation. The *Carmarthen Journal* saw it as 'a pregnant and portentous symptom of the age' and one of 'the multiform tribes of political quacks that infest British society'.[5] To Sir John Walsh, Conservative MP for Radnorshire, the League

---

[1] *Y Dysgedydd*, June 1846, p. 189. Quotations from sources in the Welsh language have been translated.
[2] *Merthyr Star*, 4 Feb. 1860.
[3] *Cardiff and Merthyr Guardian*, 20 Feb. 1858.
[4] *Carnarvon and Denbigh Herald*, 26 Nov. 1842.
[5] *Carmarthen Journal*, 30 July 1841, 26 Jan. 1844.

was one of 'those great joint-stock companies which had produced
such important effects on the policy and destiny of the country
... how many more of those associations would it take to crush
the independence of Parliament—to subvert the stability of the
Government, or to effect the dismemberment of the Empire?'[6]
Other movements were similarly denigrated. Thus, to the Anglican
periodical, *Yr Haul*, Liberationists were little different from Chartists: 'John Frost and Co. eyed the possessions of the aristocracy,
and the Disestablishment Society eyes the possessions of the
Church.'[7]

The pressure organizations studied in this book are essentially
of the crusading type, pursuing specific goals, as distinct from
those constituted in order to protect and promote particular economic interests.[8] The campaigns invariably assumed a moral character, invoking emotive language against such evils as the Corn
Laws, Nonconformist disabilities, and the corrupt and unrepresentative nature of the political system. Accordingly, the support of
ministers of religion, and especially in Wales Dissenting ministers,
was much valued and frequently cultivated, for this was thought
to bestow the sanction of righteousness on the cause.

Reform societies and movements sought to put pressure on
Parliament and government to move in specific directions. Objectives could be positive or negative; positive in the sense of placing
progressive legislation on to the statute book (as in the case of
parliamentary reform), negative in the aim of erasing laws which
imposed restrictions on particular sections of the community (as
in the case of Liberationist reform or women's rights). Pressure
groups might also be formed simply to safeguard the status quo,
often to counter the activities of other groups (the Anti-League
in response to the Anti-Corn Law League or the Church Defence
Institution in reply to the Liberation Society).

Popular reform societies operated intermittently in Britain in
the late eighteenth and early nineteenth centuries. They were,
however, considered dangerous and unnecessary; Parliament was
thought to be the only theatre of political discussion and decision-

---

[6] *Hansard's Parliamentary Debates*, Third Series, LXXXIII, col. 591, 9 Feb. 1846.
[7] *Yr Haul*, Jan. 1866, pp. 27–8.
[8] Some, like the A.C.L.L. and certain trade unions, embodied elements of both. For
a brief typology of nineteenth-century pressure groups, see P. Hollis (ed.), *Pressure from
Without in Early Victorian England* (1974), pp. vii–viii.

making. Thus, during the French Wars such societies were prohibited by repressive government legislation. With avenues of constitutional protest inadequate, economic and social pressures often
led to outbursts of violence, sporadic and localized, rather than
organized reform bodies. Alternatively, opinion was expressed
through requisitioned public meetings and petitioning, which
meant only transient vigour. In contrast, the permanence of reform
societies, mobilizing various channels of agitation, obviously represented a much more formidable type of pressure. It was not until
the 1830s that these became typical of pressurizing agencies in
Britain. National organizations took the lead, subsidiary societies
forming essential components in the strategy. Thus, in 1841, the
Nonconformist newspaper, seeking to launch a complete suffrage
movement, advocated 'the formation of some central society ...
which shall have affiliated associations over the whole surface of
the country'.[9] Or, conversely, as one Welsh radical urged in
the 1860s: 'Form yourselves into little clubs for the purpose of
more effectively carrying out the principles of reform, and join
ourselves to such leagues as are formed in London, Manchester
and elsewhere.'[10]

In mid century, inspired by the apparent triumph of the Anti-
Corn Law League in 1846, reform movements were very much
part of the political scene. Indeed, by the 1860s agitation was
considered respectable and even healthy. It was seen as an agency
of social control, allowing the expression of grievances which might
otherwise lead to violence. Gradually, in the 1870s and 1880s,
organizations associated with the Liberal Party began to act as
instruments of pressure, seeking to induce the national leadership
to endorse specific policies and, by the end of the century, party
machines dominated the political landscape, with reform societies
increasingly superfluous. Where pressure groups did operate they
were by this time highly proficient in techniques and organization,
drawing on the experience of earlier campaigns. Accordingly, they
were now charged with distorting public opinion, of being, in
a sense, anti-democratic, whereas in previous decades they had
been hailed as the democratic expressions of the public will. Even
a prominent Welsh Liberationist could observe in 1883: 'Societies

[9] *Nonconformist*, 29 Dec. 1841.
[10] *Star of Gwent*, 1 Sept. 1866.

and paid agents are multiplying terribly in our days, and not without reason the public have lost confidence in them. They think more of the salary than the work.'[11]

This book concentrates on the period from 1840 to 1886. In Wales, the late 1830s were years of unprecedented popular protest with Chartism attracting mass support. The abortive Newport Rising of November 1839 marked the climacteric and its aftermath is an appropriate starting-point for this study. One of its effects was to weaken the revolutionary thread in British radicalism and to direct Chartists towards effective legal methods of pressure, improved organization and greater unity, exemplified in the formation of the National Charter Association in 1840. The Rising itself has recently been the subject of two scholarly studies.[12] The purpose of this work is to examine the character and operation of certain pressure groups and popular reform movements in Wales over most of the following half-century, a critical period in Welsh political and social history. The terminal date of 1886 also seems opportune, coming in British politics shortly after important measures of parliamentary reform and witnessing the dramatic Liberal Party split over Irish Home Rule. Moreover, Welsh politics changed significantly after 1886 with the emergence of a powerful Welsh Parliamentary Liberal Party and the creation of the North Wales Liberal Federation in December 1886 and a similar body in south Wales the following month, with most local Liberal associations affiliating to them. This new organizational structure served to unite the rather dispersed elements of Welsh radicalism and to a large degree superseded existing pressure groups, above all marking the end of the ascendancy of the Liberation Society in Wales.

Although a diversity of reform movements appears and often reappears in the following pages, this is of necessity a fundamentally political story. While groups might call themselves non-political, they were all seeking objectives that could only be brought about by parliamentary legislation and thus unavoidably became involved in politics. Two areas of reforming activity dominate the book, political Dissent and parliamentary reform. The main pressure group of the former was the Liberation Society though

---

[11] *Y Cronicl*, Jan. 1884, pp. 35–6.
[12] David J. V. Jones, *The Last Rising* (Oxford, 1985); Ivor Wilks, *South Wales and the Rising of 1839* (1984).

others, like the National Education League, advanced causes specifically related to Nonconformist interests. A multiplicity of organizations promoted varying schemes of parliamentary reform during
the nineteenth century. Free trade, and especially the anti-Corn
Law movement, was another important early Victorian campaign.
It also constituted part of the recurrent theme of attack on the
power of the landed class. As the century progressed trade unionism took firmer root in Wales and became more politically involved, and there were also increased efforts for the direct representation of labour in Parliament and for women's rights. I have
tried to examine these themes in some depth. Throughout this
period other agitations abounded, extolling the merits of multi-
farious causes—temperance, anti-slavery, peace, public health,
republicanism, land and administrative reform, and more—while
local concerns represented a further complication. Inevitably,
some of the reform movements can only be touched upon here.

I have divided the period from 1840 to 1886 into three chronolo-
gical sections: 1840–50, 1850–68, 1868–86. Within each period
the aim is to distinguish and analyse the basic issues and to outline
the context in which the various reform societies operated. This
procedure creates difficulties, the main danger being that the pressure groups appear to be distinct and somewhat disparate movements. This was far from the reality, for there was considerable
overlap in personnel, ideology and organization, and in agitational
technique and strategy. I have tried to illuminate these links and
to convey the interrelationship of grievances, concerns, ideas and
emotions which were surely present in the minds of individuals
and communities. The book comprises a collection of studies on
related topics; such is the nature of the subject matter that some
repetition of content and theme is inescapable.

The title of the book requires some explanation. The 1832
Reform Act evoked the slogans 'Register! Register! Register!' and,
reflecting a widespread disillusionment and the desire for further
reform, 'Agitate! Agitate! Agitate!'[13] Increasingly though,

---

[13] 'Cynhyrfer! Cynhyrfer! Cynhyrfer!' ('Agitate! Agitate! Agitate!') was the plea adopted
in the late 1830s by Revd David Rees of Llanelli, editor of the Independent periodical,
Y Diwygiwr (see Apr. 1838, p. 122; Sept. 1843, p. 288). Under his direction this journal
urged agitation in support of radical reform, most especially the redress of Nonconformist
grievances and the advance of democratic principles. For David Rees, see Iorwerth Jones,
David Rees, Y Cynhyrfwr (Swansea, 1971).

reformers placed the emphasis on the formation of local committees and societies to direct opinion and actively to support national agitations, and accordingly the cry was 'Organise! Organise! Organise!'[14] The section headings broadly suggest society's changing perception of pressure groups over the successive subperiods.

In the early decades of the nineteenth century only a minority of Welsh people were continuously and deeply concerned about politics. During the period upon which this book concentrates Wales experienced an unprecedented growth in political consciousness. Political education was in part afforded through the functioning of reform movements. This study seeks to assess this contribution and to address certain other questions. Why were movements supported, or opposed? Who provided the leadership, membership and adherence? What were the links between local organizations and central executives in England? Fundamentally, therefore, the objective is to derive information on the political life of Victorian Wales primarily through exploring one particular avenue.

---

[14] See, for examples, *Western Vindicator*, 23 Nov. 1839; *English Chartist Circular*, 1841, 1, Nos. 15, 16; *Northern Star*, 10 Aug. 1850; *London News*, 10 July 1858.

Part 1
1840–1850
'Disturbers of the Poor Man's Peace'

I

WELSH SOCIETY AND POLITICS IN THE FORTIES

The half-century or so before 1840 was a seminal period in the development of modern Wales. The dynamic forces of demographic change, industrialization and religious Nonconformity combined to transform Welsh society, introduce new complexities and divisions and, critically for the purposes of this study, fashion political consciousness.

According to the census returns of 1841 the thirteen counties of Wales contained 1,045,073 people, a dramatic increase of 457,828 or 78 per cent on the 1801 figure. Every county experienced an increase in each decennial census until 1841. Rapid population growth continued during the forties, almost 120,000 being added in the decade up to 1851. Such expansion exerted tremendous pressure on the rural economy and from the 1840s there was large-scale migration to the industrial areas of Wales and increasing depopulation in rural counties. The mid-century demographic statistics also graphically portray the impact of rapid industrialization on parts of north and south Wales, resulting in the emergence of two very contrasting cultures. Most of the country, especially the northern and central regions, remained rural though harbouring scattered enclaves of industry, principally woollen mills in Montgomeryshire, copper-mines in Anglesey and lead-mines in Cardiganshire. The most striking evidence of industrialization in Wales in the 1840s was the string of iron communities at the heads of the valleys in east Glamorgan and west Monmouthshire, from Hirwaun to Blaenafon with Merthyr Tydfil as the focal point: this area produced more than one-third of total British iron manufacture in 1839. Elsewhere in the south, the Swansea-Llanelli-Neath region dominated British copper-smelting; indeed, Swansea was a major metallurgical centre with diversified interests extending well beyond copper. As yet, coal was mined primarily to service the iron and copper-works and the industry was underdeveloped. Industry was not confined to the south Wales coalfield. Along the English border in Flintshire and Denbighshire there were important ironworks and collieries, while in the north-west the slate industry grew extensively in Caernarfonshire and Merioneth, particularly around Bethesda and Llanberis. Accordingly, some Welsh communities experienced spectacular rises in population in the first half of the nineteenth century and Wales became a country with large towns. By far the largest was Merthyr, with 46,378 inhabitants in 1851, the second, Swansea, at 21,253, not amounting to even half Merthyr's size.[1]

Linked to industrialization and urbanization was improvement in the markedly deficient communications of Wales. Most significantly, the 1840s brought large-scale railway construction and by mid century a dozen or so railways had been completed, penetrating the inland valleys and providing links with England; slowly, the railway network was extended into the rural regions. The coming of the railway was of central importance in the economic, social and political life of Wales. It gave a great stimulus to industry, opened up new markets for farmers and facilitated migration to the industrial areas. It also helped erode localism and insularity. 'This country will soon be one neighbourhood', wrote a commentator in the mid forties.[2] Another contemporary observed:

> Railways have brought, within a few hours' distance of London, places which ... were a week or fortnight's journey away. For every stranger who traversed our hills and dales ... a hundred are now wandering amongst them. Liverpool, Manchester, Bristol, and other places, are now the market

[1] For the growth of industry in Wales, see C. Baber and L. J. Williams (eds.), *Modern South Wales: Essays in Economic History* (Cardiff, 1986); A. H. Dodd, *The Industrial Revolution in North Wales* (Cardiff, 2nd. edn., 1951); E. W. Evans, *The Miners of South Wales* (Cardiff, 1961); A. H. John, *The Industrial Development of South Wales, 1750–1850* (Cardiff, 1950); A. H. John and Glanmor Williams, *Industrial Glamorgan from 1700 to 1900* (Cardiff, 1980); J. Lindsay, *A History of the North Wales Slate Industry* (Newton Abbot, 1984); J. Morris and L. Williams, *The South Wales Coal Industry 1841–75* (Cardiff, 1958).
[2] Thomas Evans, *The Background to Modern Welsh Politics, 1789–1846* (Cardiff, 1936), p. 233, citing *Y Diwygiwr*, June 1846.

towns of districts, whose inhabitants ... were esteemed oracles if they had performed a pilgrimage to either of them once in the course of their lives.[3]

Among the 'strangers' increasingly appearing in Wales from the 1830s and 1840s were lecturers and agents representing reform movements based in England, while the spread of communications also fostered the rapid dissemination of literature and ideas.[4] Despite the increasing complexities introduced by the advance of industrialization, the growth of communications and the impact of demographic change, the social structure of Wales in the forties remained fundamentally as it had been for many generations. Pre-eminent, in both rural and industrial regions, were the owners of often vast landed estates, the aristocrats and the 'lesser gentry', whose economic power made their ascendancy almost unchallengeable. These families also controlled the parliamentary representation, even after the passage of the Reform Act of 1832, and held complete authority in the administration of justice and local government until the advent of local democracy in the 1880s. Apart from those estates containing mineral deposits, landowners derived most of their income from the rents paid by tenant farmers, for throughout the nineteenth century only a small proportion of the cultivated land in Wales, as little as ten per cent, was actually owned by the farmers who worked it.[5] With the economic developments of the late eighteenth and nineteenth centuries some landed families turned to industry and commerce to reinforce their wealth and social position. At the same time, there emerged in the industrial regions a new entrepreneurial class, who dominated their communities as much as the gentry did in the rural areas.

Rural society was founded on degree and place with an accepted chain of subservience and, despite increasing tensions and resentments, it remained in the forties essentially deferential—socially, economically and politically. Even in the rural towns the grip

---

[3] A. J. Johnes, *The Principality: or The Wants of Wales Considered* (1851), p. 25.
[4] Improved communications linked Wales with the markets of industrial England. Within Wales, travel northwards or southwards remained laborious. For instance, the Chartist lecturer R. G. Gammage, visiting Wales in 1852, had to walk the twenty-six miles from Builth Wells to Llanidloes, there being no regular conveyance. *People's Paper*, 24 July 1852.
[5] For rural society, see D. W. Howell, *Land and People in Nineteenth-Century Wales* (1978); D. Jenkins, *The Agricultural Community in South-West Wales at the Turn of the Twentieth Century* (Cardiff, 1971); I. G. Jones, *Explorations and Explanations: Essays in the Social History of Victorian Wales* (Llandysul, 1981), Chs. 3, 4; D. Williams, *The Rebecca Riots: A Study in Agrarian Discontent* (Cardiff, 1955).

of the local landed families held firm. The new industrial communities, on the other hand, were structured very differently from both the farming areas and the rural towns. They were stratified above all by class, though the concept was only coming into usage at this time. Though it was slow to develop there was, by the 1830s and 1840s, beneath the enormously influential ironmasters, a recognizable middle class comprising professional, industrial and commercial elements, forming an increasingly significant group in certain parts of Wales. Merging into the lower middle class and distinct from the mass of the workers were the skilled craftsmen and tradesmen. Generalizations on class divisions are hazardous but certainly class awareness, interests and prejudices played a role in a number of nineteenth-century reform agitations. In industrial areas people were more class-conscious, more resentful of the injustices of the social system and readier to turn to political activity to redress their grievances. At the same time, of course, these areas were far more conducive to political organization, discussion and involvement.

Mid-nineteenth century Welsh society exhibited a glaring and widening gulf between the privileged, mainly English-speaking, Anglicized gentry and the impoverished Welsh-speaking mass of the population. With the former retaining allegiance to the Church of England and the latter flocking to the Nonconformist chapels, religion represented a further and crucial facet to the social division. 'For the last fifty years', proudly asserted one Welshman in 1846, 'we have been practical and efficient church extensionists. From the highest peak in our land, to our lowest valleys, we have studded the country with chapels and schoolrooms.'[6] The Census of Religious Worship of 1851 confirmed such claims, recording that over eighty per cent of those attending religious institutions in Wales on 30 March of that year went to Nonconformist chapels.[7] Membership statistics and adherence estimates are unreliable and caused much dispute; but clearly the Calvinistic Methodists had greatest strength, followed by the Independents (or Congregationalists, as they were often termed), the Baptists and the Wesleyan Methodists, in that order.

[6] *Nonconformist*, 8 Apr. 1846.
[7] *Census of Great Britain, 1851: Religious Worship, England and Wales. Report and Tables* (1853), pp. 122–5.

The Religious Census revealed other important statistics. First, in terms of accommodation and the use made of it, Wales was far more religious than England. In Wales 75.5 per cent of the population could be seated in places of religious worship as compared with 51.4 per cent in England. The figures for attendants are less accurate, but it has been calculated by one historian that the proportion of the population of the two countries together which attended on Census Sunday was 24 per cent, while for Wales alone it was 34 per cent.[8] At the same time, it must not be overlooked that a significant majority of the people of Wales, almost two-thirds, did not attend religious service on that particular Sunday. But the impact of Nonconformity on Welsh life is unmistakable. Because they were religious centres the chapels were the focuses for much else too and the Sunday schools, chapel societies, temperance organizations, choirs and music, and other social activities became embedded in Welsh society, rural and industrial. Passionate preaching was fundamental to Nonconformity but the influence of ministers extended far beyond the pulpit. They became active in social and political life and were accepted popular leaders in the community. Religion was a highly pervasive force in Victorian society, initiating controversies and influencing attitudes. Nonconformists were frequently at the forefront of movements seeking to affect public opinion and pressure the legislature. Some reform organizations, most obviously the Liberation Society and the National Education League, promoted specifically Nonconformist causes, while others, like the Anti-Corn Law League, the Complete Suffrage Union and the United Kingdom Alliance, in adopting a moral posture against the evils of the Corn Laws, the political system and alcohol respectively, had a clear appeal to that section of society. These were, of course, particularly relevant factors in Wales with its numerical preponderance of Nonconformists. Increasingly, too, the Nonconformist press addressed itself to social and political issues.

Indeed, at a time when the serious inadequacies of schooling and the prevalence of illiteracy were starkly evident, the press represented a potent means of informal education. A whole crop of Welsh-language periodicals appeared in the 1830s and 1840s. Religious themes predominated and, in fact, many were closely

[8] See I. G. Jones, op. cit., pp. 216–35.

connected with particular denominations and had a limited audience. Others, however, like *Y Diwygiwr* (described by *The Times* as 'a violent radical Welsh monthly magazine'[9]), *Yr Amserau* and *Y Cronicl*, discussed social and political affairs and gained a wide and enthusiastic readership. The growth of the periodical press was central to the evolution of Nonconformist radicalism. At the same time, the number of English-language newspapers printed in Wales increased, making a dozen by 1850, while journals published in England, often radical in nature, also circulated. Clearly, the press was an increasingly powerful opinion-forming force in Wales, despite the formidable problems of distribution, stamp and paper duties, and widespread illiteracy. To what extent Wales was literate in mid century is very difficult to ascertain. The circulation figures of journals are a doubtful gauge at a time when Welsh society remained largely based on oral culture. The influence on the community of a small number of literate men, reading to illiterate groups, could be far-reaching. Similarly, in such a culture, listening to a lecture or a sermon was often a stimulating experience. The diffusion of knowledge and ideas in these ways is incalculable.

Much of Wales remained cut off from English publications and other influences because of language. Welsh was the almost universal medium of communication in most parts of the country in the forties and, despite powerful and varied forces operating against it, continued in widespread use throughout the century (the census of 1891 recorded that 54.4 per cent of the people of Wales spoke Welsh[10]). This presented a peculiar problem for English-based reform movements in their overtures to the Principality and restricted their ability to disseminate information. 'Our language has proved an insuperable barrier against any systematic and regular communication with our brethren in England', bemoaned one Nonconformist radical in the 1840s.[11] To be thoroughly effective, literature had to be translated into Welsh. So, too, with public speakers. 'Some English Chartists came', reported

[9] *The Times*, 17 Aug. 1843, cited in E. T. Davies, *Religion and Society in the Nineteenth Century* (Llandybïe, 1981), pp. 44–5.

[10] *Census of England and Wales, 1891*.

[11] *Nonconformist*, 14 Jan. 1846. '… Considerable numbers refuse to recognise the English language, and cling to their native tongue with the strongest devotion …', commented R. G. Gammage in the 1850s. R. G. Gammage, *History of the Chartist Movement* (1854), pp. 68–9.

Merthyr's Morgan Williams to the 1842 Chartist Convention, 'but they [the local people] had no confidence in them because they were English.' He went on: 'The great, and the only want, throughout the districts which I represent is that of lecturers who understand the two languages; it was not so material that they should be eloquent men, as that they should be able to lay down the principles in language all could understand.'[12] As well as greatly widening a movement's audience in Wales such efforts helped to allay feelings of suspicion, though an undercurrent of mistrust frequently persisted.

Reform agitations in the 1840s and in subsequent decades were in part prompted, sustained and determined by the character of Welsh society and the prevailing economic climate. At the same time, traditions of grievance, tension and protest, in some areas reaching back into the previous century, were an inescapable element in these agitations. Violence was a familiar reaction. Food and enclosure riots were common in the eighteenth and early nineteenth centuries, while violence was also a typical weapon in industrial and political disputes.[13] But alongside such direct action constitutional forms of agitation developed.

The American War of Independence marks the genesis of political radicalism in Wales but of greater significance in diffusing democratic principles was the French Revolution. Driven underground during much of the French Wars, political agitation came to life again after 1815. Radical literature, including translated extracts from William Cobbett's *Political Register* and Henry Hunt's speeches, circulated in Wales and parliamentary reform was the subject of a number of public meetings and petitions. Generating far more concern in the late 1820s were repeal of the Test and Corporation Acts and Catholic emancipation. Dissenting congregations throughout Wales petitioned heavily on these issues. Participation in the parliamentary reform movement of 1831-2 followed, though some Nonconformist leaders continued to exert a formidable influence against involvement in political affairs.

In some parts of Wales there had been evidence of political consciousness among working people long before the reform crisis

---

[12] *Northern Star*, 14 Jan. 1846.
[13] For violent protest at this time, see D. J. V. Jones, *Before Rebecca: Popular Protests in Wales, 1793-1835* (1973).

of 1831–2. For most people of this class, however, interest and involvement in politics began in this decade and certain industrial communities experienced political activity for the first time, the stimulus and direction commonly being provided by locally organized reform societies. The model was often Thomas Attwood's Birmingham Political Union, itself much influenced by Daniel O'Connell's successful Catholic Association of the 1820s. Attwood emphasized class co-operation, middle- and working-class elements uniting in action. In some places this occurred; elsewhere, working men exhibited independence, radicalism and militancy. Founded to lead this working-class movement was the National Union of the Working Classes, launched in London by two future Chartist leaders, William Lovett and Henry Hetherington, which campaigned for universal male suffrage, the secret ballot and annual parliaments. Offshoots of both the Birmingham and London organizations were established in the industrial regions of south and central Wales.[14]

Independent political action by working people brought mob violence and rioting in parts of Wales in 1831–2. Most sensationally, in June 1831, thousands of workers, galvanized by political tension and acute economic depression, broke into insurrection in Merthyr Tydfil.[15] But increasingly thereafter the trend was towards organization and education. In Merthyr itself, the year 1831 saw the formation of political unions and trade union lodges—branches of the National Association for the Protection of Labour—while 1834 saw the birth of Wales's first bilingual working-class newspaper, *Y Gweithiwr / The Workman,* under the editorship of Morgan Williams. The one surviving issue includes a fierce attack on 'a bloated clergy ... and a stupid and imbecile aristocracy' and, referring specifically to the evils

[14] For radicalism in the late eighteenth and early nineteenth centuries, see Gwyn A. Williams, *Artisans and Sans-Culottes: Popular Movements in France and Britain during the French Revolution* (1968); idem, 'The making of radical Merthyr, 1800–36', *Welsh History Review,* 1, No. 2 (Dec. 1961); idem, 'Locating a Welsh working class: the frontier years', in D. Smith (ed.), *A People and a Proletariat: Essays in the History of Wales, 1780–1980* (1980); idem, 'South Wales Radicalism: the first phase', in S. Williams (ed.), *Glamorgan Historian,* 2 (1965); idem, *When Was Wales?* (1985), pp. 167–72; D. A. Wager, 'Welsh politics and parliamentary reform, 1780–1832', *Welsh History Review,* 7, No. 4 (Dec. 1975); I. G. Jones, 'Wales and parliamentary reform', in A. J. Roderick (ed.), *Wales Through the Ages, Vol. 2* (Llandybïe, 1960); D. J. V. Jones, *Before Rebecca;* I. W. R. David, 'Political and electioneering activity in south-east Wales, 1820–51' (University of Wales MA thesis, 1959).

[15] See Gwyn A. Williams, *The Merthyr Rising* (1978); D. J. V. Jones, *Before Rebecca,* Ch.6.

of the Corn Laws, prophetically warned: 'The wind is now asleep on the waters, but how long we cannot say ... The crisis is coming.'[16] Within a few years working-class resentment over the 1832 Reform Act, allied with a mixture of social and economic grievances, provided a rich field for the growth of Chartism.[17] In Wales the movement first took root in Carmarthen, where a branch of the London Working Men's Association was established by the radical solicitor, Hugh Williams, early in 1837. Similar societies followed, particularly in the woollen towns of Montgomeryshire and in the valleys of Monmouthshire and Glamorgan. But the growth was slow until a startling efflorescence in 1839. 'You have no alternative but to unite', declared the Pontypool Working Men's Association early in that year, 'form associations, agitate the Principality throughout. Let not a single parish, hamlet, city, town or village be without its association.'[18] And indeed, at that very time, stimulated by the efforts of English emissaries like Henry Vincent or local Welsh ones like John Frost and William Edwards in Monmouthshire, large numbers of ironworkers and colliers were enlisting, the number of radical societies was multiplying and Chartism in south Wales became a mass movement, whereas the early associations had been dominated by tradesmen, artisans and the lower middle class. In Monmouthshire alone, it was claimed that between November 1838 and January 1839 twenty Chartist branches were founded.[19] By November 1839 the Chartist leader, Zephaniah Williams, estimated that 'Glamorgan and Monmouth Shires contained 50 associations, and in each from 100 to 1,300 Members ...', a total of perhaps 25,000.[20] In south Wales, the year 1839 unmistakably

[16] *Y Gweithiwr / The Workman* (no. 4), 1 May 1834 (copy in Public Record Office, H.O. 52/25, photocopy at NLW).

[17] For Chartism in Wales, see D. Williams, *John Frost: A Study in Chartism* (Cardiff, 1939); idem, 'Chartism in Wales', in A. Briggs (ed.), *Chartist Studies* (1959); D. J. V. Jones, 'Chartism in Welsh communities', *Welsh History Review*, 6, No. 3 (June 1973); idem, 'Chartism at Merthyr: a commentary on the meetings of 1842', *Bulletin of the Board of Celtic Studies*, XXIV, Part II (1971); idem, *The Last Rising*; A. V. John, 'The Chartist endurance: industrial south Wales, 1840–68', *Morgannwg*, XV (1971); O. R. Ashton, 'Chartism in mid-Wales', *The Montgomeryshire Collections*, 62, Part I (1971); I. Wilks, op. cit.

[18] *Cardiff and Merthyr Guardian*, 9 Feb. 1839.

[19] *Silurian*, 23 Feb. 1839.

[20] NLW Tredegar Park Muniments, 40/2, Zephaniah Williams to A. McKechnie, 25 May 1840; see D. J. V. Jones, *The Last Rising*, pp. 64–5.

saw mounting tension, with conflict between employers and work-men, the arrest of radical leaders, and arming. The climax was, of course, the disastrous Newport Rising in November.

Nonconformists were as disappointed as working-class radicals with the 1832 Reform Act. The narrow franchise and the continu-ing control of Parliament by Anglican landowners offered little prospect of the redress of Nonconformist grievances. Thus, this section of the community had a compelling interest in the advance of democracy. '. . . We are Dissenters in principle', a Pontypool minister emphasized to his south Wales colleagues, 'and we have given up all hope of redress of grievances except we adopt the People's Charter which involves a redress of all the grievances of the nation.'[21] Undeniably, Welsh Nonconformity had close links with Chartism, though Unitarians were the only religious body in Wales to come out publicly in support of the movement. The Independent *Diwygiwr* voiced general approval, insisting that the Charter was consistent with Christianity and urging the forma-tion of working men's associations. At the same time it counselled middle-class alliance and denounced violent tactics.[22] Indeed, men like the Revd David Rees of Llanelli, editor of *Y Diwygiwr*, and other publicists such as Revd Samuel Roberts ('S.R.') of Llanbryn-mair were stirring Nonconformists into political action on a number of fronts in these years.

Until the 1840s the 'older Dissenters', the Baptists and Independ-ents, took the lead in political agitation, while the Methodists, under the powerful influence of John Elias, eschewed such activity, confining themselves to spiritual affairs. Thus, when political unions were formed in Merthyr in 1831, the Calvinistic Methodists 'strenuously exerted themselves to induce their members to aban-don those societies'.[23] However, during the thirties and forties, the affinity between Methodism and Anglicanism was eroded—in origin, Methodism had been a revitalizing movement within the Anglican Church and did not break with it until 1811—and it gradually moved into line with the other Nonconformist bodies, certainly on political questions bearing on their religious worship, and later even allying against the political system itself. The impact of the Oxford or Tractarian Movement within the Anglican

---

[21] *Silurian*, 11 May 1839.
[22] *Y Diwygiwr*, Dec. 1839, p. 372; Feb. 1839, pp. 58–60.
[23] *Hansard*, X, col. 1128, 5 Mar. 1832 (Col. Thomas Wood, MP for Breconshire).

Church from the mid 1830s, with its emphasis on ritualism which smacked of Catholicism, was one important factor in this development for it alarmed Methodists as much as the 'older Dissenters'. Another was participation in the reform movements and controversies of early Victorian Britain.

The celebrated Welsh Nonconformist radical, Revd Henry Richard, described Wales in the first decades of the nineteenth century as in a 'season of political apathy'.[24] By 1840 a very different political era was at hand, the product of immense change in Welsh society. The forties were a decisive decade in the widening of popular politics. Reform and protest movements were conspicuous and agitational techniques were learned. Both middle- and working-class activists pressed for further parliamentary reform while others, expecting much of the reformed Parliament, launched further movements, the most sophisticated and efficient of which was the Anti-Corn Law League. Of particular significance in Wales was the role played by the various campaigns, in alliance with a flowering radical periodical press, in the politicization of Nonconformity. Moreover, from 1844 there existed a highly political and increasingly powerful pressure group, the British Anti-State-Church Association or, as it became popularly known, the Liberation Society, specifically representing Nonconformist interests.

[24] H. Richard, *Letters on the Social and Political Condition of Wales* (1867), p. 79.

II
REPEAL OF THE CORN LAWS

The Corn Law of 1815 stipulated, most significantly, that no foreign wheat was to be imported until the home-grown price had reached eighty shillings per quarter; similar regulations affected barley and oats. At the end of the Napoleonic Wars, Parliament, dominated by the landed interest, sought to protect British farmers from cheap foreign corn. The motive was not solely self-interest, for the desirability of being independent of foreign food imports in time of war was a major factor in the legislators' minds. Subsequent measures in 1822, 1828 and 1842 introduced and modified a sliding scale of import duties according to the domestic price. The whole body of protective legislation for agriculture was repealed in 1846.

From the time of enactment there were protests demanding repeal, but before 1839 this agitation never became a national issue. In these years, repeal movements in Wales, as elsewhere, were indigenous, localized and spasmodic affairs, taking the form of public meetings, petitions and press editorials; they were countered by similar protectionist activities.[1] The question finally emerged nationally in the severe distress caused by a series of poor harvests from 1838 and, more significantly, with the availability of effective leadership in the shape of the Anti-Corn Law League (A.C.L.L.), whereby discontent could be co-ordinated and channelled into a formidable agitation. In September 1838 an Anti-Corn Law Association was formed in Manchester; within six months, it had developed into the National Anti-Corn Law League. Dominated by Lancashire middle-class reformers, its objective was 'total and immediate repeal' of the corn duties.[2]

[1] T. H. Williams, 'Wales and the Corn Laws, 1815–46' (University of Wales MA thesis, 1952), Part I, pp. 24–6, 52, 58; R. I. Parry, 'Yr Annibynwyr Cymraeg a Threth yr Ŷd, 1828–45', *Y Cofiadur*, 19 (Mar. 1949), pp. 20–32; T. Evans, *Background to Modern Welsh Politics*, pp. 163–6.

[2] For the history of the anti-Corn Law movement, see N. McCord, *The Anti-Corn Law League, 1838–46* (1958); A. Prentice, *History of the Anti-Corn Law League, 1838–46* (2 vols., Manchester, 1853); D. G. Barnes, *History of the English Corn Laws, 1660–1846* (1930); N. Longmate, *The Breadstealers* (1984). The main material relating to Wales has been assembled by I. G. Jones in 'The anti-Corn Law letters of Walter Griffith', *Bulletin of the Board of Celtic Studies*, XXVIII, Part I (1978), pp. 95–128.

The League's influence was extensive, penetrating all areas of the country. For seven years, between 1839 and 1846, it kept the question of the Corn Laws before both the public and Parliament and played an important supporting role in the decisive parliamentary struggle which ultimately secured repeal. Significantly, the League also exerted a wider influence, and this was certainly so in Wales, where it provided political education and political experience, teaching techniques of propaganda, organization and agitation. In the mid nineteenth century it was, as John Jenkins, its agent in south Wales, observed, 'the greatest and most perfect reform organisation in history',[3] the most advanced political pressure group the country had yet seen.

The inception and early operations of the League were greeted in Wales with apparent indifference. Public attention focused overwhelmingly on the Chartist movement, which was at its height in 1839, while the Welsh press gave little coverage to free trade. No Welsh representative attended any of the League's meetings in the first year of its existence as a national movement, and of the mass of repeal petitions sent to Parliament in the early part of 1840 only a handful emanated from Wales.[4] Anti-Corn Law activity in Wales was, therefore, minimal before the appointment of Walter Griffith as League lecturer in April 1840. On commencing work, he was most forcibly struck by public ignorance on the question. In his own words, he was 'breaking up the Fallow ground'.[5] Towards the end of his first tour of the Principality, Griffith concluded: 'In Wales the agitation against the corn laws is quite a new thing...'[6]

A native of Caernarfonshire, Griffith moved to Manchester in the late 1830s where he came in contact with the nascent A.C.L.L. The ability to lecture in Welsh as well as English, allied to great industry and dedication, made his contribution to the agitation in Wales an immense one. His driving force was a confirmed and unflagging belief in the cause. The League Council

[3] John Jenkins, *The Ballot and Ministerial Reform: What Ought to be Done? A Letter to the Hon. F. Henry F. Berkeley, MP for Bristol...* (1852), p. 10.
[4] See I. G. Jones, 'The anti-Corn Law letters of Walter Griffith', pp. 96–8.
[5] A.C.L.L. Letter Book (L.B.), 4, No. 611, Walter Griffith to John Ballantyne (Secretary of the League), 30 May 1840.
[6] *Anti-Corn Law Circular (A.C.L.C.)*, 14 Jan. 1841. The *A.C.L.C.* was founded in April 1839 as the organ of the League. In April 1841 its title became the *Anti-Bread Tax Circular (A.B.T.C.)* and finally, in September 1843, *The League*. For Walter Griffith, see I. G. Jones, 'The anti-Corn Law letters of Walter Griffith', pp. 95–100, and references therein.

had originally advertised for 'the services of those who are strongly convinced of the immoral and irreligious character of the corn law, and who could conscientiously advocate its total and immediate repeal as a Christian duty'.[7] He unquestionably met these requirements. Convinced that God was on his side, Griffith saw himself as the evangelist of a righteous crusade. Writing in June 1840 he declared: 'I am full of spirit in the cause; and sometimes I feel like the Apostle Paul and I could say, I count not my life valuable to me in this great cause.'[8]

Griffith delivered his first lecture at Rhosllannerchrugog in May 1840. The following month was spent canvassing the counties of Flint and Denbigh. Once an area had been thoroughly covered—tracts liberally distributed, a nucleus of supporters cultivated and, where possible, lectures and meetings held—the agent would remove to another district. In this way, Griffith had traversed the whole of Wales by February 1841. In the latter half of 1842, he conducted a second tour. The intervening period was also an active one. He delivered many lectures in north Wales, was a leading figure behind an Anti-Corn Law Ministerial Conference held at Caernarfon in December 1841, and a Welsh-language periodical, *Cylchgrawn Rhyddid*, under his directorship, was established in the same town. During 1843 and 1844 Griffith's activities, now restricted through illness, were confined to the northern parts of the Principality. The lecturer's main exertions corresponded to the first of two distinct phases, roughly separated at the end of 1842, of the A.C.L.L.'s operations in the country as a whole and certainly in Wales. Early efforts concentrated upon propaganda, aimed specifically at winning over public opinion to repeal. The objective in later years was to convert this sentiment into practical terms, which meant intervention in parliamentary constituencies and elections.

The experiences of Walter Griffith illustrate the reception of the A.C.L.L. in Wales. In his immediate task of promulgating the cause he faced powerful opposition from several quarters. The Established Church was often a source of hostility, accusing Nonconformist ministers of turning chapels into political meeting-houses when they allowed Griffith their use. In reply, Leaguers

---

[7] *A.C.L.C.*, 15 July 1841.
[8] A.C.L.L., L.B., 5, 643, Walter Griffith to Ballantyne, 13 June 1840.

taunted Church leaders with denying cheap bread to the pea-
santry. At Ruabon, the local parson published a pamphlet condemning the activities of the A.C.L.L.[9] Others denounced the
movement from the pulpit and refused the use of churches for
meetings. The most widespread and influential opposition to
Griffith came from local landowners. Local corporations, frequently under their control, refused the use of town halls, and
innkeepers would not let rooms for fear of arousing landowner
hostility.[10] Acquiring meeting-places became one of Griffith's
major problems. In the summer months, he could speak in the
market square, on the sea-shore, and even address men when
leaving the local works, but in winter this was often impractical.
Sometimes, as at Tywyn, landlords were accused of hiring trouble-
makers to disturb meetings.[11] A more regular complaint by Griffith, however, was the power exercised against expression of sympathy with the League. In some areas, he was certain that the
people wished actively to support the movement but were afraid
of reprisals from the local 'nobility'.[12] In certain localities,
Griffith faced most serious opposition from the other great agitation of the day, Chartism. His meetings were sometimes interrupted or even 'captured' by Chartists, as were those of other
League emissaries. Relations between the two movements varied
from locality to locality and, indeed, within localities. Nevertheless,
a preponderance of Chartists, certainly in the early 1840s, saw
the free trade agitation as a threat to their own chances of success;
thus opposition was directed more towards the League itself than
towards its doctrines.[13]

In spite of this considerable and varied opposition, there were
circumstances that favoured an anti-Corn Law agitation in Wales.

[9] *A.C.L.C.*, 15 July 1841.
[10] A.C.L.L., L.B., 5, 666, Walter Griffith to George Wilson (Chairman of the League),
25 June 1840; 671, same to Ballantyne, 1 July 1840; 672, same to Wilson, 2 July 1840;
683, same to same, 10 July 1840; 722, same to Ballantyne, 6 Sept. 1840; *Silurian*, 9 Oct.
1841; *A.C.L.C.*, 25 Sept. 1841; *Carnarvon and Denbigh Herald*, 19 Feb. 1842. Griffith Evans,
the Merioneth gentleman-farmer (described by his nephew as 'First lecturer on the Corn
Laws and Christian Unity in N. Wales') also spoke of the hostility of local aristocrats,
who branded him 'a spouting demagogue' and used their influence in the denial of town
halls, public houses, chapels, and churches. Bangor MS 235, University College of North
Wales, Bangor; *Carnarvon and Denbigh Herald*, 19 Feb. 1842; R. I. Parry, op. cit., p. 61.
[11] *A.C.L.C.*, 10 Sept 1840.
[12] Ibid., 25 Feb. 1841; *A.B.T.C.*, 18 July 1843; A.C.L.L., L.B., 4, 606, Walter Griffith
to Ballantyne, 28 May 1840; 5, 650, same to Wilson, 16 June 1840; 659, same to same,
20 June 1840; 706, same to same, 23 July 1840.
[13] For a further discussion of this theme, see below pp. 47–50.

In the first place, scattered throughout the country there were numerous middle-class liberals who were ready contacts for local activity. Of more significance was the aid of Dissenting ministers and the power they were able to exert over their congregations. It was this support which gave the A.C.L.L. real influence in Wales. From the first, the League had sought to infuse a moral, religious spirit into the movement, depicting the Corn Laws as inhumane, anti-Scriptural and oppressive, as, for example, did a resolution adopted at a meeting of Caernarfonshire Congregational leaders in 1841:

> ... the present corn laws are impolitic in principle, unjust in operation, and cruel in effect, they are condemned throughout the sacred volume; they are opposed to the benignity of the Creator, and they are at variance with the very spirit of Christianity.[14]

The Welsh response to the League's exhortations in this direction was manifest in chapels freely granted for Walter Griffith's lectures, pulpit announcements on their occurrence and, on occasion, in sermons and prayer in support of the cause. In other instances, ministers distributed League literature and appeared on public platforms with the agent. Anti-Corn Law petitions frequently came from chapel congregations in Wales. Official Nonconformist bodies, like the Monmouthshire Baptists and the Caernarfonshire and Merioneth Independents, gave their seal of approval to the A.C.L.L. Yet, support from Dissenting denominations in Wales was not universal. Certainly, the Independents and Baptists were everywhere conspicuous. Not so the Methodists, as Walter Griffith observed: 'The Wesleyan and Calvinistic Methodists will give no help; and not only that, they speak in many places very much against our cause.'[15] These had long shunned political agitation. Neither body was won over to official participation in the movement. The A.C.L.L., certainly in the Caernarfon district, attracted several Calvinistic Methodist ministers and sections of their congregations, but the Wesleyan Methodists always remained aloof.

The League's efforts to enlist the active support of the Dissenting denominations in the free trade movement culminated in August

---

[14] *A.B.T.C.*, 9 Sept 1841. As early as October 1839, the League had issued an 'Address to the Dissenting Clergy of Great Britain' in the *A.C.L.C.* (1 Oct. 1839).
[15] A.C.L.L., L.B., 4, 606, Walter Griffith to Ballantyne, 28 May 1840.

1841, when nearly 700 ministers of religion assembled at Manchester to discuss the Corn Laws and came out overwhelmingly in opposition to them. A substantial number of Welsh ministers attended, some authorized by their congregations to do so, most self-appointed.[16] The lead offered to local opinion in this way obviously elicited a good response in many areas. Prayer meetings and public gatherings were the prevalent features of anti-Corn Law activity in Wales in the weeks following the Manchester conference. Their frequency and support suggest that A.C.L.L. sympathy was not lacking amongst Dissenting congregations. Similar conferences of ministers were held in other parts of the country, including one conducted in Wales in November 1841 at Caernarfon, a meeting organized by the local branch of the League. The enterprise earned the unqualified approval of the majority of the Welsh periodicals and was welcomed by many of the local townspeople, a large number of whom contributed to the assembly's expenses. Lasting three days, the conference attracted ministers from throughout north Wales and brought strong condemnation of agricultural protection, particularly on religious, moral and humanitarian grounds. Few concrete provisions were made; but ministers were to participate more fully in local agitation, for the Corn Laws required 'a more emphatical and effective denunciation than can be given to them from the pulpit'.[17] All in all, the conference was an impressive demonstration of the convictions of north Wales Dissenting ministers on the question. For the League, it served as important propaganda material and strengthened relationships between a large body of provincial sympathizers and the central organization.

League agitation in its early years gave a strong emphasis to petitioning as a means of pressurizing the government. Wales responded readily, as Walter Griffith found on his first tour. Petitioning reached its height in the early months of 1842, when the League launched a new campaign for total repeal, in opposition to Peel's modification proposals. By March, 3,000 petitions had

---

[16] Reports on Welsh representation differ in both number and personnel; it seems about twenty-five attended. *Cynhadledd o Weinidogion y Gwahanol Enwadau Cristionogol yn Manchester* (n.d., *c.* 1841); *Y Dysgedydd,* Oct. 1841, pp. 324–6; *A.B.T.C.,* 12 Aug., 2 Nov. 1841; *Silurian,* 7 Aug. 1841; N. McCord, op. cit., pp. 103–7.
[17] *Carnarvon and Denbigh Herald,* 12 Feb. 1842. For the conference, see ibid., 18, 25 Dec. 1841; A. Prentice, op. cit., Vol. I, pp. 276–7.

been presented,[18] and more were received after this date. Almost 100 were contributed by Welsh localities at this time. The bulk came from the industrial centres of both north and south, although some rural areas also participated. Caernarfon confirmed its position as the centre of the A.C.L.L. in Wales by getting up eleven petitions.[19]

Petitioning was one expression of public opinion, but it lacked continuity, as the Manchester leaders frequently emphasized:

> Local organisation is of essential importance; and to this point we would direct the immediate attention of our friends. Our publications, our lectures, and our leaders, can do much, but they cannot do all. They are and must be comparatively inefficient without a well trained band of local auxiliaries.[20]

Much of the responsibility for inspiration in this field fell, as often, upon the shoulders of the lecturers. Thus, the first anti-Corn Law society in Wales was established at Llangollen in May 1840. Soon afterwards, organizations sprang up in other parts of north Wales, all under the initial direction of Walter Griffith. But the formation of such associations was no easy matter. According to Griffith, Welsh people were both reluctant and unable to organize locally:

> As for forming Associations, they are wholly inexperienced; they have no taste for such a thing. They are ready to assist the cause with their prayers, with their names to petitions, and with their mites towards a public collection, but they say they have no time, nor the power of forming Associations.[21]

Indeed, not only was a high degree of commitment needed for an effective anti-Corn Law society, but particularly in rural areas it might also represent a solid stance against local power and influence. There was a considerable difference between adding one's name to a petition as a singular objection and regularly supporting a repeal association, sometimes in contradiction to landlord influence. Furthermore, agitation in some districts centred on the Dissenting minister and the chapel and, in this way, the formation of a local organization was perhaps superfluous.

---

[18] A.B.T.C., 10 Mar. 1842.
[19] Carnarvon and Denbigh Herald, 12 Feb. 1842.
[20] A.B.T.C., 27 Dec. 1842.
[21] Ibid., 8 Oct. 1840, quoting from a letter dated 3 Oct. 1840.

The quantity of petitions presented by chapel congregations is instructive here. Of the eleven submitted to Parliament from Caernarfon in February 1842, nine came from Dissenting chapels.[22]

Nevertheless, a number of free trade associations were formed in Wales, although no precise figure can be given. In 1840 these were most conspicuous in north-east Wales. Later, important ones were established at Caernarfon, Carmarthen, and Swansea. The immediate necessity was obviously to attract members. Canvassing of the locality extended to the establishment of associations in nearby towns and villages, as in the Holywell area in 1840.[23] As the Manchester Council stipulated, petitioning was to be 'the first and principal labour of every Anti-Corn Law Association'.[24] Other key functions included making arrangements for lectures and assisting in the circulation of tracts and other literature. One of the most flourishing in Wales was the Caernarfon association, due substantially to the efforts of Revd William Williams ('Caledfryn') and other committed individuals, and the presence over lengthy periods of Walter Griffith. In February 1842 its membership reached 300,[25] though local adherents to the cause numbered many more. Walter Griffith's lectures in the town usually attracted around a thousand, while signatures to petitions in Caernarfon in early 1842 were treble this figure.[26] At the same time, the branch was responsive to national conferences and fund-raising projects, and showed particular zeal in founding a free trade periodical, *Cylchgrawn Rhyddid*, in the autumn of 1840, and at the end of the following year organizing the conference of ministers in the town.[27]

[22] *Carnarvon and Denbigh Herald*, 12 Feb. 1842.
[23] A.C.L.L., L.B., 5, 650, Walter Griffith to Wilson, 16 June 1840; *A.C.L.C.*, 18 June 1840.
[24] *A.C.L.C.*, 23 Jan 1840.
[25] *Carnarvon and Denbigh Herald*, 22 Jan. 1842.
[26] Ibid., and 12 Feb. 1842.
[27] The two Caernarfon representatives at the A.C.L.L. deputies' meeting in London in February 1842, Revd William Williams ('Caledfryn') of Caernarfon and Griffith Evans of Maesypandy Farm, Talyllyn, were both nominated in the foundation of the Executive Committee (Revd Ellis Hughes, an Independent minister, also attended as the Holywell delegate). *A.B.T.C.*, 10 Feb. 1842; A. Prentice, op. cit., Vol. I, pp. 303–6. 'Caledfryn', Independent minister at Caernarfon, 1832–48, was a prominent League activist in north Wales, addressing public meetings, organizing petitions and assisting in the foundation of *Cylchgrawn Rhyddid*, and succeeding Walter Griffith as editor in February 1841. *Carnarvon and Denbigh Herald*, 8 Aug. 1846; *Cylchgrawn Rhyddid*, 15 Feb. 1842; A.C.L.L., L.B., 5, 703, Revd William Williams to League Council, 21 July 1840. For a testimony to his work on behalf of the movement, see *Carnarvon and Denbigh Herald*, 8 Aug. 1846.

Indeed, this period represented the high point of League activity in Wales. North Wales, and more particularly Caernarfon, led the movement. In 1842, Welsh participation in the A.C.L.L. agitation began to decrease, as epitomized by events at Caernarfon. The declining circulation and ultimate end of *Cylchgrawn Rhyddid* were symptomatic of the dwindling public interest in the movement. Meetings of the Caernarfon branch of the League ceased. Speaking in the town in early 1843, Walter Griffith urged the community to be, once more, 'active and energetic'. He was able to rejuvenate the cause with the formation of a committee to collect subscriptions for the recently launched £50,000 fund, but the revival was short-lived and Caernarfon contributed little to this appeal. Nor did it contribute much to the electoral registration campaign and later money-raising schemes. While the leading figures in the Caernarfon Association no doubt retained their repeal sympathies, active commitment virtually ended. As elsewhere, other controversies acted as distractions; most obviously at Caernarfon, Nonconformist ministers turned towards their specific Dissenting grievances.

The year 1842 marked an important change in the League's strategy. Rather than the mere creation of a public opinion in favour of repeal, it now sought to exert greater pressure and therefore looked more towards Parliament and electioneering; as the *Monmouthshire Beacon* observed, the use of itinerant lecturers and the diffusion of pamphlets diminished and Leaguers became 'traffickers in the composition of county votes, and canvassers for registration operations'.[28] In Wales this policy led to declining popular support and a change in the geographical location of A.C.L.L. activity. South Wales, centred on Swansea, played an increased role, while, in the north, Holywell superseded Caernarfon. The shift is in part to be explained by the greatly diminished role of Griffith and the employment of a south Wales agent, John Jenkins of Swansea, a former Unitarian minister and schoolmaster, subsequently founder and editor of the *Swansea and Glamorgan Herald* and later a barrister.[29] This appointment was part of the League's reorganization scheme of 1842. This set up twelve regions for England and Wales as a whole, each with its own full-time agent. Wales was divided into north and south, under Griffith and Jenkins respectively. Monmouthshire was included in the border 'Iron Districts' under A. W. Paulton, one of the earliest A.C.L.L. lecturers and subsequently editor of *The League*. He made very few visits to the county. Other League officials occasionally visited Wales. Griffith made only a handful of lecturing appearances from 1843 onwards, but Jenkins was active in the League's service for some three years from the middle of 1842. He addressed many meetings and was involved in fund-raising, distribution of propaganda and electoral registration. In addition, the League wished to subdivide the regions into sections under local registrars. Some were appointed in Wales, in places like Monmouth, Abergavenny and Swansea,[30] but evidently this was not done systematically throughout Wales.

Two major facets of the League's new policy are discernible: enquiry into the nature of the electorate and then manipulation of it. From the first, the League had sought to acquire a thorough knowledge of the size, composition, influence and sympathies of each county and borough. In November 1840, for example, William Norton, a Carmarthen brewer, supplied such information on the local borough to George Wilson.[31] This was also part of the lecturers' task. Such investigations were now considered more important and by its later years the A.C.L.L. had amassed an incomparable collection of information on conditions in virtually every constituency.

Influencing the outcome of an election was a more complex operation, however. Persuasion of voters to support repeal candidates relied on the League's ability to produce and disseminate propaganda, for the process entailed the distribution of tracts to electors all over the kingdom. In this respect, it was able to make

---

[29] From 1843 onwards, Griffith was overwhelmed by personal tragedy and died in 1846. See I. G. Jones, 'The anti-Corn Law letters of Walter Griffith', p. 100. For John Jenkins, see ibid., pp. 99–100 and the references therein. If Griffith's dedicated efforts on behalf of the A.C.L.L. can be determined with some precision because of the quantity of available information, the same cannot be said of Jenkins's. Only the letters sent to the League in the early years have survived and therefore this period can be followed more closely than the later.

[30] *A.B.T.C.*. 1 Dec. 1842, 11 April 1843.

[31] A.C.L.L., L.B., 5, 790, William Norton to Chairman of the A.C.L.L., 13 Nov. 1840.

excellent use of the cheap, national and efficient postal service which was introduced in 1840. In parts of Wales, certainly in Carmarthenshire and Glamorgan, local agents were also very active, distributing hundreds of electoral parcels.[32] Elsewhere the bulk of the burden fell on its two lecturers. It is impossible to assess the influence of these electoral packets. It seems that Welshmen readily accepted them, though whether their directives were followed, or even closely read, is another matter.

The League's electoral campaign went far beyond propaganda. In particular, it recognized the importance of electoral registration which in later years was presented as the focal point of agitation: 'The registration courts must be the future battleground of the League.'[33] The fundamental aim was to 'improve' the registers in favour of repeal, in borough and county constituencies, by the inclusion of as many supporters as possible and the exclusion of as many opponents. The first part of the task was ascertaining the political views of voters on the register, usually through laborious door-to-door enquiries. Registers were then scrupulously examined and, at the annual revision, protectionists were objected against on the basis of the slightest technical flaw in the voter's description. At the same time, the registrations of free traders were carefully checked and, wherever necessary, corrected to protect the vote. Efforts were also made to get those favourable to repeal on the electoral roll by encouraging them to qualify for the franchise by purchasing the appropriate property qualifications, especially the forty-shilling freehold in the county constituencies. Accordingly, League lecturers and agents extolled the virtues of property ownership not only in extending the franchise but in terms of financial investment and gaining a stake in the country. In the years after 1843, correspondents in many Welsh districts reported to the League Council on local electoral registration. The reported gains were small and, in any case, numbers are open to interpretation. Sometimes they are estimates of likely successes. More often, it is difficult to distinguish between the activities of local Liberals and activities conducted specifically to promote repeal. Nevertheless, some light is shed on A.C.L.L. operations

---

[32] *Cambrian*, 23 June 1843, 16 Feb. 1844.
[33] *The League*, 28 Sept. 1844. The registration campaign for parliamentary electors is discussed in detail in N. McCord, op. cit., pp. 148–55.

in the Principality. Holywell, Carmarthen and Swansea were the most active Welsh centres in the registration campaign for Parliamentary electors. In October 1844, Holywell free traders fought a keen battle with local protectionists in the Flintshire Registration Court.[34] In south Wales, John Jenkins closely involved himself in the details of constituency politics.[35]

The final step was, of course, to translate this groundwork into an electoral victory. Should none of the candidates avow free trade principles, repealers could either pressurize one to do so or bring forward a candidate themselves. The issue was not always as straightforward as this. For instance, David Morris, Whig MP for Carmarthen Boroughs, was apparently a repealer but unable to support this cause in the Commons because his seat was dependent upon an important landowner 'giving him twelve or fourteen votes'.[36] Other constituencies, particularly county ones, were still under traditional agricultural influence and unfavourable to A.C.L.L. electioneering. John Jenkins became disillusioned:

> In calculating the probability of the return of a candidate in the Principality, no account needs to be taken of the opinion or feelings of the constituents,— that is quite beside the question; and if an agent were dispatched on such a mission of enquiry, he need only go to each contributory, cast up the number of electors under the control of the representative Whig and Tory landlords of the neighbourhood, and he might then safely conclude that the return will be in accordance with the majority which the one or the other party can command.[37]

Thus, in Wales, Leaguers did what they could in the circumstances. In the general election of 1841, Walter Griffith was addressing meetings on the eve of the poll in Caernarfonshire.[38] The main avenue of repeal support, however, was the Nonconformist press. *Cylchgrawn Rhyddid* urged its readers to vote for Lord George Paget and free trade in the Caernarfon Boroughs.[39] In south-east Wales,

[34] *The League*, 12 Oct. 1844.
[35] *Monmouthshire Merlin*, 4 Oct. 1844.
[36] A.C.L.L., L.B., 5, 790, William Norton to Chairman of the A.C.L.L., 13 Nov. 1840.
[37] J. Jenkins, op. cit., p. 19.
[38] *A.B.T.C.*, 1 July 1841; Thomas Richards (ed.), *Er Clod: Saith Bennod ar Hanes Methodistiaeth Yng Nghymru* (Wrexham, 1934), pp. 138-9.
[39] R. G. Thomas, 'Politics in Anglesey and Caernarvonshire, with special reference to the Caernarvon Boroughs' (University of Wales MA thesis, 1970), p. 191.

Revd David Rhys Stephen, the Newport Baptist minister, in his *Morgan Llewelyn's Journal*, depicted the Monmouthshire election as a simple choice between 'a bread-taxer' and 'a candidate who will untax the poor man's loaf'.[40] Other periodicals, like the Independent *Y Diwygiwr*, linked it with Dissent; it called for 'free religion and bread'.[41] Nevertheless, free trade candidates generally did badly in Wales in the general election of 1841.

Between 1842 and 1846, two by-elections occurred, again with only moderate involvement by local Leaguers. In Carmarthenshire in 1842, D. A. Saunders Davies, a protectionist, was returned unopposed. Even the *Welshman*, which had consistently urged that a free trade candidate be brought forward, admitted that this would be only a token gesture since Davies's return was assured by 'the tutelary powers of Dynevor Castle and Golden Grove'.[42] Similarly, in Denbighshire, in 1845, the powerful Sir Watkin Williams Wynn, again a protectionist, was returned unopposed, although local repealers did seize the occasion to promote their cause.[43]

Wales, then, was not unaffected by the electoral campaign of the A.C.L.L., though it was inevitably a limited involvement. The latter years of the League's life were publicly quiescent ones; electioneering was often an inconspicuous process. Some commentators were critical of the policy. To *Y Dysgedydd*, removing the matter from the public eye could lead only to 'levity and indifference'.[44] The League therefore frequently justified its strategy:

> It does not matter how great the popular majority is in favour of unrestricted commerce; if these be not a majority at the poll it is valueless. Then, Free Trade is not a question to be carried by popular enthusiasm like a Reform Bill, but rather by hard facts and hard arguments operating in the minds of men, and leading to steady, deliberate and resolute action.[45]

The Welsh press stressed, too, that the agitation was now of a different but equally effective order, and continued to report

---

[40] *Morgan Llewelyn's Journal*, 3 July 1841.
[41] *Y Diwygiwr*, July 1841, quoted by I. W. R. David, op. cit., p. 159.
[42] *Welshman*, 30 Dec. 1842.
[43] *The League*, 17 May 1845.
[44] *Y Dysgedydd*, July 1844, p. 210, quoted by T. H. Williams, op. cit., Part II, p. 104.
[45] *The League*, 4 Oct. 1845.

League activities; but there was none of the enthusiasm generated by public meetings and itinerant lecturers. Not surprisingly, popular interest and support for the A.C.L.L. in Wales steadily declined from the heights of 1841–2.

After 1842 the League's major provincial activity centred on fund-raising, and indeed the reorganization of that year was largely intended to augment finances. Hitherto, local groups or individuals were relied upon to forward whatever sums they could. In Wales, this meant donations from a few scattered sympathizers only. Even Caernarfonshire, which was the hub of A.C.L.L. activity in 1841–2, contributed little or nothing. In the various districts set up in 1842, local officials were appointed for the registration of members. Six registrars were soon recruited in Flintshire and Denbighshire; later, two others were approved at Monmouth.[46] Administrators were doubtless engaged in other areas, too, judging from the applications for membership cards from various places in Wales. The actual numbers enrolled are uncertain. The enrolment of as many as 180 persons at a single meeting in late 1842 at a market town like Monmouth suggests that in some areas figures were substantial.[47] As ever, they varied considerably, from a dozen at most at Hay-on-Wye to several hundred in the Holywell district.

It is possible to be more precise about financial contributions after 1842, when the campaign for registration of members was superseded by new enterprises. Between 1842 and 1846, the League launched a series of massive fund-raising schemes, with successive targets of £50,000, £100,000 and £250,000. Welsh contributions totalled £200, £91 and £213 respectively.[48] Closer analysis suggests certain conclusions. Allowing for the distortion created by the remarkable donations from Holywell (£177) towards the £250,000 fund, contributions from Wales steadily fell in the period 1842–6. It is also evident that subscriptions to the £100,000 target came from individual supporters scattered in all parts of the Principality, often giving £1 or so, rather than a

---

[46] *A.B.T.C.*, 11 Aug., 1, 13 Dec. 1842.
[47] *Monmouthshire Merlin*, 3 Dec. 1842.
[48] Figures compiled from lists appearing in the *A.B.T.C.*, 31 Jan. 1843 to 2 May 1843, and *The League*, 7 Oct. 1843 to 4 July 1846. In addition, in May 1845, the League organized a bazaar in London as another money-raising project. Collections, comprising varying items, were made at Wrexham, Carmarthen, Swansea and Aberystwyth, while several individuals elsewhere made donations. *The League*, 25 Jan., 8 Feb., 1 Mar., 12, 19 Apr., 3, 17 May 1845.

large number of small sums forwarded by the local collector to Manchester, as was the case with the £50,000 target. This is symptomatic of the decrease in popular League support between 1842 and 1846; more and more the emphasis fell upon the more committed in provincial regions.

The geographical distribution of Welsh subscriptions indicates that the League made its deepest impression in manufacturing towns. From 1842 onwards the industrial areas centred on Holywell and Wrexham supplanted Caernarfon as the heart of A.C.L.L. support in north Wales. In the south, the most active and sustained repealers were located in Carmarthen and Swansea. The A.C.L.L. never attained a position of strength in the iron communities of Glamorgan and Monmouthshire, although it is likely that there was a substantial number of free traders in the region. Loyalty to Chartism was a potent factor here. Nor were the agricultural areas ever converted to repeal. A minority of farmers was persuaded by the League's assurance that free trade would bring economic benefits to them as well as to industry, but overwhelmingly they remained true to the age-old traditions of loyalty and subservience to the local landowner.

The reception afforded to the A.C.L.L. in various localities can in part be explained by political tradition, economic activity and local influence. But the importance of individual supporters was often significant, also. Who, then, supported the League in Wales? We have already noted a fundamental alignment—Dissenting ministers, particularly Independents and Baptists, and middle-class liberals, on the one side, and the gentry and Anglican Church, on the other. The League also made an appeal to movements associated with Dissent. Thus, Walter Griffith received valuable assistance from local temperance men. He often attended and addressed their meetings and, in turn, they helped to arrange his public lectures and to distribute tracts. In short, teetotallers were the 'best friends of repeal'.[49] The alliance was obviously based on religious and moral grounds. There was also the common enemy, for Griffith frequently suffered interruption from those

---

[49] *A.C.L.C.*, 19 Nov. 1840. Some teetotallers put the affinity thus: 'Our society brings the people to drink water, and yours brings them plenty of bread with it.' Ibid.

under the influence of alcohol.[50] Similarly, some overtures were made to youth. At Holywell, Griffith addressed meetings of the local Young Men's Association, and theological college students at Pontypool, Brecon and Carmarthen were attracted to the League.

An occupational analysis of prominent Leaguers in Wales reveals that the principal support came from the 'respectable classes'—Dissenting ministers, skilled tradesmen, shopkeepers, professional men, factory and mine-owners.[51] The main supporters of the Caernarfon Anti-Corn Law Association were two drapers, a grocer, solicitor, printer, reporter, architect, chemist, flour dealer, miller, ironmonger and a corn dealer. At Swansea, the movement was led by four drapers, a surgeon, jeweller, banker, bookseller, ironmonger and a mechanic. In Holywell, it was championed by the families of local mine-owners, while activity at Carmarthen owed much to the enthusiasm of the Norton brothers, William and Henry, who were brewers. Dissenting ministers were involved in all four centres.

The support of families like the Mathers, Eytons and Salisburys in north-east Wales gave the cause influential backing. Elsewhere, too, substantial gentlemen were conspicuous—men like Samuel Holland, the quarry-owner of Plas Penrhyn, Merioneth, Sir Love Jones-Parry, squire of Madryn, near Pwllheli, Summers Harford of the Sirhowy ironworks and Colonel Biddulph of Chirk Castle. Several MPs—Sir Josiah John Guest, Merthyr, John Henry Vivian, Glamorgan, and William Bulkeley Hughes, Caernarfon Boroughs—also gave the A.C.L.L. their support. Local officialdom was sometimes sympathetic; in December 1845, for example, the magistrates and council at Queensferry petitioned for repeal.[52]

What of the working classes? An occupational analysis suggests that generally the working classes were not prominent or, indeed, committed Leaguers. They were certainly not in the forefront

[50] At Flint, in 1840, he was 'afraid at first of keeping a meeting' for the town was 'in a state of drunkenness and the people were very disorderly, which I understand is the case almost every Whitsuntide ...' When a meeting was convened the local constable stayed in the hall to defend the speakers. A.C.L.L., L.B., 4, 640, Walter Griffith to Wilson, 12 June 1840.

[51] The analysis, of 186 persons in all, comprises mainly subscribers to A.C.L.L. funds, but it is supplemented by prominent spokesmen at League meetings. The occupational structure is based on *Pigot's Directory* (1835), *Slater's Directory* (1851) and references in the local press.

[52] *The League*, 13 Dec. 1845.

of societies, meetings or subscriptions. Yet this could be misleading. It was invariably the most influential who were chosen as local officials and speakers. Similarly, there were people who, while wishing to support the League financially, were simply unable to do so, a point made by the Abersychan Baptist minister, Revd Stephen Price. Although repeal had made a favourable impression in the area, he regretted that 'the iron trade is so depressed we can't do much towards the Fund here'.[53] Others, of course, readily adhered to the objective of the A.C.L.L. but were reluctant to make a financial sacrifice. Indeed, Walter Griffith noted a large working-class membership in both the Llangollen and Holywell Anti-Corn Law Associations, in a three-tier division of nobility, tradesmen and working class.[54] Moreover, in industrial south Wales working-class suspicion and hostility towards the anti-Corn Law movement diminished in time and by 1844–5 it was accepted even in Chartist strongholds like Merthyr. It could now claim, with greater justification, to represent both middle- and working-class opinion and not, as was often alleged, the selfish interests of Manchester manufacturers. Nevertheless, the A.C.L.L. was essentially a moneyed and middle-class campaign.

How great an impact did it make on the Welsh populace? In this respect, it would be erroneous to neglect or underestimate the degree of pro-Corn Law sentiment prevalent in Wales, for, clearly, the A.C.L.L.'s splendid organization and range of activity often gave a somewhat distorted impression of public opinion. The most obvious fear of protectionists was that economic ruin would follow repeal. Anglesey farmers in mid 1841 petitioned for retention of the Corn Laws, believing that Wales was particularly needful of protection as the corn grown there was inferior to that of other parts of the country.[55] Wider economic repercussions were also forecast. Sir John Walsh, the most vehement protectionist among Welsh MPs, argued:

> The agricultural Members of that House were ... the representatives of a great national interest, upon which the prosperity of all classes was founded, and therefore they contended that no change could be made

---

[53] *A.B.T.C.*, 1 Dec. 1842.
[54] A.C.L.L., L.B., 4, 606, Walter Griffith to Ballantyne, 28 May 1840; *A.C.L.C.*, 18 June 1840.
[55] *North Wales Chronicle*, 1 June 1841.

detrimental to its condition which would not also prove injurious to all other branches of industry.[56]

It was the A.C.L.L. itself, however, which bore the brunt of protectionist attacks. Inevitably, its leaders were accused of being 'only desirous of filling their own purses', aiming at wage reduction.[57] The very existence of the League was also challenged. To Sir John Walsh it constituted a threat to 'stable, regular government' and could prove 'destructive of the independence and utility of representative government'.[58] 'We trust', cautioned the *Cardiff and Merthyr Guardian*, 'that a vigilant watch will be set upon those roving vagabonds, whether Chartists, or Socialists, or Anti-Corn Law Leaguers, the disturbers of the poor man's peace and the fomentors of sedition. Of these we believe the anti-corn law leaguers to be the worst and most unprincipled.'[59] The authorities, too, saw something dangerous, even sinister, in the League. In 1844, the Home Office told Colonel Love, the commander of troops in south Wales, that 'Repeal Emissaries in the South Wales area must be carefully watched'.[60] The agitation was subjected to much sensationalism, yet many Leaguers certainly viewed the campaign as an opportunity to strike at the power of the upper classes and to produce a more equitable society. Clashes with local dignitaries, and in addition the misery and poverty encountered on his journeys, induced Walter Griffith to write bitterly:

> You are aware that the *Welsh* are in general very *fiery*, and so am I at present, yea, more so than ever, in going from one place to another, seeing

[56] *Hansard*, LXXXIV, col. 1555, 17 Mar. 1846.
[57] Ibid. This conviction was most forcibly expressed in a printed handbill, circulated in south-west Wales in mid 1841. Place Newspaper Collection, Set 8; Handbill addressed 'To the Pembrokeshire Farmers' and signed 'R', Narberth, 25 May 1841.
[58] *Hansard*, LXXXIII, col. 592, 9 Feb. 1846; W. O. Stanley, Anglesey, expressed a similar view, ibid., LXXXIV, col. 718, 2 Mar. 1846.
[59] *Cardiff and Merthyr Guardian*, 20 Aug. 1842.
[60] Home Office Letters and Papers (HO) 41/18; quoted in D. Williams, *The Rebecca Riots*, p. 153. Cobden himself wrote to his brother-in-law, Hugh Williams, the Carmarthen solicitor: 'We seem ... to be on the verge of a social disorganisation, which may lead God knows whither—the people are not to blame—they have borne too much and too patiently. It is to be deplored that they don't know their real oppressors—they attack shopkeepers and masters, and let the aristocracy escape—at least for the present they are on the wrong scent.' WSRO, Cobden Papers 57, Cobden to Hugh Williams, 15 Aug. 1842. Williams was also apparently 'active in the service of the League'. Col. Love to Home Office, 6 Jan. 1846, HO 45/1431; quoted in D. Williams, *The Rebecca Riots*, p. 153.

the nobility, the aristocratic landowners and bread taxers, rolling in wealth, drinking wine and eating venison, while the fair daughters and the once hearty sons of Cambria are trodden to the dust by the (well termed) Satanic corn law.[61]

The case against repeal was propounded in sections of the press in Wales. Protectionists, however, did not organize themselves as a national movement until the formation of the Central Agricultural Protection Society or the 'Anti-League' (A.L.) in February 1844 aimed at counteracting the influence of its rival by stimulating and compounding pro-Corn Law sentiment in the country. It made immediate progress with the growth of a number of local units and the influx of substantial funds.[62] In February 1844, the Chepstow Agricultural Protection Society was established, and it soon became part of the newly formed county association.[63] Others, centred at Brecon, Cowbridge, Welshpool, and Mold, followed.[64] The largest landowners and farmers were everywhere prominent: men like the Duke of Beaufort and Joseph Bailey in Breconshire, C. R. M. Talbot, MP, in Glamorgan and Crawshay Bailey, MP, in Monmouthshire. The movement was noticeably confined to the most Anglicized counties of Wales, areas where the A.C.L.L. had not been particularly active, where the Welsh periodicals did not circulate widely, and which were in close proximity to already established associations. No protectionist activity is discernible in the western regions of the Principality.

In Wales, the initial burst of protectionist enthusiasm in the early months of 1844 was succeeded by apparent inactivity. No further meetings or agitation are reported for the remainder of the year. Lord John Russell's commitment of the Whigs to free trade in his 'Edinburgh Letter', followed by the clarification of Sir Robert Peel's intentions, changed this. Without the support of either party in Parliament, the A.L. appealed once more to the country. At Raglan, 500 landowners and farmers attended a meeting under the auspices of the Monmouthshire Association

---

[61] *A.C.L.C.*, 8 Apr. 1841.

[62] See G. L. Mosse, 'The Anti-League 1844–6', *Economic History Review*, XVII (1947); M. Lawson-Tancred, 'The Anti-League and the Corn Law crisis of 1846', *The Historical Journal*, III (1960); T. H. Williams, op. cit., Part III, pp. 2–23.

[63] *Monmouthshire Beacon*, 3, 17 Feb., 9 Mar. 1844.

[64] Ibid., 16 Mar. 1844; *Cambrian*, 16 Feb. 1844; *North Wales Chronicle*, 5 Mar. 1844; *Carnarvon and Denbigh Herald*, 30 Mar. 1844; *Chester Courant*, 26 Mar. 1844.

in February 1846.[65] More significantly, protectionists in Brecon-shire determined to demonstrate their feelings by ousting the county member, Colonel Thomas Wood. In the spring of 1846, a requisition signed by 533 constituents called upon Wood to resign his seat because of his recent support for Peel's measures, and invited Joseph Bailey to stand at the next election, an offer that was duly accepted.[66] In the Commons, the member, once 'the very Nestor of Protection', was singled out as a prime example of a Tory who had betrayed local opinion and his own conscience in order to follow the party lead.[67]

Elsewhere, protectionists took the opportunity in the general election of 1847 to register their protest against members con-sidered to have betrayed their manifesto pledges. This was most forcibly displayed in Monmouthshire, where efforts were made by the Protection Committee to replace Lord Granville Somerset by his brother Captain Edward Somerset as the second member. The attempt narrowly failed.[68] In a number of other Welsh consti-tuencies candidates styled themselves 'Protectionist'.[69]

The organization and effectiveness of the protectionist move-ment were never comparable with those of the A.C.L.L. This is in part attributable to the failures of the A.L.'s national leader-ship. It made its greatest impact in Parliament. In Wales, activity was certainly limited. There are, of course, other guides to pro-Corn Law sentiment over these years. We have already noted that protectionists battled with free traders in the registration courts of several constituencies. In addition, open reaction against the A.C.L.L., most obviously demonstrated in the refusal to make town halls and other public rooms available to League agents, is a pointer. Furthermore, the A.C.L.L.'s lack of financial support, both quantitatively and geographically, and the existence of few sustained A.C.L.L. societies in Wales may not have been wholly due to apathy.

---

[65] *Silurian*, 14 Feb. 1846.
[66] NLW, Maybery Collection, 6701, Address of Col. Wood to the Electors of the County of Brecon, 15 Apr. 1846.
[67] *Hansard*, LXXXIV, cols. 724 5, 2 Mar. 1846; see also, ibid., cols. 1464 5, 17 Mar. 1846.
[68] NLW, Tredegar Park MSS, 71/269; *The League*, 9 May 1846.
[69] The controversy remained alive in the following decade. In 1851, for example, the Bridgend Protectionist Society was active in the Glamorgan election. I. W. R. David, op. cit., p. 170.

A useful guide to assessing public sympathies lies in the reception
of repeal and protectionist views in the press. In its propaganda
campaigns, the A.C.L.L. made unprecedented efforts in the distribution of tracts and newspapers. In Wales, Walter Griffith and
others translated some of these into the Welsh language to increase
their effectiveness. Griffith wrote his own pamphlet, *Treth y Bara*
('The Bread Tax') in July 1840. The League published, in English,
a flysheet edition of Samuel Roberts's essay on 'Agriculture'.[70]
Men like Dr O. O. Roberts, surgeon, of Bangor and Dr Thomas
Thomas, the Pontypool Baptist minister, wrote tracts attacking
the Corn Laws.[71] The A.L. also circulated a bulk of literature,
but it never used the Welsh tongue or achieved the extent of
dissemination of League propaganda. As elements in affecting public opinion, these pamphlets were important and yet had their
limitations. In particular, they tended to appeal primarily to
already committed supporters. A more significant factor was,
therefore, the local press, designed to attract the ordinary reader.
The editorial stance of the newspaper was, of course, often a
reflection of local opinion, but equally, it could direct it, and meetings, petitions and associations were sometimes the response to
such a lead.

Such 'independent' support for the A.C.L.L. was therefore invaluable and, accordingly, the leadership advised each lecturer 'to
write letters to the newspapers, and ... make himself acquainted
with all the liberal journals'.[72] Walter Griffith certainly made use
of the Welsh periodical press, regularly contributing articles and
letters to the most sympathetic of them, such as *Seren Gomer, Ystorfa
y Bedyddiwr* (both Baptist), *Y Dysgedydd* and *Y Diwygiwr* (both Independent). The circulation of such magazines, though considerable,
was nevertheless confined to the particular religious denomination—in Griffith's words, they were not 'universal'.[73] In addition,
on the protectionist side there were significant forces led by *Yr
Haul, Y Brytwn* and *Y Protestant.*

It was therefore felt that there was a need to establish a Welsh-
language publication to advocate liberal views and to support the

[70] S. Roberts, *Pleadings for Reforms* (Conwy, 1881), p. 27.
[71] Dr T. Thomas, *A Proper Consideration of the Cause of the Poor* (Pontypool, 1841); Dr O.
O. Roberts, *Facts for Farmers or Agriculture and the Corn Laws* (1841).
[72] *A.B.T.C.*, 22 Sept. 1842.
[73] A.C.L.L., L.B., 5, 691, Walter Griffith to Wilson, 15 July 1840.

A.C.L.L. in particular. The instigation for this venture came from prominent Leaguers in north Wales. 'Caledfryn' was particularly enthusiastic and seems to have undertaken much of the practical organization.[74] The first issue of the paper, published under the title *Cylchgrawn Rhyddid*, appeared on 1 October 1840.[75] Walter Griffith was its first editor, succeeded in February 1841 by 'Caledfryn'. It carried general discussions of the Corn Law question, translations from League publications and circulars, and news from Manchester and the rest of the country. Locally, résumés of Griffith's lecturing work and other anti-Corn Law activity were reported. *Cylchgrawn Rhyddid* primarily served the growing body of League supporters in north-west Wales. But it also aimed at a wider audience. It was 'principally devoted to the annihilation of the Corn Laws, but was diversified with the usual variety that characterises the periodical publications of the present age'.[76] In the first year of its existence, circulation was 4,350 and in the second, 2,600,[77] though the readership would have been considerably higher.

From the English-language newspapers published in Wales, the A.C.L.L. received rather less support than it did from the periodicals. In north Wales, the movement acquired considerable support from the *Carnarvon and Denbigh Herald*, while, in the south, the *Silurian* and *Welshman* were, according to Walter Griffith, 'true friends of the cause'.[78] To Griffith, the *Cambrian* was neutral, but by 1842 it was undoubtedly strongly in favour of repeal, as were the *Monmouthshire Merlin* and the *Pembrokeshire Herald* on its inception in 1843. On the protectionist side, there was a formidable phalanx, including the *North Wales Chronicle*, the *Monmouthshire Advertiser*, and the most zealous advocate of organized opposition to the A.C.L.L., the *Monmouthshire Beacon*.

Wales had considerable sympathy with the repeal movement and the A.C.L.L., even though there was also a substantial body of opinion in favour of Corn Law retention. The Principality was

---

[74] Ibid., 703, William Williams to League Executive, 21 July 1840.
[75] Published as a four-page monthly at Caernarfon by James Rees, Heol-Fawr, price 2*d.* (later 3*d.*) and running until 15 April 1842 (19 numbers). No. 1 is available at the National Library of Wales, Nos. 5–19 at the British Newspaper Library, Colindale.
[76] *Carnarvon and Denbigh Herald*, 15 Aug. 1840.
[77] *Report from the Select Committee on Newspaper Stamps, Parliamentary Papers* (PP), 1851, XXVII (558), reprinted in Irish University Press's *Newspapers*, I, Appendix, pp. 572–3.
[78] *A.C.L.C*, 14 Jan. 1841.

not, however, a major stronghold of A.C.L.L. support. It was never a large contributor to the coffers of the central body or a centre of agitation. Activity in Wales was not distinct from the League but very much dependent upon it for guidance and inspiration. In many areas, local agitation enthusiastically burst forth with the appearance of Griffith or Jenkins or one of the other League agents, only to prove ephemeral once they had gone. Activity was, therefore, discontinuous, except at Caernarfon for a time. A graphic portrayal of A.C.L.L. operations here would reveal a pyramidal pattern. Elsewhere, in strong League centres like Holywell, Carmarthen, and Swansea, it would be a cyclical one with peaks of action being reactions to external stimuli—the appearance of a League official or the launching of major fund-raising schemes. Self-determined action, in anything more than petitioning, was rare and confined to periods of particular strength, as at Caernarfon, for a time, when local free traders directed their own agitation and levied their own subscriptions to be deployed in local work. Even then, however, the bond with central authority remained tight through the presence of Griffith and frequent correspondence between the two tiers.

Wales's contribution to the A.C.L.L. was, therefore, a modest one. Arguably, what the League did for Wales was of greater significance. It provided a model in the application of techniques of political agitation. It also had a role in the development of political consciousness. In particular, its deliberate appeal to religious Dissent was of critical importance, and it was this which made the real impression in Wales; the height of the League's influence in the Principality coincided with its most fervent efforts to attract Dissenting support.

III

PARLIAMENTARY REFORM

I THE NATIONAL CHARTER ASSOCIATION

'We regret they [the Welsh Chartists] should have given vent to their feelings in the way they have, because it was in no way calculated to forward the cause of the People's Charter.'[1] Thus wrote a columnist in the Chartist *Western Vindicator* in the wake of the events at Newport on 3–4 November 1839; deficient in organization and discipline, though not in numbers and bravery, was the writer's verdict. And indeed, the rising did have detrimental effects on the movement, particularly in south Wales. The transportation and imprisonment of many Chartist activists did much to weaken the cause, while the experience, or the fear, of a rigorous gaol sentence may also have served to dampen ardour. Moreover, the numbers of troops, police and magistrates increased in south Wales and, frequently through the employment of spies, the authorities kept a close watch on, and impeded, radical activity. Mid Wales was similarly affected, as a local Chartist explained: '. . . with the troubles of that year—the violence, arrests, imprisonment, etc.—the people of Newtown, as in many other places, allowed the cause to lapse'.[2]

The strength and determination of the opposition were unmistakable. Lack of progress in the face of false hopes and exaggerated optimism was equally dispiriting. Inevitably, some left the movement in disillusionment while violence frightened away others. 'The Chartists are come', the cry of one agitated Abersychan observer on that eventful Sunday night, and the conveyed 'impression of something terrible and indescribable' echoed loud and long.[3] 'Terror and panic have seized the minds of the peaceably disposed population to an extent I could not have believed possible', wrote a correspondent from 'the Mining Districts' to Lord Bute.[4] Symptomatically, the inhabitants of the small market town

[1] *Western Vindicator*, 30 Nov. 1839.
[2] *Northern Star*, 29 Jan. 1842.
[3] *Western Mail*, 25 Jan. 1902.
[4] Bute Papers, xx, 73.

of Crickhowell, just off the major coalfield, speedily convened a public meeting to devise 'some means for the protection of life and property in the district'; as in other communities, large numbers of special constables were promptly sworn in.[5] By the early 1840s, the word 'Chartism' frequently evoked images of violence, bloodshed and revolution in the public mind. The *Welshman* in 1841 spoke of 'tens of thousands to whom the very name "Chartist" has hitherto been associated with madness, outrage and danger to the peace of society'.[6]

In the aftermath of the Newport March, the clergy denounced Chartist activities in sermon and in print. The Revd Evan Jenkins, vicar of Dowlais, led the attack but Nonconformists participated too.[7] 'The disturbance at Newport will be a lasting stain on our character. Welshmen, alas, condemned for high treason!', thundered Revd John Elias, the Calvinistic Methodist 'Pope'.[8] In some localities ministerial indignation was publicly demonstrated in exclusions from membership of their congregations, thereby inducing Chartist 'revenge and malice'.[9] The press also did much to align public opinion against the Chartist movement. Previously sympathetic newspapers like the *Silurian* and the *Cambrian* backed away while their Tory counterparts entered into fierce condemnation. 'With those lying incendiaries the Chartists ... we can hold no terms. Their creed is rebellion, their practice bloodshed, murder and confiscation', ran one typical, vitriolic outburst from the *Cardiff and Merthyr Guardian* in the early forties. Yet at the same time, lengthy periods of ignoring Chartist activities characterized the policy of this and other papers: 'The "bad preeminence" which our District has acquired by the numerous signatures contributed to the Chartists' petition, requires that we occasionally recur to the subject.'[10] Severe criticism also came from some of the Welsh-language periodicals. *Y Drysorfa*, the monthly

[5] *Silurian*, 30 Nov. 1839.
[6] *Welshman*, 22 Jan. 1841.
[7] Revd E. Jenkins, *Chartism Unmask'd* (1840). See also, D. Williams, *John Frost*, pp. 323–6; D. J. V. Jones, 'Chartism in Welsh communities', p. 243; idem, *The Last Rising*, pp. 223–4. At the same time, Anglicans sought to link the insurrection with Nonconformity, *Yr Haul*, for example, assailing its arch-enemy, *Y Diwygiwr*, for inciting agitation. See Revd J. Vyrnwy Morgan (ed.), *Welsh Religious Leaders in the Victorian Era* (1905), pp. 148–50.
[8] E. Morgan, *Valuable Letters, Essays and other Papers of the late Reverend John Elias of Anglesea* (Caernarfon, 1847), p. 196, cited by C. Turner, 'The Nonconformist response', in T. Herbert and G. E. Jones (eds.), *People and Protest: Wales 1815–1880* (Cardiff, 1988), p. 93.
[9] *A.B.T.C.*, 25 Aug. 1842.
[10] *Cardiff and Merthyr Guardian*, 27 Aug. 1842.

magazine of the Calvinistic Methodists, expressed sorrow that the poisonous principles and spirit of the movement should have found their way into 'peaceful Wales', while the Wesleyans, in the *Eurgrawn Wesleyaidd*, declared that the Chartist points were opposed to Christianity.[11] The Independents and Baptists were generally less disparaging. Nevertheless, *Y Diwygiwr*, reflecting on 'the sorrowful, deplorable and shameful events that have recently occurred', lamented in December 1839: '... our country has been stigmatised—our nation is in disgrace ... In Newport, in Wales, the stench of the destructive massacre has not dispersed and the awful desolation of civil war is evident.'[12] To this and other journals the futility of violence and the necessity for constitutional action had been tragically confirmed.

The Newport débâcle left Chartists in a quandary. 'We move morally, yet advance not! We move physically, and our motion becomes retrograde!', bemoaned the *Western Vindicator* in November 1839. 'Are we to sit quietly down, and relinquish our cause?', continued the editorial.[13] The response of some was swift and emphatic: 'they may oppress and load with chains the body, but the mind defy's them still, it scorns to be confined', wrote Charles Walters of Chepstow, from the custody of Monmouth Gaol in January 1840.[14] And indeed, if the popular support, participation and local organization of pre-Newport days were never matched again, Welsh Chartism persisted, albeit sometimes in small minorities, for a considerable number of years.

The survival is in part attributable to the role of the National Charter Association (N.C.A.), which was the dominant Chartist body during the forties and fifties. Founded in the summer of 1840 it sought to meet the movement's obvious need to make good its organizational inadequacies and provide co-ordination, unity and direction. There were several rival schemes in the offing, notably associated with 'Knowledge Chartism', 'Temperance Chartism' and 'Christian Chartism'. The N.C.A. concentrated purely on the six points, pursuing the objective through 'none but peaceable and constitutional means'. Early progress was

[11] *Y Drysorfa*, Feb.1840, p. 62; D. Williams, *John Frost*, pp. 325–6.
[12] *Y Diwygiwr*, Dec.1839, p. 365; see Glanmor Williams, *David Rees, Llanelli* (Cardiff, 1950), pp. 22–4.
[13] 'Desert not your incarcerated friends,' appealed the newspaper. 'Our counsel is—Organise! Organise! Organise!' *Western Vindicator*, 23 Nov.1839.
[14] Gwent Record Office, D/144 Misc. MS 234.

modest; only eighty-three branches took part in the executive election in June 1841. Nevertheless, despite discord and divisions, and leadership and organizational shortcomings, the Association gathered strength as journalists and lecturers unremittingly kept up their propaganda efforts; by the autumn of 1842 it claimed 401 branches and a total membership of around 50,000.[15]

The N.C.A. was formed at a conference of twenty-three delegates at Manchester in July 1840. David John, jun., the Merthyr blacksmith-journalist, was the single representative from Wales and he gave strong support to the new organization. Speaking on behalf of the Chartists of Merthyr, Aberdare, Pontypridd, Newport and Pontypool, he stated that his 'constituency' desired two things in particular: 'the establishment of a Central Board for the government of the whole, and the distribution of political tracts for the enlightenment of the people'.[16] Over the following months Chartist meetings in various parts of south Wales testified to the rejuvenation of the cause. Local organization was sluggish though; a list of 299 N.C.A. branches published in the *Northern Star* in December 1841 included only eight in Wales—at Aberdare, Abergavenny, Blackwood, Cardiff, Merthyr, Monmouth, Newport and Porthyglo (Pontypridd).[17] Others were apparently formed later in such places as Swansea, Morriston, Tredegar, Chepstow, Newtown, Llanidloes, Holywell and Mold. Largely inconspicuous pockets of Chartists, lacking formal organization, undoubtedly existed in other localities. Nevertheless, Morgan Williams's report to the Chartist Convention of April 1842 and the survey of N.C.A. secretary, John Campbell, a few months later pointed to the paucity of organized societies in Wales.[18] Welsh links with the N.C.A. were cemented by the election of Morgan Williams to the executive in June 1841, and again the following year. In these years there were also a large number of appointments from south-east Wales to the General Councils of the Association. Ties between the branches and the national executive were furnished by written correspondence, visits from appointed lecturers, delegate conferences and, critically, through the *Northern Star*. Relationships varied,

[15] See J. T. Ward, *Chartism* (1973), pp. 143–5.
[16] *Northern Star*, 25 July 1840.
[17] Ibid., 24 Dec. 1841.
[18] Ibid., 25 June, 9 July 1842; *Udgorn Cymru*, 18 June 1842.

however, and some Chartist societies no doubt had very tenuous links with the central administration. In late 1842 the Merthyr N.C.A. had ten wards, the strongest being at Georgetown, which had thirteen discussion classes. Each ward had a nominated collector to transmit money to the central treasurer.[19] No other Welsh area rivalled this depth of organization. N.C.A. branches took great pride in their democratic processes; the appointment of different chairmen at meetings and functions represented tangible expression of the democratic ideal. Policy decisions were the preserve of the total membership, though of course under the influence of national recommendations. In the early 1840s thriving N.C.A. branches met weekly or more frequently. Some, like those at Abergavenny and Monmouth, had their own rooms. In other places, public houses, beerhouses, schoolrooms or members' homes were used. Larger meetings took place in the open air or in the local hall, if permitted by its administrators, usually the town clerk. Branch meetings no doubt devoted a good deal of time to the collection of dues.[20] A large number of local associations paid little or nothing to central funds; the *Northern Star* frequently published lists of defaulting localities. Apart from financial business, branch activity might involve the reading aloud and discussion of correspondence and newspaper articles, both from radical journals like the *Northern Star* and from unfriendly publications like *The Times*, the *Bristol Mercury* and the *Monmouthshire Merlin*. Treatment by the respectable press was an abiding concern of Chartists; William Miles, a dismissed miner, even suggested that the Merthyr Association bring a libel action against *The Times*.[21] Discussion at meetings also centred on the raising and use of funds and on agitational progress and methods; periodically, there was the election of delegates and executive officials, locally and nationally. Special occasions brought formal celebration. Thus at a public dinner in Newtown in October 1843 in honour of the local radical, Thomas Powell, 'speeches were made, and democratic toasts, songs and recitations were given'.[22] Merthyr

[19] D. J. V. Jones, 'Chartism at Merthyr', p. 233; K. Strange, 'The condition of the working classes in Merthyr Tydfil, *circa* 1840–50' (University of Wales Ph.D. thesis, 1983), p. 421.
[20] HO 45/453, Chartist meetings on 16 and 23 July 1843 and specimen N.C.A. membership card.
[21] Ibid., Chartist meeting, 23 July 1843.
[22] *Northern Star*, 28 Oct.1843.

Chartists held an annual festival on Christmas Day to commemorate the initiation of their agitation. They remembered their heroes, too, celebrating the birthday of Thomas Paine, for example, while they buried their dead with full honours and a display of solidarity.[23]

In Merthyr, admission to branch meetings was by N.C.A. membership card only: the problem of spies remained a perennial one. The numbers present were therefore a reasonable estimate of association size, though fully paid-up memberships were quite another matter. In 1843 Merthyr attendances usually totalled between 250 and 300, though references were frequently made to the disappointing numbers attending, indicating higher figures a year or two previously. Elsewhere in Wales, membership would not have been comparable. Branch sizes varied and are difficult to pin-point, though scattered references afford some index. It seems that membership totals in most Welsh localities in 1842 were small, below fifty. Newport, Abergavenny, Pontypool, Swansea and Newtown probably exceeded this, with Aberdare and Merthyr being the largest. In January 1842 Aberdare had a total of 93 members; two months later it had increased to 120.[24] Numbers inevitably fluctuated widely over a period of time. Chartist support was, of course, always much broader than membership and subscription figures. Even the hostile *Cardiff and Merthyr Guardian* placed the Merthyr crowd greeting Morgan Williams's return from the 1842 Convention at 5–6,000.[25] At public meetings in 1843 the Merthyr N.C.A. could still attract an attendance of over 1,000. Similarly, the Newport and Abergavenny societies were gaining audiences of 600 and 250 respectively, at a time when paid-up memberships could be numbered in tens. Each Chartist society could therefore draw on a large body of adherents who would readily attend public meetings and sign petitions but who would be indisposed to make regular financial contributions and hold membership cards. At Pontypool many persons would not enrol apparently 'for fear their employers might know it, and they lose their work in consequence'.[26]

[23] Ibid., 6 Jan., 3 Feb.1844 (funeral of David John, jun.).

[24] Ibid., 15 Jan., 5 Mar. 1842; cf. Dorothy Thompson, *The Chartists* (1984), Appendix, pp. 341–68, figures for N.C.A. membership cards taken out in one year between 1839–42; Aberdare, 440; Merthyr, 1,100; Newport, 400.

[25] *Cardiff and Merthyr Guardian*, 14 May 1842.

[26] *National Vindicator*, 27 Nov. 1841.

The social composition of N.C.A. rank and file is difficult to ascertain. Study in industrial south Wales suggests the involvement of a broad section of trades and occupations,[27] although the substantial 'floating' support would no doubt include a significant proportion of miners, colliers and labourers. Local leadership is more easily distinguishable. Branch executives were dominated by tradesmen and shopkeepers with a sprinkling of professional men and some miners and labourers too. In 1841 prominent members of the Monmouth association included three shoemakers, a watchmaker, blacksmith, plasterer and labourer.[28] While it was essentially a working-class movement, the middle-class influence in Chartism is undeniable. The involvement of Nonconformist ministers contributed here. Men like Thomas Davies, the Merthyr Baptist, John Davies of Aberdare and Benjamin Byron of Newport, two Independents, and the Unitarians William Williams and John Jones, both of Aberdare, and David John, sen., of Merthyr strongly supported Chartism though they utterly rejected physical force. The affinity between Nonconformity and Welsh Chartism was displayed in other ways. Chartists founded chapels in south Wales, vehemently attacked the Anglican Church and employed biblical argument in their cause.[29]

Indeed, the Chartist survival was aided, in no small measure, by the breadth of interest of the activists. The police force, 'a useless body which was not wanted', was a common target.[30] The inhumanity of the New Poor Law aroused deep resentment. 'Unjust' industrial legislation like the Master and Servants Bill of 1844 was opposed; the Factories Bill of 1843, however, was acceptable 'as an instalment', Dissenters' protest meetings sometimes being overturned, as at Newtown.[31] Merthyr and Swansea Chartists were at the forefront of protest meetings in 1846 against the proposed revival of the militia. Welsh Chartists also took an interest in Irish affairs, supporting repeal of the Act of Union and denouncing coercive measures, and nationalist leaders visited

---

[27] A. V. John, 'The Chartist endurance', pp. 28–9; D. J. V. Jones, 'Chartism at Merthyr', pp. 235–6.

[28] *Northern Star*, 1 May 1841.

[29] See D. J. V. Jones, 'Chartism in Welsh communities', p. 253.

[30] *Cardiff and Merthyr Guardian*, 29 Jan.1842; see also D. J. V. Jones, 'Chartism at Merthyr', p. 239.

[31] *Northern Star*, 6 May 1843, 20 Apr. 1844; see also, A. V. John, op. cit., p. 27.

the Principality.[32] Parochial matters, like a desire to keep the price of meat down, were important too.[33]

Nevertheless, the six points were always the fundamental commitment. In this respect the preoccupations of N.C.A. branches revolved around winning as much popular support as possible and exploiting the various avenues of pressure open to non-electors. In the propaganda compaign, use of the printed word, and, in particular, of Chartism's own press, was obviously central. *Udgorn Cymru* and its sister paper, the *Advocate and Merthyr Free Press*, published by Morgan Williams and David John, jun., were two of many Chartist journals launched in Britain in these years. Combined circulations reached 1,500 a month at one stage; readership would have been considerably higher. Merthyr Chartists carried them around the town and into the public houses not only for sale but for public readings. The papers were subsidized by members of the local N.C.A.[34] Radical organs published in England circulated too. Henry Vincent's *National Vindicator* had agents in Newport, Merthyr, Pontypool and Monmouth.[35] But most influential was the *Northern Star*, controlled by the N.C.A.'s dominant figure, Feargus O'Connor. To many Chartists this was the oracle; the much-maligned George Cudlippe's interventions at public meetings in Swansea invariably involved lengthy readings from this source. Chartist tracts were also translated into the Welsh language and distributed.[36]

Equally vital in invigorating support was, of course, oratory. Speech-making and debate played a vital role in Chartist activities. Prominent local figures like William Edwards of Newport and George Williams of Cardiff lectured to various branches but Merthyr leaders proved the most prolific agents, frequently speaking in towns and villages in the area. Emissaries were even dispatched as far as north and west Wales, the latter particularly at the height of the Rebecca Riots in 1843. In September 1840 the N.C.A. provisional executive appointed Isaac Rogers of

[32] HO 45/453, fol. 23; *Monmouthshire Merlin*, 16 June 1843.
[33] NLW, Tredegar Park MSS, 71/139, H. J. Davis to Octavius Morgan, 9 June, 12 Oct. 1841.
[34] HO 45/54, fol. 19. *Udgorn Cymru* ran for forty issues, from March 1840 to October 1842, the *Advocate and Merthyr Free Press* for only five, from July to November 1840.
[35] *National Vindicator*, 18 Sept. 1841, 12 Feb. 1842.
[36] Miniken–Vincent MSS, Vin.1/1/23; see also, D. J. V. Jones, 'Chartism at Merthyr', p. 231, n.1.

Merthyr as missionary for south Wales.[37] The Principality was frequently visited by outside speakers, especially from Bristol and Bath: 'restless and designing strangers who inflicted so much injury in the country' in November 1839.[38]

Such visits could occasion displays of strength and vitality, as when Henry Vincent, 'an old and long-tried friend', lectured in Merthyr in June 1841. In the usual fashion, placards announcing the event had been posted around the town during the previous week and a rousing reception was arranged. A local newspaper report detailed the scene:

> The day came, hundreds of persons of every age and sex seemed as if anxiously expecting his entrance. Almost a quarter to four o'clock, a large procession of his friends, the Chartists, preceded by a band of music, moved off to the Taff Vale Railway Station-House, as it was expected Mr Vincent would arrive by the four o'clock train. The train arrived, bearing Mr Vincent, who was greeted with immense cheering, and was immediately handed to a car, in which several of the Chartist leaders were sitting. The procession moved through High Street (Mr Vincent standing the whole in the car), and was adorned by a tri-coloured flag, and banner, bearing Chartist inscriptions ...[39]

Sentiment had of course to be translated into pressure. Petitioning was a frequent if largely fruitless resort. 'They might as well petition the Rock of Gibraltar as the House of Commons', David John, jun., told the N.C.A. Convention of 1840.[40] And indeed, despite the collection of over 3,300,000 signatures the National Petition of 1842 was summarily dismissed by the Commons, by 287 votes to 49. Wales contributed over 48,000 names,[41] almost 22,000 emanating from Merthyr, a 'folly and wickedness' which the local newspaper found incomprehensible.[42] Beyond enactment of the six points, petition pleas varied. A recurrent theme of the decade, however, was the liberation of Frost, Williams and Jones. Many thousands of signatures were collected towards this cause

[37] Northern Star, 3 Oct.1840.
[38] Monmouthshire Merlin, 2 Jan.1841.
[39] Silurian, 12 June 1841.
[40] Northern Star, 25 July 1840.
[41] Ibid., 16, 23 Apr., 7 May 1842; Udgorn Cymru, 23 Apr. 1842. For a breakdown of the signatures, see A. V. John, op. cit., p. 27, note 20.
[42] Cardiff and Merthyr Guardian, 14 May, 3 Sept. 1842.

which increasingly attracted a broader section of local communities.[43] In March 1846, for example, petitions were presented
to Parliament from Newport Town Council and from Abergavenny containing half of the jurymen who had originally con-
victed the three.[44] Chartist associations displayed banners bearing
painted likenesses and meetings frequently ended with cheers for
the 'Exiled Patriots'.

A less orthodox but endemic form of N.C.A. agitation was interference in public meetings, to 'enforce a discussion of our rights
and claims, so that none may remain in ignorance of what we
want, nor have an opportunity of propagating or perpetrating
political ignorance and delusion'.[45] Anti-Corn Law functions were
a frequent target but varied gatherings were assailed. Welsh Chartists were active in late 1841, for example, intervening in meetings
celebrating the recent birth of the Prince of Wales.[46] The conversion of meetings into Chartist rallies furnished a demonstration
of strength but it is difficult to see any deeper value; indeed, sabo-
tage of this kind must have embittered sections of public opinion.

'. . . Wherever convenient and practicable . . . forward Chartist
candidates at every election', ran one of the 'Means for the Attainment of the Great End' agreed by the founding delegates of the
N.C.A. at Manchester in July 1840.[47] And indeed, at the 1841
general election there were two Chartist candidatures in Wales,
at Merthyr and in the Monmouth Boroughs. Since few Chartists
could vote, a contest was futile, but participation allowed a display
of numerical strength and the propagation of principles at the
hustings. These aims were achieved at Merthyr, Morgan Williams
triumphing over Sir Josiah John Guest on a show of hands, declining to go to a poll and withdrawing.[48] In the Monmouth Boroughs,

---

[43] See, for example, ibid., 17 Aug. 1844; also, A. V. John, op. cit., p. 26.
[44] *Hansard*, LXXXIV, col. 868, 10 Mar. 1846 (T. S. Duncombe).
[45] *Northern Star*, 1 Aug. 1840.
[46] Ibid., 27 Nov. 1841; *Monmouthshire Merlin*, 20, 27 Nov., 25 Dec. 1841; *National Vindicator*, 4 Dec. 1841.
[47] *Northern Star*, 1 Aug. 1840.
[48] *Cambrian*, 2 July 1841; Earl of Bessborough (ed.), *Lady Charlotte Guest: Extracts from her Journals, 1833–52* (1950), pp. 121–4. Six years earlier, in the 1835 election, Morgan Williams had been 'the architect' of Guest's victory over the Tory solicitor, William Meyrick. See Gwyn A. Williams, 'The Merthyr election of 1835', *Welsh History Review*, 10, No. 3 (June 1981). But subsequent events showed that 'he was not what he then professed to be — a friend of the people' (*Cardiff and Merthyr Guardian*, 3 July 1841). For Morgan Williams, see *Dictionary of Welsh Biography down to 1940* (1959), p. 1059.

however, Chartist involvement was badly bungled and counter-productive. Uncertainty over the choice of Chartist candidate, whether William Edwards, the Newport radical, or the remarkable Dr William Price of Pontypridd, brought confusion at the Monmouth hustings and bitter recrimination afterwards. In the evening, rival Chartist factions burnt effigies of leading actors in the drama and houses were attacked in Newport. Troops were called out at midnight to restore order. The result of the poll conducted a few days later compounded the fiasco; R. J. Blewitt 476 votes, W. Edwards nil. The whole episode invited ridicule.[49]

In the weeks before the election, the Newport N.C.A. branch had written to Blewitt to invite him to explain his parliamentary conduct to one of their meetings. Such challenges were rarely accepted and clearly there were limits to the degree that parliamentary candidates could be pressurized by non-electors. But Newport Chartists seemingly had some success. In supporting the complete suffrage motion in the Commons in April 1842, Blewitt announced that he was doing his 'duty to a large body of constituents who have sought me out'.[50] Electoral pressure also involved questioning candidates at the hustings, as George Cudlippe, the Swansea Chartist, did to John Henry Vivian in 1847.[51] Local politics offered distinct possibilities and Chartists at Merthyr, Newport, Swansea and elsewhere influenced and acquired posts in local government.[52]

Exclusive dealing was another legitimate method of pressure, though this was sometimes backed by intimidation. In late 1843, for example, Merthyr Chartist leaders determined upon reprisals following the trials of Rebeccaites in Cardiff. David Ellis told the 300 or so members assembled at the Three Horse Shoes Inn in early November that 'no one should buy any article whatsoever from any of the jurymen for twenty years—this is the period John Hughes, the Rebecca leader, was transported for'. The Council of the Merthyr N.C.A. subsequently issued a list of blacklisted

[49] *Silurian*, 3 July 1841; *Cambrian*, 9 July 1841; *Northern Star*, 13 Aug. 1841; *Monmouthshire Merlin*, 3, 10, 17 July 1841; *Monmouthshire Advertiser*, 3 July 1841; see also, D. Williams, *John Frost*, pp. 329–30.
[50] NLW, Tredegar Park MSS, 57/282; *Hansard*, LXII, col. 982, 21 Apr. 1842.
[51] *Cambrian*, 30 July 1847; *Swansea and Glamorgan Herald*, 4 Aug.1847. 'I see this will be a one-sided Parliament, a rich man's Parliament', was Cudlippe's retort on failing to gain a hearing.
[52] See A. V. John, op. cit., p. 37.

shopkeepers in the area and circulated leaflets threatening to 'scotch any one' who bought goods from these men.[53] Similarly, a response to the desperate distress of 1841 was to fix a maximum price on meat (on veal, mutton and lamb) and the issue of threats to transgressors apparently secured effectiveness.[54]

Economic hardship, embittered by the threat of wage reductions, initiated a wave of strikes in Staffordshire and Lancashire in August 1842. Chartist leaders did not originate the so-called 'plug plot' but as it spread they sought to take advantage. Merthyr and Aberdare Chartists jointly agreed to go on strike 'until the Charter became the law of the land'.[55] This seems to have been the only area of support in Wales; unsuccessful overtures were apparently made from Merthyr to the Ebbw valley.[56] Lacking leadership and unity and encountering speedy and harsh action by the authorities, the general strike quickly collapsed at a local and national level. Chartists were widely victimized. The *Cardiff and Merthyr Guardian* reported that upwards of a hundred well-known Chartists were discharged from ironworks in the neighbourhood, many of whom subsequently paraded the streets 'with placards in their hats, soliciting alms'; the inscriptions read: 'In England, a free and Christian country, we are turned out to starve, for being Chartists.'[57]

A division between moral- and physical-force Chartism can be a misleading simplification. Activists often moved between the camps, reacting to events. Nevertheless, at times, debate within Chartist associations inevitably centred on the question of constitutional or violent action. In the early forties there was evidence of the collection of arms in several parts of the coalfield and another rising was feared.[58] A physical-force faction had always existed among Merthyr and Aberdare Chartists; certainly the fact that participation from this area in the Newport March of 1839 was

[53] HO 45/453, Col. Love to Home Office, 18 Nov. 1843. The Chartist Association was in communication with the Rebeccaite solicitor, the Chartist Hugh Williams, at this time.
[54] Bute Papers, XX, 164.
[55] *Silurian*, 27 Aug. 1842.
[56] Bute Papers, XXII, 20.
[57] *Cardiff and Merthyr Guardian*, 10 Sept.1842; see also, D. J. V. Jones, 'Chartism at Merthyr', p. 232; and Walter T. Morgan, 'Chartism and industrial unrest in south Wales in 1842', *National Library of Wales Journal*, X, No.1, (1957), pp. 12-16.
[58] D. Williams, 'Chartism in Wales', p. 243.

limited cannot be adequately explained as a rejection of revolutionary action.[59] The period following the collapse of the August
1842 strike brought increased support for armed rebellion among
Merthyr Chartists with disillusioned leaders such as William Miles,
Matthew and David John, jun., and David Ellis evidently moving
in this direction. The reports of spies, albeit somewhat alarmist,
testified to this.[60] At the same time, moderates led by Morgan
Williams, long the epitome of moral force, and William Gould
continued to reject this strategy and there was talk of Merthyr
Chartists splitting into two associations. During the years 1842–3
arms clubs were formed in the area and there were rumours of
an insurrection. It did not occur, the difficulties and the risk presu-
mably being too great, but the situation was threatening enough
in November 1842 for Feargus O'Connor to warn Merthyr Chartists against a repeat of the Newport affair.[61] He was similarly
anxious the following year that Welsh Chartists should not become
involved in the Rebecca Riots, something which certainly had
its advocates within the Merthyr Association.[62] O'Connor gained
assurances that Merthyr and Swansea Chartists would have
nothing to do with the rioting; he then strenuously repudiated
any connection with Rebecca in the columns of the *Northern Star*
and apparently chose not to tour south Wales as he had intended,
fearing accusations of collaboration.[63]

Much local N.C.A. activity was, of course, a response to national
events. The existence and operations of the other great pressure
organization of the day, the A.C.L.L., were an important aspect
here and Chartist societies, and individuals within societies, reacted
differently. The views of national Chartist leaders on free trade
and the League varied considerably and were sometimes inconsis-
tent.[64] Feargus O'Connor and John Campbell, the N.C.A. secretary, led a minority party in advancing standard protectionist arguments against repeal, contending in particular that low wages
would be the inevitable consequence. A more popular faction

---

[59] D. J. V. Jones, *The Last Rising*, p. 117.
[60] For a detailed discussion, see idem, 'Chartism in Merthyr'.
[61] Idem, *The Last Rising*, p. 220. Physical force remained very much a weapon in industrial disputes on the coalfield in the 1840s and 1850s.
[62] D. Williams, 'Chartism in Wales', pp. 245–6; idem, *The Rebecca Riots*, pp. 150–2.
[63] *Northern Star*, 12, 19 Aug. 1843.
[64] For a full discussion of this theme, see Lucy Brown, 'Chartism and the Anti-Corn Law League', in Asa Briggs, *Chartist Studies*, pp. 342–71.

condemned the League as a rival diversionary movement. While holding repeal sympathies, these Chartists saw their own programme as paramount. Many, like Bronterre O'Brien, believed that under the existing political and social system repeal would be at best ineffectual, at worst injurious to working men, while a most powerful determinant was mistrust, even repugnance, of manufacturers who dominated the A.C.L.L.

At a provincial level, attitudes were similarly equivocal, a theme seized upon by Chartist adversaries like the *Cardiff and Merthyr Guardian*.[65] A small number of Welsh Chartists in Merthyr, Newport and elsewhere strongly disputed the supposed benefits of repeal. At the hustings in Merthyr in 1841 Morgan Williams poured scorn on his opponent's advocacy of abolition of the Corn Laws: 'cheap bread meant cheap labour ... they [employers] would lower the wages of workmen to meet the lowered price of corn.' He continued in protectionist vein: '... free trade was all a fallacy ... The French made gloves which could be sold in London at a cheaper rate than the English could do it, and the consequence was that the English glovers were starving while the French were well employed.'[66]

On the other hand, radical leaders in south Wales had long denounced the injustice of the Corn Laws and thousands of Merthyr workmen, for example, had signed repeal petitions in the early 1830s.[67] Thus, some Chartists like Thomas Griffiths, secretary of the Abergavenny N.C.A. branch, threw themselves wholeheartedly into the repeal agitation and became paid League agents. Elsewhere, too, there is evidence of compromise between Chartists and Leaguers. But most Welsh Chartists fiercely insisted that the six points were the real answer to their grievances. Any other reforms were peripheral and thus undesirable diversions.[68] In 1839 Newport Chartists argued that, though the Corn Laws were 'unjust and iniquitous', without universal suffrage 'there can

[65] *Cardiff and Merthyr Guardian*, 14 Feb. 1842.
[66] Ibid., 3 July 1841. During the election one north Monmouthshire observer noted the lack of 'any excitement whatever respecting "cheap bread"', which 'does not form even a topic of conversation'. NLW, Tredegar Park Muniments, H. J. Davies to Octavius Morgan, 25 May 1841.
[67] G. A. Williams, 'The making of radical Merthyr, 1800–36', pp. 174–5; A. H. John, *The Industrial Development of South Wales*, p. 93.
[68] Merthyr Chartists were urged 'not to be led away with any Corn-Law repealers or any such thing but stick to the Charter alone'. D. J. V. Jones, 'Chartism at Merthyr', p. 240.

be no amelioration of the condition of the people ... there would be more suffering than at present'.[69] Committed repealers in the Merthyr Chartist leadership, like David John, jun., and David Ellis, apparently toed this line. Some found it an inappropriate stance to sustain. Thus John Dickenson of Newport argued in 1841 that Corn Law modification or abolition would 'prove a good wedge for the Charter' whereas two years earlier, as he seconded a Chartist amendment at an anti-Corn Law meeting, the repeal agitation had been 'a delusion'.[70]

The experiences of the A.C.L.L. lecturer Walter Griffith in Chartist strongholds are illuminating. At Llanidloes in September 1840 local Chartists granted him a fair hearing but subsequently pronounced that the Charter was more relevant to their needs: 'The chartists behaved themselves well. They all supported me quietly, but at the same time they thought chartism *better*.'[71] Further south, his reception was far less agreeable. His Swansea lecture was constantly interrupted,[72] while in the Merthyr-Aberdare area, so entirely and aggressively did Chartists reject his efforts to expound repeal, that Griffith decided against holding a meeting for fear of disturbance, limiting his activities to distributing tracts (where they would be accepted) with a view to returning at a future date.[73] These fears were confirmed when two years later he revisited Merthyr and his lecture was 'captured' by the Chartists.[74] Attempts by Independent ministers to hold repeal meetings in north Monmouthshire in the summer of 1841 were regularly balked by Chartist infiltrators.[75] Anti-Corn Law functions were also disturbed by Chartists in such places as Newport, Sirhowy and Blackwood.[76]

---

[69] *Monmouthshire Merlin*, 16 Feb. 1839. A League activist from Morriston recalled that though the working classes wanted cheap bread they considered other reforms 'paramount' and believed the repeal movement to be of an 'interested character'; thus 'the bona-fide working man always held aloof'. *Labour Standard*, 16 July 1881.

[70] *Monmouthshire Merlin*, 16 Feb. 1839, 12 June 1841.

[71] A.C.L.L., L.B., 5, 722, Walter Griffith to Ballantyne, 6 Sept. 1840.

[72] *A.C.L.C.*, 8 Oct 1840. At Swansea, George Cudlippe consistently proposed Chartist amendments at League meetings, in spite of their unpopularity. *Monmouthshire Merlin*, 12 June 1841; *Cambrian*, 22 Apr. 1843.

[73] A.C.L.L., L.B., 5, 750, Walter Griffith to Ballantyne, 17 Oct. 1840. 'We'll have nothing at all to do with your repeal question', the lecturer was sharply told. Ibid., 742, 14 Oct. 1840.

[74] *A.B.T.C.*, 27 Dec. 1842; *Cambrian*, 30 Dec. 1842.

[75] *A.B.T.C.*, 25 Aug. 1842. '... they opposed us with all their might, disturbing our meetings most shamefully.'

[76] T. H. Williams, 'Wales and the Corn Laws', Vol. III, p. 28; *Silurian*, 23 Feb. 1839.

The frequency and vehemence of the clashes greatly diminished after 1843, as Chartist strength declined and the League's campaign continued inexorably. Moreover, the League could call upon its formidable organization, expertise and financial resources to attack vacillating Chartist attitudes. It was certainly not difficult to strike at the protectionist elements and O'Connor was frequently taunted as the upholder of monopoly, an accusation not easily refuted, as he found in his celebrated open debate with Richard Cobden in 1844. By 1845 the Irishman had made an about-turn on the issue and the December Chartist Conference officially dropped hostility to repeal. Yet, certainly in Wales, this marked no great victory for the A.C.L.L. over the N.C.A. While gaining some genuine working-class support, it did not win substantial numbers of the industrial workers of mid and south Wales over from Chartism. In April 1843 when an A.C.L.L. lecture by John Jenkins was held in Merthyr's Market Square, Chartists sought to disrupt it by convening a counter-meeting in the same place.[77] At Newtown, as late as April 1844, Chartists seized a repeal meeting addressed by J. J. Finnigan, one of the two able working men specifically appointed by the League to counter Chartist opposition.[78] Later in the same year a Chartist public meeting in Merthyr was still being told that the free trader was 'the greatest enemy of the working man'.[79] Even in February 1846, with local Chartist leaders Matthew John, William Gould and David Ellis now openly advocating repeal, John Jenkins had to rebuff 'insinuations directed against the League'.[80] Chartist suspicion of the middle-class-dominated A.C.L.L. was rarely absent.

'THE WELCH CHARTISTS. Where are they? What are they doing? Are they still alive?' asked the *Northern Star* in June 1843.[81] And indeed, most Welsh N.C.A. branches evidently had a transient existence in the forties. 'After a long slumber Chartism has again

---

[77] *Cardiff and Merthyr Guardian*, 29 Apr. 1843; *Silurian*, 29 Apr. 1843. Anti-Corn Law petitions comprising almost 7,000 signatures from Merthyr and Dowlais followed. *Cambrian*, 12 May 1843; cf. a petition of 10,640 from Merthyr the following year calling for the Charter and a pardon for Frost, Williams, and Jones. *Cardiff and Merthyr Guardian*, 17 Aug. 1844.
[78] *Shrewsbury News*, 13 Apr. 1844; N. McCord, *The Anti-Corn Law League*, p. 73.
[79] *Monmouthshire Merlin*, 20 July 1844.
[80] *Cambrian*, 13 Feb. 1846. On tactical grounds these Chartists now spoke out against insisting upon immediate and total repeal, accepting Peel's more cautious plan, 'lest the abolition of the Corn Laws be deferred ten or twelve years and lest the useless Whigs be returned to power'. *Silurian*, 14 Feb. 1846. See also, N. McCord, op. cit., pp. 200-2.
[81] *Northern Star*, 3 June 1843.

reared its giant form in the aristocratic district of Pontypool', reported the *National Vindicator* in November 1841.[82] In mid Wales the National Petition of 1842 inspired a reawakening: 'Recently ... a few friends whose souls burned within them at seeing the apathy of the people have stirred themselves into a revivalist action ...'[83] Such references to impermanence are common. Even in Merthyr, a Chartist public meeting in July 1844 was told: 'There are some who think that Chartism is dead, and who sneeringly ask what has become of its agitation. If they think that Chartism is dead they are greatly mistaken, the overheated minds and exciting enthusiasm have, it is true, subsided, but they have given way to calmer, more enlightened and determined feelings ...'[84] In some localities, Merthyr most obviously, organized Chartism had a continuity; elsewhere it lapsed into obscurity in the middle years of the decade. Nevertheless, if formal Chartist associations expired, the spirit and ideology of the movement among minority groups survived. The Education Commissioners of 1847 reported the existence of societies and secret clubs at Llanidloes and Newtown for teaching and discussing the theories of Paine, Volney, Owen and Carlile; newspapers and publications, propounding 'infidel and seditious principles', were widely read too.[85] Political agitation and 'the spirit which engendered and fed the onslaught on Newport' also remained a force in the industrial areas of Monmouthshire and Glamorgan. In July 1844 a lieutenant in south Wales noted that the district appeared in a quiet state 'but no one can answer ... that the Chartists are really tranquil'.[86]

In the mid 1840s the Chartist movement took a new direction, the O'Connor-inspired land scheme seeking to tackle the sufferings of the new industrial society by settling operatives on smallholdings. A number of estates were purchased and in total over £100,000 was subscribed by 70,000 members. But by the middle

---

[82] *National Vindicator*, 27 Nov. 1841.
[83] *Northern Star*, 29 Jan. 1842.
[84] *Monmouthshire Merlin*, 20 July 1844.
[85] *PP*, 1847, XXVII, *Report of the Commissioners of Inquiry into the State of Education in Wales*, pp. 533–4.
[86] HO 45/642.

of 1848 only 250 operatives had been settled and, beset by conti-
nual financial problems, the enterprise collapsed.[87] Merthyr
proved the most ready and ardent source of support for the scheme
in Wales. As early as August 1843 David Thomas had urged
upon an N.C.A. meeting in the town 'the necessity for the people
to return to the land'.[88] A branch was formed in Merthyr in
1845; later two more were added. Welsh branches were categor-
ized under the Merthyr District and in 1847 included Buckley,
Cardiff, Chepstow, Garndiffaith, Llanelli, Monmouth, Newport,
New Radnor, Swansea, and Tredegar as well as Merthyr itself.
Societies were subsequently set up in a number of other centres
while there were Land Company shareholders elsewhere too.[89]
Evidently, the plan evoked its greatest response on the rim of
the coalfields. Support from Wales reached its peak in 1848 when
a sum of over £172 in shares and expenses was subscribed;
Merthyr provided almost £76 of this figure. The rapid decline
in the Company's fortunes was mirrored in the Welsh contribution
of only £35 in the following year. Several Merthyr shareholders
and a Monmouth man were successful in acquiring allotments
under the scheme.[90]

The participation of local N.C.A. members in Land Company
branches was a predictable one, though the degree of this involvement is not wholly clear. Certainly the activities of land societies
portrayed many of the features of local Chartist associations. Standard radical works on agriculture by Cobbett and O'Connor were
read and discussed. Meetings were also addressed by occasional
visiting lecturers and Merthyr men once more acted as missionaries. Representatives from Merthyr and Chepstow visited the
various estates and returned with glowing reports. Land societies
inevitably acted as centres for political discussion too and Chartist
business may well have been conducted at meetings.[91] In Merthyr

[87] For a detailed discussion, see J. MacAskill, 'The Chartist Land Plan', in A. Briggs
(ed.), op. cit.; A. M. Hadfield, *The Chartist Land Company* (Newton Abbot, 1970); W. H.
G. Armytage, 'The Chartist Land Colonies, 1846–8', in *Agricultural History*, 32 (1958);
J. Saville's edition of R. G. Gammage, *History of the Chartist Movement* (1969), pp. 48–62.
[88] *Northern Star*, 19 Aug. 1843.
[89] Local branches, or at least Company members, at Abergavenny, Blaina, Brecon, Dowlais, Ebbw Vale, Llanidloes, Llantwit Fardre, Melingriffith, Mold, Montgomery, Neath,
Newbridge, Newtown, and Raglan. See Dorothy Thompson, *The Chartists*, Appendix, pp.
341–68.
[90] For more details on these points, see A. V. John, op. cit., pp. 31–3.
[91] See, e.g., *Principality*, 21 Sept. 1847.

in 1848 there were distinct Chartist and land organizations but on occasions they held joint meetings and co-operated in political action.[92] At the same time there seems to have been a considerable amount of membership overlap in Wales.[93] For example, prominent Land Company supporters like John Williams, the Newport sailmaker, Thomas C. Ingram, the Abergavenny shopkeeper, and David Morgan, the Merthyr mason, had earlier been involved in local N.C.A. activities—in 1847 Morgan was secretary of the Merthyr District of the Land Company, having previously served as secretary of the N.C.A. For a time, the attentions of many Chartist supporters were diverted away from politics. But far from acting as a damaging distraction the adventure provided a timely boost to waning Chartist fortunes, particularly in organizational terms, local N.C.A.s often having lapsed into inactivity. The increased circulation of the *Northern Star* was symptomatic of a widespread invigoration. In many areas old enthusiasms were rekindled and redirected.

In 1847–8 economic crisis at home and revolution abroad were the most potent factors behind the stirring, though short-lived, revival of Chartism in its purely political aspect. In Wales, as elsewhere, die-hards, supplemented by younger converts, surfaced 'to unfurl the Chartist flag again', often after a lengthy period of quiescence. Meetings were held in a number of places including Merthyr, Newport, Swansea, Monmouth, and Menai Bridge in support of the third National Petition. N.C.A. branches were certainly reorganized at Merthyr, Newport, and Swansea and possibly elsewhere too.[94] A committee was formed and a subscription fund launched at Menai Bridge where the local magistrates and clergy used 'every means' to stop the movement.[95] Indeed, activists everywhere met opposition, the respectable press rarely being sympathetic. The *Swansea and Glamorgan Herald*, under the editorship of ex-A.C.L.L. agent, John Jenkins, though passionately advocating a secret ballot agitation, spurned Chartism, censuring Parliament

[92] *Northern Star*, 1 Apr., 20 May 1848. One of the land branches named Emmett's Brigade indicates a strong Irish influence and indeed Merthyr Chartists called for repeal of the union of Britain and Ireland. *Cardiff and Merthyr Guardian*, 15 Apr. 1848; *Swansea and Glamorgan Herald*, 12 Apr. 1848.

[93] See A. V. John, op. cit., pp. 32–3.

[94] *Northern Star*, 18 Mar., 8 Apr., 13 May 1848; *Principality*, 28 Mar., 28 Apr. 1848; *Cambrian*, 28 May 1848.

[95] *Northern Star*, 8 Apr., 1 July 1848. The initiative for Chartist activity may well have been the outside influence of contract workmen constructing the new railway bridge.

for 'tossing the Chartists into unmerited importance'.[96] The *Cardiff and Merthyr Guardian* was predictably abusive, referring to 'seditious ragamuffins, demagogues and spouters of treason',[97] while the *Cambrian* also spoke of 'the venom of demagogues'.[98] There was less explicit disparagement too; thus, for example, Merthyr Chartists reportedly dispersed 'to test the strength of Barclay and Perkin's stout'.[99] Forthright support was voiced by the recently founded but short-lived *Principality*, which viewed enactment of the Charter as the best insurance against violence, and 'the safety valve of the nation'.[100]

Merthyr once more emerged at the forefront of the Welsh movement. 'The Republic for France and the Charter for England', headlined their placards.[101] At one time meetings were being held nightly and the town supplied the only delegate from Wales, David Thomas, a cooper, to the Chartist Convention in London in April. Old activities were resumed. Subscriptions to the N.C.A. recommenced, lectures were delivered by men like William Gould, the Merthyr grocer, and J. W. Manning, the Cardiff tailor. Chartist missionaries from England addressed meetings in Merthyr, Swansea, and Newport. George Cudlippe, the Swansea stalwart, 'strutted the streets' for hours on end, urging the people to support the cause. The old spirit was rekindled too, manifested in a Chartist amendment at a Merthyr public meeting to congratulate the Queen on childbirth. Local Chartists began to put restrictive dealing into practice again, shunning those shopkeepers who did not support the movement. In some cases, retribution, dismissal from employment for Chartist activity, was apparently again the price.[102]

At a national level, the summer months of 1848 were characterized by Chartist indecision on whether to resort to violence and fear of such an occurrence by the public at large, features whose interplay caused much uncertainty and misrepresentation. On no

---

[96] *Swansea and Glamorgan Herald*, 22 Mar. 1848.
[97] *Cardiff and Merthyr Guardian*, 22 Apr. 1848, quoted in A. V. John, op. cit., p. 33.
[98] *Cambrian*, 28 Apr. 1848.
[99] Ibid., 24 Mar. 1848. 'The Press is the enemy of the working classes', declared Swansea Chartists. Ibid., 28 Apr. 1848.
[100] *Principality*, 14 Apr., 7 June 1848.
[101] *Swansea and Glamorgan Herald*, 22 Mar. 1848.
[102] *Northern Star*, 1, 8, 15 Apr., 20 May, 17 June 1848; *Principality*, 28 Apr. 1848; *Cambrian*, 21, 28 Apr., 5 May 1848; *Cardiff and Merthyr Guardian*, 22, 29 Apr. 1848; *Swansea and Glamorgan Herald*, 17 May 1848; HO 40/59, fol. 301.

occasion was this truer than at the Kennington Common mass meeting of 10 April, a peaceful demonstration but widely depicted as the raising of the revolutionary flag. On the eve of the event a fearful young Aberaeron chemist recorded his prayer that the 'Lord will keep our land from the horrors of insurrection and bloodshed which at present extends throughout the continent'.[103]

There was fear of insurgence in south Wales, too, and alarmist letters were sent to the Home Office. A correspondent from Swansea cited 'a house in Gardner Street in this Town, the common rendezvous of the Chartists and the resort of characters of the worst description' as a hive of seditious activity. In particular, Cudlippe was inciting the lower orders 'to acts of mischief' and needed to be vigilantly watched.[104] Indeed, the authorities were alive to possible disorder. On Home Office advice the mayor of Newport rejected a requisition for a public meeting supporting the National Petition. The resurgence of Chartism in Merthyr was accompanied by the swearing in of special constables, the military being put on standby and the presence of police, spies and magistrates at local meetings.[105]

No serious outbreak of violence occurred in Wales at this time. Yet there was tension. Merthyr's David Thomas told the National Convention that 'his constituents had desired him to remain until the Charter was gained ... and although they were moral force men now they would soon be converted to physical force men'.[106] Evidently, local leaders were sometimes stretched in keeping members and the loose following in check. Dissentients at Merthyr sometimes called their own meetings, the 'official leadership' consisting of men like William Gould, Matthew John, and Henry Thomas (apparently a sworn constable in these months) dissociating themselves from the proceedings. Accordingly, the *Cardiff and Merthyr Guardian* drew a distinction between 'the leaders of the more respectable and better conducted advocates of the People's Charter' and 'the lower order Chartists of Chinatown' ('the celestial empire').[107]

---

[103] NLW, Olive Mary Jones Collection, Diary of William Griffith, 1847–58, 4 Apr. 1848.

[104] HO 40/59, fol. 301. The writer urged confidentiality; if the communication were to become public knowledge, 'I should not consider my person safe for a single hour'.

[105] *Northern Star*, 1, 8 Apr. 1848; *Principality*, 14 Apr. 1848; *Swansea and Glamorgan Herald*, 12 Apr. 1848; HO 41/19, fol. 89.

[106] *Northern Star*, 8 Apr. 1848.

[107] *Cardiff and Merthyr Guardian*, 17 June 1848.

In 1848–9 the issue of relations with the middle class once again came to the fore. Chartists sought middle-class assistance but with little success. Frustration was inevitable; thus George Morgan, stone-cutter and prominent Merthyr N.C.A. member, urged intimidation to 'compel the middle classes to register their votes in favour of the Charter'.[108] At the same time, radical MP Joseph Hume's 'Little Charter' was dividing Chartists. This proposed household suffrage, the secret ballot, equal electoral districts and triennial Parliaments. Merthyr Chartists fiercely opposed any compromise: 'Nothing short of the whole hog, bristles and all will satisfy us ... several attempts within the last four or five months to introduce a 3-legged animal to us ... found us determined to manfully oppose the trash.'[109] Elsewhere, however, Welsh Chartists were prepared to make concessions. At a Newport reform meeting, veteran campaigner William Edwards supported Hume's programme 'as half a loaf was better than none' and the local newspaper praised the large number of Chartists present for not throwing 'any impediment in the way of business'.[110]

The year 1848 saw renewed Chartist hopes followed by mounting exasperation, particularly after the rejection of the National Petition in April. This brought insurrectionary plotting and disturbances in some parts of the country accompanied by resolute government action; by the autumn many leaders had been arrested. These months sealed the reality, that Chartism as a genuine national force was dead. At a local level, many associations clearly folded amidst the widespread disillusionment. In Wales, organized Chartism, which had reappeared only on a limited scale in 1848, certainly did not have a prolonged, continuous existence. Probably in Merthyr alone did local N.C.A. activity extend beyond a matter of months at that time. Nevertheless, the movement in Wales, as in other regions, survived among resilient knots of partisans throughout the following decade.

II THE COMPLETE SUFFRAGE UNION

Most study of pressure group politics in the early 1840s has inevitably concentrated on the operations of the A.C.L.L. and the

---

[108] Ibid., 25 Mar., 22 Apr. 1848.
[109] *Northern Star*, 2 June 1849, quoted in A. V. John, op. cit., p. 34.
[110] *Monmouthshire Merlin*, 17 June 1848.

N.C.A. The former was dominated by middle-class liberals and businessmen, while Chartism, though subject to important middle-class influence, was closely identified with the working class. The National Complete Suffrage Union (C.S.U.) sought to reconcile the two classes in a campaign for the democratic demands of the Chartists, from which repeal of the Corn Laws would follow. In the words of one of its founders, Revd Edward Miall, editor of the *Nonconformist*, the foremost newspaper of radical Dissent, the aim was 'the fusion of all the more orderly and progressive workers of the Anti-Corn Law League with the moral force Chartists for political rights'.[111]

The C.S.U. was an offshoot of the A.C.L.L., the prime mover being Joseph Sturge, a Birmingham corn merchant and prominent Leaguer. Following disappointments at the general election of mid 1841, he became increasingly disturbed about the League's future prospects, disputing its ability to achieve repeal under the existing electoral system. He found an influential ally in Edward Miall who, at this time, was expounding complete suffrage principles in the *Nonconformist*, in a series of articles entitled 'Reconciliation of the Middle and Working Classes'. In organizational terms the movement originated at the Manchester Anti-Corn Law Convention of November 1841, when Sturge initiated a discussion on the 'essentially unsound condition of our representative system' and invited delegates to sign 'the Sturge Declaration', a manifesto calling for a 'full, fair and free exercise of the elective franchise'. A number of the signatories went on to form the Birmingham C.S.U. which, at a delegate conference in April 1842, developed into a national body campaigning for the six points of the Charter. Objects and rules were promptly published, tracts issued, public meetings held, lecturers dispatched to the provinces and the *Nonconformist* officially adopted as the movement's organ. Arrangements were also made for establishing branch associations. At the founding conference it was reported that fifty or sixty were in the process of formation; fifty-one localities were actually represented at the gathering. The number of branches increased during

[111] A. Miall, *Life of Edward Miall* (1884), p. 84.

the remainder of the year, though they probably never numbered more than a hundred.[112]

In Wales, complete suffrage won its most favourable reception from the Nonconformist press. To periodicals such as *Y Dysgedydd*, *Y Diwygiwr* and *Seren Gomer* it should be the single aim of public agitation, a prerequisite for other reforms:

> If you wish for effective reform in state and church—if you wish to lessen the taxes—if you wish for good order in the colonies—if you wish to annihilate war and promote peace—if you wish for educational progress for the nation—if you wish for free trade—if you wish for support for the aged—and if you wish to save the kingdom from destruction, you must form branches of, and support the principles of, the Complete Suffrage Union, and not rest until its attainment.[113]

Such sympathy, however, was not translated into widespread organized support. Indeed, on its own acknowledgement, the central executive did 'scarcely anything ... to advance the cause' in Wales despite its view that 'a large amount of democratic opinion pervades the country',[114] and only six branches seem to have been established—at Tredegar, Tywyn, Ruabon, Newport, Pontypool, and Abergavenny. The Union's minutes also reveal interest from Aberystwyth, Caernarfon, Montgomery, Newtown, and Llanidloes, while a number of other areas contained keen supporters. The formation of associations at Newport, Pontypool, and Abergavenny owed much to the visit of an official lecturer, Revd Thomas Spencer, an Anglican minister from Bath, in October 1843. Elsewhere, they were indigenous efforts.

Local societies concentrated first on propaganda. Thus the Pontypool C.S.U. determined on 'lectures to be delivered monthly, tracts distributed and every means used to make the principles become universally disseminated'.[115] Similarly, at Abergavenny and Newport, local canvassing was pronounced the immediate intention. In Merioneth, Griffith Evans of Maesypandy Farm,

---

[112] *The Rise and Progress of the Complete Suffrage Movement* (Tracts of the C.S.U., No. 3, Birmingham 1843), pp. 14–15; *Report of the Council of the C.S.U. for the year ending 30 April 1843* (Birmingham, 1843), pp. 5–6; S. Hobhouse, *Joseph Sturge: His Life and Work* (1919), pp. 69–72.
[113] *Y Dysgedydd*, Feb. 1843, p. 65; see also, *Seren Gomer*, Introduction, 1842, p. iv; Iorwerth Jones, *David Rees, Y Cynhyrfwr*, p. 207.
[114] *The Complete Suffrage Almanack for 1844*, p. 51.
[115] *Nonconformist*, 1 Nov. 1843.

Tal-y-llyn, was lecturing in several parts of the county in the summer of 1842 while the Ruabon association appointed three Dissenting ministers as 'speakers' to outline the nature of their society at local meetings.[116] To carry out such activities efficiently required sound organization, hard-working officials, regular committee meetings and subscriptions to finance local activity. Thus the inaugural meeting in Abergavenny agreed upon the following resolutions:[117]

1 That a complete suffrage union now be formed for the town of Abergavenny and its vicinities.

2 That all persons subscribing not less than two pence per month be members of the Union, and constitute a committee—seven of whom to form a quorum.

3 That a committee meet every fourth Tuesday, from the present Tuesday in the Temperance Hall at 8 o'clock in the evening, to admit new members and report progress.

4 That the town be divided into districts, and canvassed for members to join the union, both electors and non-electors indiscriminately.

C.S.U. branches in Wales also resolved upon electoral action— the pressurizing of candidates and MPs, registration work, and the promotion of suitable candidates.[118] In Monmouthshire concerted action between the towns was initiated though, in fact, the Boroughs' member, R. J. Blewitt, supported Sharman Crawford's complete suffrage motions in Parliament on several occasions, earning him the commendation of local radicals.[119] In reality, there was little scope for electoral activity, at least on a parliamentary level, in 1842–3; the next general election lay several years ahead, in 1847.

Ties between Welsh branches and the national executive in Birmingham were loose and, indeed, the central executive did not seek to impose tight control on branches. It called for no financial contributions, and levies, as at Abergavenny, were to cover only local costs. Rather, it offered federation. Evidently, Welsh branches looked to Birmingham for guidance only, wishing to retain their independence, as Monmouthshire supporters made

[116] Ibid., 11 May 1842; *Seren Gomer*, Nov. 1843, p. 328.
[117] *Nonconformist*, 15 Nov. 1843.
[118] Ibid., 17 Aug., 1 Nov. 1843; NLW, Tredegar Park MSS, 40/60A.
[119] *Monmouthshire Merlin*, 19 Jan. 1844; *Sentinel*, 2 Mar. 1844; C.S.U., Minute Book of the Committee for General Purposes, 5 Feb. 1844.

clear: 'We are not yet prepared to join your union but think it better to mature our own, previous to such a step.'[120] Little information is available on the operations of Welsh complete suffrage associations and, in all probability, they were short-lived. Membership is also difficult to ascertain. At Abergavenny, about 900 attended Spencer's lecture, one-tenth of whom enrolled;[121] it is unlikely that memberships elsewhere in Wales much exceeded this.

The C.S.U. was essentially a middle-class initiative and accordingly, everywhere in Wales, except at Tredegar, middle-class representatives, particularly shopkeepers and Nonconformist ministers, played a leading role. 'The greater part' of the Pontypool sympathizers reputedly consisted of 'middle-class electors who had hitherto shown but little sympathy with the suffrage movement'.[122] Such developments gave commentators optimism. At Newport, the participation of the once 'resolute upholders of things as they are' was hailed as a significant advance in public opinion.[123] Indeed, from the outset, Joseph Sturge had aimed to attract 'that part of the philanthropic public who do not commonly mix in politics'.[124]

After a tour of northern England and Scotland by a deputation headed by Joseph Sturge in 1842, it was reported: 'Everywhere they found the friends of the temperance reformation and the independent minds among religious communities, standing forth as supporters of the cause.'[125] This was certainly echoed in Wales where complete suffrage had close links with Nonconformity and temperance. Revealingly, at Tywyn the agitation was fomented by a civil and religious liberty committee rather than an orthodox C.S.U. branch. According to Joseph Roberts, the Aberystwyth draper, supporters of the movement in his district were 'what you may call religious Chartists'.[126] In Newtown, interest in complete suffrage was stimulated by a lecture in April 1842 by John Collins, the prominent Birmingham radical, representing the

[120] *Nonconformist*, 1 Nov. 1843; *Sentinel*, 4 Nov. 1843.
[121] *Nonconformist*, 15 Nov. 1843; *Silurian*, 4, 25 Nov. 1843.
[122] *Nonconformist*, 1 Nov. 1843.
[123] Ibid.
[124] Place Papers, XXII, Add. MSS 27,810, fol. 99.
[125] *Report of the Council of the National C.S.U. . . .*
[126] *Nonconformist*, 17 Aug. 1842; C.S.U., Minute Book, 15 Aug. 1842.

Chartist Church Society.[127] Nonconformist ministers were fore-most in the Abergavenny, Pontypool, Newport, and Ruabon socie-ties and overwhelmingly prominent were Baptists. Other local C.S.U. supporters had similar connections. At Pontypool, the stu-dents of the Baptist College joined the Union. According to the superintendent of police in the area, the local Baptists were 'strong Chartists' and it was they who organized Spencer's lecture in the town.[128] In Abergavenny, chairman, secretary and treasurer of the local association were all deacons at Frogmore Street Baptist Chapel.[129] The secretary of the Ruabon association and Joseph Roberts of Aberystwyth were Baptists. The movement was endorsed by two of the denomination's most influential organs, *Seren Gomer* and *Y Gwir Fedyddiwr* (later, *Y Bedyddiwr*). Central to the appeal was the religious tone of much C.S.U. argument. Sturge 'seldom made a speech without putting forward the distinctively Christian grounds upon which he acted' and argued that universal suffrage was 'the birthright of men, the inalienable gift of God, proved by the whole tenor of sacred history'.[130] Union tracts also frequently sought to reconcile democracy with Christianity. Hand-bills advertising a complete suffrage address by Revd Thomas Spencer of Bath, at Pontypool in October 1843, spoke of a lecture 'in relation to the Genius of Christianity, and the principles of the British Constitution'.[131]

The C.S.U. stood for universal male suffrage, the secret ballot, and the other points of the Chartist programme but emphatically condemned violent action. Sturge insisted upon 'the utter hopeless-ness of carrying the object by any other means than those recom-mended by the Complete Suffrage Union, namely, by purely moral, Christian and peaceful means'.[132] In the words of Griffith Evans, pioneer of the movement in Merioneth, addressing the Dolgellau branch of the Religious Freedom Society: 'We do not want to use any weapons, only the force of principles. The air of these meetings is too pure for Chartists to breathe.'[133] Complete

[127] NLW, MS 12888E, E. R. Horsfall-Turner, 'Chartism in Montgomeryshire'. This is a rough, uncompleted draft by a local historian, written in the last year of his life (1936). See Asa Briggs, *Chartist Studies*, p. 231, n.1.
[128] HO 45/453, fols. 124, 177.
[129] NLW, Minor Deposits, 1207 B.
[130] H. Richard, *Memoirs of Joseph Sturge* (1864), pp. 296, 327.
[131] HO 45/453, fol. 176.
[132] *Nonconformist*, 14 Sept. 1842.
[133] *Y Dysgedydd*, Nov. 1839, p. 351.

suffragists at Pontypool and Ruabon published their condemnation of physical force. In 1842–3 the term 'Sturgeism' was coined in this context.[134] Such emphasis on peaceful and constitutional protest was appealing in Wales where the Newport March had done much to discredit Chartism. Arguably, the agitation for popular democracy would benefit from a change of name.[135] The C.S.U. retained the six points of the Charter but rejected the Chartist label.

The C.S.U. appeal to the religious elements in the community paralleled an A.C.L.L. stratagem. There were, of course, other links. Most obviously, the complete suffrage movement was born out of disillusionment with the repeal campaign. Officially, relations between the two organizations were harmonious but suspicion was inevitable. 'Mr Sturge's movement is expressly made to supersede, and annihilate the agitation against the Corn Laws', wrote the *Free Trader*.[136] A number of prominent Leaguers in Wales—Griffith Evans in Merioneth, Joseph Roberts in Aberystwyth, Thomas Griffiths in Abergavenny, Revd Thomas Thomas in Pontypool, Revd David Rhys Stephen in Newport, and Revd Thomas Davies in Merthyr—supported and sometimes pioneered local C.S.U.s. Some no doubt supported the view that the two agitations could flourish in coexistence. In March 1842 the Caernarfon Anti-Corn Law Association declared for 'vote by ballot, extension of the franchise, and other reforms of the reform bill', and corresponded with the C.S.U. executive in Birmingham, while acknowledging the primacy of the repeal agitation.[137] Others, however, turned to the C.S.U. out of frustration with the League's progress. 'Organic must precede commercial reform', insisted Revd Thomas Thomas, 'so as to secure, by the divine blessing, the permanent commercial prosperity of the nation … There is no good expecting the removal of commercial restrictions by the present Parliament.'[138] For a time, he and other Leaguers in Wales now gave the C.S.U. pre-eminence.

As the Union was a middle-class initiative, its fundamental problem was to attract working-class support and this, of course, meant

[134] '… the country must be Sturgeised …', pronounced *Seren Gomer*, Introduction, 1842, p. iv.
[135] 'The Chartists should change their names', advised *Y Diwygiwr*, Mar. 1842, p. 98.
[136] *Free Trader*, 2 Apr. 1842.
[137] *Carnarvon and Denbigh Herald*, 2 Apr. 1842; C.S.U., Minute Book, 24 May 1842.
[138] *Nonconformist*, 20 Oct. 1841.

co-operation with the Chartists. The alliance was always a tenuous one. The proceedings of the Birmingham Complete Suffrage Conference in April 1842 developed into a struggle between Sturge's supporters and the Chartist group led by Lovett and O'Brien who wanted the adoption of 'the Charter, name and all'. The latter maintained that the Charter 'was endeared to their hearts by the memories, the hopes and even the sufferings associated with that name'.[139] On this occasion Sturge's contention that the document was synonymous with violent language and conduct held sway. A compromise was reached with the acceptance of the six points but not the name.

No such understanding was formulated at the second conference in December 1842. Once again the issue was adoption of the Chartist name, but this time the Sturgeites were outvoted and left the meeting. The conference was a tremendous blow to the Union and one from which it never recovered. Indeed, to some, the enterprise had always been impracticable: 'The National Complete Suffrage Convention, like an ill-constructed vessel, has gone to pieces in the first storm', observed the *Monmouthshire Beacon*.[140] The *Monmouthshire Merlin* took a similar if more sympathetic view: 'The amiable originator [Sturge] ... had to deal with the most overbearing and dogmatic set of men in existence'.[141] Paradoxically, most C.S.U. activity in Wales occurred in the second half of 1843 when the national movement was in decline. Indeed, the last burst of enthusiasm centred on the visit of Sturge himself to Newport in February 1844, a visit which was aimed principally at promoting the Union's new strategy, the withholding of supplies until constitutional rights had been granted. Support for the supply movement was expressed by the Newport and Pontypool associations but in practice the plan came to nothing. This effectively marked the end of complete suffrage agitation, though the Union officially remained in existence until its fusion with the A.C.L.L. in December 1845.[142]

The divisions between Sturgeites and Chartists around the conference table at Birmingham were reflected in the provinces. In

[139] H. Richard, op. cit., p. 317.
[140] *Monmouthshire Beacon*, 7 Jan. 1843.
[141] *Monmouthshire Merlin*, 7 Jan. 1843.
[142] Ibid., 24 Feb., 2 Mar. 1844; *Nonconformist*, 24 Jan., 28 Feb. 1844; C.S.U., Minute Book, 26 Feb. 1844; *The League*, 13 Dec. 1845.

some instances relations were harmonious, as at Abergavenny, where radical activity was emphatically peaceable and respectable. Apparently the town experienced no organized activities by Chartists during the excitements of 1838–9. When an N.C.A. branch was established in June 1841 its leading members were shop-keepers and the secretary was Thomas Griffiths, a schoolmaster at the local grammar school. Members supported the A.C.L.L. and eschewed intimidation: '... thank God we have no small loaf Chartists ... exclusive dealing is not known amongst us'.[143] Accordingly, Abergavenny Chartists welcomed the complete suffrage movement, sending a congratulatory address to the Union executive on its early progress.[144] On the formation of a local branch in November 1843 several Chartist leaders were prominent. Elsewhere, too, Chartists were drawn into the campaign at places like Newport, Tredegar, Llanidloes, Newtown, and even Merthyr.

If in some quarters Chartists were sympathetic to the complete suffrage overture, in others it met with outright rejection. A public meeting in Pontypridd (then known as Newbridge) in April 1842 resolved upon 'exposing the Complete Suffrage scheme and other tricks of would-be Liberals'.[145] Elsewhere, too, at Newport, Pontypool, Monmouth, and Cardiff, there is some evidence of Chartist antipathy. At Newtown, the local Chartist committee was sensitive to the charge of collusion with the C.S.U.; the visit of John Collins 'was not at the expense of Mr Joseph Sturge, either directly or indirectly ... his expenses coming to, and returning from Newtown were paid by the Chartists of the aforesaid place'.[146]

Most vociferous in denunciation were Merthyr Chartists, who opposed alliance with free traders as 'a direct step towards betrayal of the Chartist cause'.[147] Morgan Williams conveyed an unequivocal message to the 1842 Chartist Convention: 'His own opinion, and that of his constituents were in favour of the Charter, name and all; they were of the opinion that even the slightest alteration would injure the cause.' At the same assembly, Williams was foremost in opposition to compromise with the C.S.U. and, addressing the vast crowd gathered to greet his return to Merthyr, he again

[143] *Monmouthshire Merlin*, 17 July 1841.
[144] *Nonconformist*, 24 Sept. 1842.
[145] *Northern Star*, 16 Apr. 1842.
[146] Ibid., 23 Apr. 1842.
[147] J. T. Ward, *Chartism*, p. 159.

pronounced that there were 'no Sturgeites' in the locality. Subsequent branch meetings of the local N.C.A. endorsed Williams's words; a motion of censure was passed against 'any of those who deviate from a particle of the Charter, even the name'. After the second conference the Merthyr Association applauded the action of their leaders 'in bringing the People's Charter as an amendment to the imperfect document of the Sturge party'.[148]

Closer scrutiny, however, reveals that in Merthyr, as in other localities, a difference of opinion existed over the C.S.U. Several prominent Chartists were, if only for a time, attracted towards the new movement and gave it public advocacy. At the very time Morgan Williams was assuring the Chartist Convention in London that there was no Sturgeite support in Merthyr, a group of local members was actively promoting the complete suffrage cause in the Tredegar area. A public meeting near the town in April 1842, attended by over a thousand people, welcomed the C.S.U. and made provision for local action through a branch society; of the six resolutions passed, five were proposed by Merthyr men, including, most surprisingly, the militant William Miles.[149] Such activity clearly differed substantially from the line of other Merthyr Chartists and reflected the confusion which new initiatives often imparted to local radicalism.

On the whole, Chartist sympathies with the C.S.U. in Merthyr and indeed throughout Wales were brief and insubstantial. Merthyr's two delegates to the Complete Suffrage Conference of December 1842, the unemployed ironworker William Miles and the grocer Benjamin Havard, both voted for the Chartist amendment which precipitated the Sturgeite walk-out.[150] Co-operation was most authentic on the periphery of the coalfield, at Newport, Pontypool and, most especially, at Abergavenny. It was not easy to create an alliance in the ironworks communities where the overwhelming power of the masters was in stark contrast with the hardships and poverty of the large body of miners and ironworkers, making for greater class consciousness and sharper

[148] *Northern Star*, 16, 23, 30 Apr. 1842, 7 Jan. 1843; *Udgorn Cymru*, 23 Apr. 1842; *Glamorgan, Monmouth and Brecon Gazette and Merthyr Guardian*, 14 May 1842; *Cambrian*, 20 May 1842.

[149] NLW, Tredegar Park MSS, 40/60A; Walter T. Morgan, 'Chartism and industrial unrest in south Wales in 1842', p. 11; see also, David Rees, a miner, addressing a Merthyr N.C.A. branch meeting in August 1842, quoted in D. J. V. Jones, 'Chartism at Merthyr', p. 240.

[150] *Northern Star*, 14 Jan. 1843.

class divisions. Moreover, in such communities, apart from Merthyr, the middle class was confined to a small group of shop-keepers and mining agents. Where occupational structure was more diversified, as in a market centre such as Abergavenny, class anta-gonism was less overt and co-operation had greater possibilities.

The C.S.U. thus induced divisions of varying proportions in the ranks of Welsh Chartists. Those who gave their support saw no inconsistency with previously held convictions. They remained steadfast to the six points, and the prospect of middle-class alliance towards those ends made the new venture appealing. At the same time, in Scotland and in parts of England, the Union was against Feargus O'Connor, and Joseph Sturge was seen as an alternative leader. Welsh Chartists for the most part remained faithfully O'Connorite, and O'Connor for much of the time was hostile to the Sturgeites. Thus, the Newport branch of the N.C.A., debat-ing the complete suffrage issue in March 1842, pronounced its unqualified faith in O'Connor: '... we are determined to resist all his enemies, and stand by him until death, considering his enemies foes of humanity, and to the cause of freedom.'[151] The loyalty was sometimes colourfully demonstrated, as at Aberga-venny where a local activist christened his son Henry Feargus O'Connor Haines, 'to commemorate the unflinching champion of people's rights'.[152] On complete suffrage Welsh Chartists may well have argued as did their Bristol comrades:

> ... if the question is between Feargus O'Connor and Joseph Sturge, the decision must be years of toil in favour of Feargus O'Connor ... but for Joseph Sturge we may ask, what do we know of him?—answer, that he was a free trader only, till he found that he could not carry free trade without the Chartists.[153]

Such reasoning had a compelling logic.

If the influence of O'Connor and the *Northern Star* led to implac-able attitudes in many areas, at root mutual suspicion between the middle and lower classes was rarely absent; this was the funda-mental reason for the failure of the C.S.U. Chartists most specifi-cally questioned the motives of complete suffrage leaders, suspecting an A.C.L.L. trick: '... these men meant only to stifle

[151] Ibid., 12 Mar. 1842.
[152] Ibid., 17 July 1841.
[153] Ibid., 4 June 1842.

the Chartist movement that they might bring on the only question they really had at heart, the Repeal of the Corn Laws.'[154] For their part, the middle classes were similarly unprepared for co-operation. Sturge himself expressed dismay at the prejudice amongst his 'own class'.[155] Fear of violence was a factor. At Llanid-loes in 1840 Walter Griffith, the A.C.L.L. lecturer, observed: 'The middle class here have great prejudice against any agitation at present, because the *chartist* made so much riot.'[156] These senti-ments were echoed in Merthyr, where a correspondent to the local newspaper observed: 'The Whig portion of the middle class stand aloof from the violent advocates of ultra-liberalism, and seem quite indisposed to form an alliance with infidels and anarch-ists, under any name.'[157]

The 1830s had seen the rift between the middle and working classes, born in working men's disillusionment with the great Reform Act, widened by Whig rule over the following years and sealed by the Chartist activities of the latter part of the decade. Some years would have to pass before the suspicion and bitterness thereby engendered would fade.

---

[154] Ibid., 14 May 1842.
[155] Place Papers, XXII, Add. MSS 27,810, fol. 128.
[156] A.C.L.L., L.B., 5, 722, Walter Griffith to Ballantyne, 6 Sept. 1840.
[157] *Cardiff and Merthyr Guardian*, 22 Oct. 1842.

IV

RADICAL DISSENT

Nonconformists in Wales, as elsewhere, were strongly attracted to the anti-Corn Law, parliamentary reform, anti-slavery, peace, and temperance movements, and often played prominent roles locally. At the same time, there was a long tradition, albeit a discontinuous one, of agitation to secure redress of peculiarly Dissenting grievances, relating to such issues as marriage, burial, parochial tithe, and Church rates. In 1844, a new era of this campaign opened with the foundation of the British Anti-State-Church Association (A.S.C.A.), the Liberation Society as it later came to be known, the most influential and directly political of Dissenting pressure groups.

A succession of societies seeking to promote or to safeguard Nonconformist interests had operated since the 1730s. Each made intermittent appeals to the provinces and made some impact on Wales, undertaking extensive propaganda activities through the dissemination of pamphlets and addresses and generating branch associations, though of a transitory nature, in a number of places.[1] By the 1830s, Dissenting protest in many parts of Wales also took the form of the concerted refusal to pay Church rates. The bitterness aroused by such controversies did much to radicalize Dissent, one aspect of which was the shift of focus away from individual grievances towards an attack upon the citadel itself and a call for Church-State separation. Spearheading a more militant Dissent in Wales was a new generation of Nonconformist ministers, including men like Hugh Pugh, William Williams ('Caledfryn'), William Rees, Thomas Thomas, David Rees, and Samuel Roberts, all born in the early years of the century. As early as 1833, Hugh Pugh, the Merioneth schoolmaster and Independent

[1] I. G. Jones, 'The Liberation Society and Welsh politics, 1844–1868', in idem, *Explorations and Explanations: Essays in the Social History of Victorian Wales* (Llandysul, 1981), pp. 238–42; O. Parry, 'The parliamentary representation of Wales and Monmouthshire during the nineteenth century—but mainly until 1870' (University of Wales MA thesis, 1924), pp. 166–7; R. T. Jones, 'The origins of the Nonconformist disestablishment campaign, 1830–40', *Journal of the Historical Society of the Church in Wales*, 20, No. 25 (1970), pp. 65–71; T. M. Bassett, *The Welsh Baptists* (Swansea, 1977), p. 147.

minister, founded the Penllyn and Edeirnion Young Men's Association to provide instruction in the principles of Dissent and Liberalism, and he published *Catechism yr Ymneillduwr*, in which he
highlighted the problems arising from the connection between
Church and State.[2] 'Caledfryn' was the leading figure in a series
of meetings demanding disestablishment held in Caernarfonshire
in the early summer of 1843, the one at Pendref Chapel, Caernarfon, being described in the local newspaper as the first ever organized in Wales for 'the express purpose of petitioning the
Legislative for separation of Church and State'.[3]

As a result of such activities, when the A.S.C.A. was founded
there was potentially a solid body of support in Wales. Indeed,
Nonconformist radicals like 'Caledfryn' reacted with indignation
when their early efforts were overlooked:

> There is great talk now-a-days with regard to the Anti-State Church Associa-
> tion in England, as if something new had happened. Welsh Ministers have
> exerted themselves on behalf of the principles advocated by the above
> institution for more than twenty years. I have thrown myself into this move-
> ment since 1832; and have sacrificed upwards of 150 l. for the promoting
> of the objects of Dissent in the Principality. I have even suffered persecution
> for my attachment to my principles as a Nonconformist.[4]

The foundation of the *Nonconformist* newspaper in April 1841 represented an important milestone in the growth of radical Dissent.
It served as a platform for repeal of the Corn Laws, for complete
suffrage and other causes, but its primary function was always
to promote religious liberty. The opening number urged reformers
'to come forward, and combine and act for an equitable and
peaceable severance of church and state; this is the great object
design of the proprietors of this paper'.[5] Political activity was
incumbent: 'To profess Christianity and to eschew politics is certainly the woman's head and the fish's tail of moral obligation.
Nothing could be more grotesque.'[6] The A.S.C.A. was formally

---

[2] *Dictionary of Welsh Biography*, pp. 812–13. Pugh's convictions brought bitter attacks on
him and a resolution was passed in a Methodist Association urging people to have nothing
to do with those who spoke against the authorities and the established institutions of
the country.

[3] *Carnarvon and Denbigh Herald*, 17 June 1843. According to *Y Cronicl*, Nov. 1883, p. 325,
the first disestablishment meeting in Wales was at Machynlleth in 1837. See also, *Nonconformist*, 27 Nov. 1878.

[4] NLW, MS 15404C, Revd William Williams, 'A Scrapbook', 8 Mar. 1848.

[5] *Nonconformist*, 14 Apr. 1841.

[6] Ibid., 16 June 1841.

launched at a conference of some 700 delegates in London in April 1844 and, aiming at 'the liberation of religion from all governmental or legislative interference', was the embodiment of the *Nonconformist*'s exhortations. Indeed, in the Association's early years, the *Nonconformist* served as its official organ.

From the beginning the A.S.C.A. sought to incorporate all regions of the country in its organization. A council of 500 (later 600) was chosen by the localities and met every year. Fifty (later 75) members from this body were nominated to an executive committee, which met fortnightly. Both authorities were chosen triennially. Meetings to select delegates were held throughout Wales in the weeks prior to the inaugural conference and, in all, 22 men attended, 5 of whom became members of the executive committee. The first council in fact included as many as 38 representatives from Wales (plus several Welshmen holding English pastorates), reflecting the Association's willingness to accept local nominations in order to make the organization appear as geographically widespread as possible.[7]

Participation on this scale indicates that the new movement was favourably received in Wales and early activities were reported in the Welsh periodicals, if not in the English-language newspapers. In the summer of 1844 public meetings expressing approval of the enterprise were held in various parts of Wales, while in September a conference, attended overwhelmingly by representatives from the north Wales counties, was convened at Machynlleth, with Revd James Carlile, Independent minister at Hackney, attending as official representative of the A.S.C.A. Here, delegates resolved to co-operate with the Association with the proviso that Welsh members 'adopt such other local measures for the promotion of the sacred cause of religious freedom as may best suit the circumstance of their respective neighbourhoods'.[8]

The following year Carlile was deputed by the A.S.C.A. executive to lecture in north Wales, addressing meetings at Holywell, Denbigh, Llanrwst, Dolgellau, Portmadoc, and Newtown. Registrars were appointed at each place to supervise local activity, which

[7] A. Miall, *Life of Edward Miall*, pp. 95–6; *Y Dysgedydd*, May 1844, pp. 156–7, Aug. 1844, p. 254.

[8] *Nonconformist*, 9, 16 Oct. 1844, 7 May 1845; *Y Dysgedydd*, Nov. 1844, pp. 350–2; see also, I. G. Jones, *Explorations and Explanations*, p. 253.

at this early stage meant the enrolment of members.[9] It was not until February 1847 that an agent, John Kingsley, was dispatched to south Wales. He addressed audiences at Newport, Pontypool, Cardiff, Tredegar, and Swansea, establishing committees at each.[10] Shortly after, a Welsh-speaking lecturer, Revd David Rhys Stephen, was engaged to tour north and west Wales. Again, local registrars and committees were established in a number of towns.[11] In October 1848 Edward Miall made his first public appearance in the Principality, at Newport, moving on to speak at some nine locations in south Wales.[12] At the same time, committed Welsh members, like Revd Evan Jones ('Ieuan Gwynedd') of Tredegar and Revd Thomas Thomas of Pontypool, explained the Association's campaign to local audiences.[13] Such indigenous activity, however, was not widespread and clearly much depended on central initiative; as yet the organization did not extend to locally-based paid agents.

How did Welshmen react to the early exertions of the A.S.C.A.? In terms of membership and financial contributions, the initial response was limited. By December 1847, after three and a half years of existence, total subscriptions and donations from the Principality amounted to little over £24 monthly from Dissenting ministers.[14] Anticipating poor pecuniary support, the executive was unenthusiastic about Edward Miall's proposed lecture tour of south Wales in 1848. In the event, it exceeded expectations, over £75 being contributed from eight towns. Precisely because of this success, one of the society's main agents, John Kingsley, was sent to the same region in 1849. Another £50 or so was collected. In north Wales, John Carvell Williams, the A.S.C.A. secretary, raised just over £12 in October 1850.[15]

The appointment of registrars and committees gave some basis for local activity. At Tywyn, the Anti-State-Church party acquired, ironically enough, its own tithe barn to hold regular meetings.[16] But generally the establishing of committees coincided with the

[9] *Nonconformist*, 25 June, 2, 9 July 1845; *Y Dysgedydd*, Aug. 1845, p. 254.
[10] *Nonconformist*, 3, 17 Feb. 1847.
[11] Ibid., 19 May, 9 June, 7 July 1847.
[12] Ibid., Oct., Nov. 1848; *Principality*, 27 Oct., 3 Nov. 1848; A. Miall, op. cit., pp. 130–4.
[13] *Nonconformist*, 6 May 1846, 13 Oct. 1847; *Principality*, 19 Oct., 16 Nov. 1847.
[14] A.S.C.A., A/LIB/89, Secretary's Cash Book, July 1844–Oct. 1853.
[15] Ibid., 2 Nov. 1848, 3, 29 Dec. 1849, 5 Jan., 4 Nov. 1850.
[16] *Nonconformist*, 19 June 1844.

appearance of an Association representative and such bursts of enthusiasm frequently proved ephemeral. At Swansea, for instance, the formation of a local committee was claimed by successive emissaries in February 1847, June 1847, and October 1848. The employment of lecturers was an expensive business and, inevitably, visits to most Welsh localities were no more than occasional. Tracts were issued by the A.S.C.A. but, as 'Ieuan Gwynedd' emphasized, the great need was for their publication in the Welsh tongue.[17] The Machynlleth conference had set up a subcommittee to tackle this but nothing seems to have come of it.

The 1840s, then, were not years of significant popular participation by Welshmen in the society and the *Nonconformist* newspaper bemoaned the negligible results of the Machynlleth conference, while the south Wales members of the A.S.C.A. Council had done little to establish the organization in that region.[18] Yet, if Welsh Nonconformists did not throw themselves wholeheartedly into the new movement, this did not mean that they were impassive in these years. This was palpably not so, as successive controversies demonstrated. The first concerned the Factory Bill of 1843, the work of the Home Secretary, Sir James Graham, which in part provided that child education be placed under Anglican control. The reaction of Welsh Dissenters was immediate. They feared increased Anglican domination of a state-aided education system and sensed a threat to the cherished Sunday school. Rural and industrial areas were vehement in protest; at Merthyr, over 20,000 people signed petitions objecting to the bill's education clauses, while in May 1843 W. O. Stanley, MP for Anglesey, presented 279 petitions, incorporating 35,000 signatures, which reputedly covered nearly all the parishes of north Wales.[19]

In 1845 the government's decision to increase the grant to the Catholic seminary at Maynooth in Ireland provoked another burst of Dissenting passion. Public meetings all over Wales denounced the proposal and petitioned against its enactment. Even the normally taciturn Calvinistic Methodists participated in the outcry; in Cardiganshire alone, it was estimated that about 70 petitions,

---

[17] Ibid., 6 May 1846.
[18] Ibid.
[19] *Silurian*, 29 Apr. 1843; *Carnarvon and Denbigh Herald*, 6 May 1843. South-east Wales submitted nearly a thousand petitions against the bill. I. W. R. David, 'Political and electioneering activity in south-east Wales, 1820–51', p. 218.

comprising over 21,000 signatures, were being organized by that body. At the anti-Maynooth conference in London in May, Wales was represented by 25 delegates.[20] The third major 'religious' controversy in these years related specifically to Wales. This was the infamous Report of the Education Commissioners in 1847, which generated immense hostility and bitterness, among Anglicans and Nonconformists alike, in all parts of the Principality. Methodists were significantly active alongside the 'older Dissenters', producing a portentous measure of unity in the ranks of Nonconformity.

Participation in such protests, however, did not necessarily indicate A.S.C.A. adherence, though local members were invariably prominent in the controversies. Indeed, the Association represented militant Dissent and this sometimes conflicted with traditional attitudes. Some Nonconformists had qualms about its whole ethos. For its part, the A.S.C.A. leadership could be uncompromising, in 1845, for example, withdrawing from the anti-Maynooth conference because it would not come out against all establishments.[21]

The 1840s were years when the A.S.C.A. was primarily nursing potential support and establishing valuable footholds and cells of local support in Wales. Their location in this period tended towards a predominance in the south rather than north Wales (though the latter had its sympathizers, as the Machynlleth conference demonstrated) and also towards the border counties. The vast majority of subscriptions came from individuals contributing ten shillings, £1 or more, indicating a middle-class appeal though there is evidence of some working-class support.[22] The bulk of early Welsh membership came from Dissenting ministers—two-thirds of total subscriptions during the first three and a half years. Moreover, they made up all but 5 of the 42 Welsh representatives on the General Council appointed in 1844 and 8 of the 14 Welsh delegates attending the 1847 Triennial Conference.[23] Predictably, therefore, ministers provided the main source of assistance to A.S.C.A. lecturers visiting localities, offering accommodation,

[20] *Nonconformist*, 23 Apr., 21 May 1845.
[21] G. I. T. Machin, 'The Maynooth Grant, the Dissenters and Disestablishment, 1845–7', *English Historical Review*, LXXXII (1967), p. 70.
[22] A.S.C.A., A/LIB/89, Secretary's Cash Book.
[23] *Y Dysgedydd*, May 1844, pp. 156–7; *Nonconformist*, 3 May 1847.

chairing meetings and, where necessary, translating addresses. Within Dissent, the movement appealed more to the 'old Dissenters' than to the various Methodist bodies, with Baptists especially conspicuous, providing the leadership in Monmouthshire, the most responsive county at this time. Some of this A.S.C.A. support was evidently hived off from organizations like the A.C.L.L., which had attracted important Nonconformist participation.[24] Thus early activists included Griffith Evans and Revds Thomas Davies, David Rhys Stephen, Micah Thomas, Thomas Thomas, 'Caledfryn', and David Rees, men who were, or had been, enthusiastic supporters of the A.C.L.L., the C.S.U. and other reform movements.

From the first, an important feature distinguishing the A.S.C.A. from other Nonconformist pressure groups was its commitment to electoral action; here, again, the influence of the A.C.L.L., as model and inspiration, was clear, as activists readily acknowledged. Edward Miall unsuccessfully stood at the Southwark by-election of 1845, while in mid 1847 the *Nonconformist Elector* was launched to direct and co-ordinate activity prior to the general election of that year. In Monmouthshire, the Pontypool A.S.C.A. committee was active,[25] but in most areas of Wales there was little concerted Nonconformist action and the 1847 election results were disappointing. Indeed, the *Nonconformist* followed up with a series of forceful leaders on the misrepresentation of the Principality:

> The worthlessness of Welsh members is quite proverbial. With a few exceptions, they are good for nobody and good for nothing ... The fact is, that the Welsh people are not at all represented, and never will until a large extension of the suffrages takes place.[26]

Plainly, the advance of democracy was central to Nonconformist electoral success. '... Our political power must be increased before we can change the constituency of the present House of Commons,' argued Revd Abraham Jones of Merthyr, 'purge the floor

[24] Nevertheless, note the anxiety of the A.S.C.A. not to jeopardize the A.C.L.L.'s prospects of success. I. G. Jones, *Explorations and Explanations*, p. 252.

[25] *Seren Gomer*, June 1846, p. 185.

[26] Ibid., 25 Aug.1847. A by-election in the Cardigan Boroughs early in 1849 momentarily stirred Nonconformist ambitions, Edward Miall being invited to stand. He declined, citing the lack of Nonconformist electoral organization in the constituency, the shortness of time, and the power of aristocratic influence at Gogerddan. In the same election, Calvinistic Methodists entered the arena, resolving to withhold support from any candidate who would not echo their demands for ecclesiastical reform. Ibid., 10, 17, 24 Jan. 1849.

from its political shams and hypocrisies, and secure an assembly of enlightened and honest men, who shall, on the grounds of political justice and national economy dissolve the union' (of Church and State).[27] Thus Nonconformist radicals appeared on parliamentary reform platforms in the late 1840s, just as they had supported the complete suffrage movement earlier in the decade, exemplifying the *Principality*'s assertion that 'Democracy and Dissent are twin brothers, born of the same great principles'.[28] At Cardiff in 1848, A.S.C.A. members were conspicuous in supporting Hume's 'Little Charter'. Similarly, at Haverfordwest 'friends of religious liberty were prominent', while at Sirhowy Revd Noah Stephens outlined the religious reasons for universal suffrage. At Merthyr, A.S.C.A. members led by Revd Abraham Jones participated in the local parliamentary reform movement and were also behind the foundation of a freehold land society as a means of acquiring the vote to promote the cause of religious liberty. At Hirwaun in 1850 the same delegates were appointed to attend the conferences of the A.S.C.A. and the National Parliamentary and Financial Reform Association.[29]

On all counts the early progress of the A.S.C.A. in Wales was of a limited nature. Certainly there was a good deal of indifference to, and ignorance of, the society, while some Dissenters rejected its radicalism. At the same time, there existed a measure of suspicion between Welsh supporters and the Association. In 1848 'Caledfryn' was emphasizing the independent and indigenous origin of the disestablishment agitation in Wales and accusing the A.S.C.A. of ill-using and neglecting the Principality. The 'English champions of Nonconformity' were simply using the Welsh to bolster their attacks upon the established Church and would contribute nothing to their voluntaryist campaign: '... many of them have not given a farthing for the last twelve months towards any case'.[30] Activists like 'Caledfryn' were clearly looking for a reciprocal relationship and not a submissive one.

---

[27] Ibid., 30 Nov. 1849.
[28] Ibid., 7 Dec. 1849. 'Help forward the suffrage whenever you can,' advised Edward Miall, 'help forward the Separation of Church and State whenever you can; but if you cannot do both, help forward the suffrage, and the other will be secure.' R. Masheder, *Dissent and Democracy* (1864), p. 144.
[29] *Principality*, 12 May, 16, 23 June, 14 July 1848, 30 Nov. 1849, 12 Apr., 3 May 1850.
[30] NLW, MS 15404C, Revd William Williams, A Scrapbook, 8 Mar. 1848.

The immediate efforts of the A.S.C.A. to mobilize opinion in Wales suffered from the lack of Welsh tracts and from the coolness of the English-language newspapers. It was precisely to meet the latter deficiency that the *Principality* was launched in September 1847. Printed and published originally at Haverfordwest by its proprietor, David Evans, it presented itself as a national newspaper for Welsh Nonconformists. As an advocate of religious and political liberty and as a mouthpiece for the A.S.C.A., the *Principality* sought to fulfil a similar role to that of the *Nonconformist* in England.[31] These aspirations were never realized, however, despite a move to Cardiff in April 1848. It ran for another sixteen months but was little more than a local journal from early 1849. The proprietor blamed its failure on the indifference of Welsh Nonconformists and also the 'party feeling and denominational jealousies—which prevail to an amazing extent'.[32] Lack of a sympathetic English-language press thus remained a serious handicap to the dissemination of A.S.C.A. principles in Wales.

Nevertheless, the late forties did constitute years of progress for the Association in Wales. The appointment of a London Welshman, John Carvell Williams, as permanent secretary in 1847 was propitious. The executive began sending more deputations to the Principality and set about supplying Welsh-language tracts. Wales also benefited from the improved organization of the A.S.C.A., particularly in the replacement of local registrars by committees and the appointment of full- and part-time lecturers to tour the country. The indoctrination of the Principality still presented peculiar difficulties. But the Association was unmistakably becoming 'a fact of some importance'[33] in British politics and Wales was increasingly affected by this advance.

---

[31] *Principality*, 7 Sept. 1847.
[32] Ibid., 23 Aug. 1850; see also, R. D. Rees, 'The Glamorgan newspapers under the Stamp Acts', *Morgannwg*, III (1959), pp. 89–91.
[33] See I. G. Jones, *Explorations and Explanations*, pp. 254–7 (quoting *Y Diwygiwr*, Dec. 1853, p. 381).

Part 2

1850–1868
'A Healthy Stimulus'

V

ECONOMIC AND SOCIAL CHANGE IN THE FIFTIES AND SIXTIES

Industrial expansion continued apace in mid-Victorian Wales. The iron industry, upon which prosperity had depended, went into slow decline, but an exuberant and rapidly expanding coal industry brought a new prosperity and with it wholesale population redistribution and the creation of a new society in the mining valleys of the south.

Coal production in Wales had steadily increased during the early decades of the nineteenth century. The situation changed dramatically from the 1840s onwards, when south Wales steam coal came into heavy demand, its high quality winning the Royal Navy's seal of approval. Accordingly, pits were opened in the valleys of the eastern and central parts of the coalfield, where this type of coal was principally to be found. By the end of the sixties the annual output of the south Wales coalfield had risen to over 13 million tons, three times the 1840 yield.

Population statistics indicated the profound changes taking place in Welsh society in the fifties and sixties. In 1851 the population of 1,163,139 was mainly rural. Twenty years later, it was 1,412,583 with a decisive shift towards urbanization, a pattern which was to become even more pronounced in the late Victorian period. The mushrooming coal-pits and levels in the south Wales valleys brought striking population growth to Glamorgan and Monmouthshire, while the Denbighshire and Flintshire figures portrayed the much more modest developments in the north-eastern coalfield. The expansion of the slate industry in the north-west brought significant population increases to Caernarfonshire and, in the 1860s, to Merioneth. Within counties, of course, there were high concentrations in certain towns and areas. Thus, for example, the Rhondda valleys, on the threshold of spectacular growth as the assault on the huge coal reserves there got under way, increased from less than 1,000 people in 1851 to almost 17,000 in 1871, while the slate town of Blaenau Ffestiniog more than doubled its population to over 8,000 in the same period. In other areas of the country the demographic trend was downward, reflecting the decline of older industries like copper in Anglesey and wool in Montgomeryshire. More fundamental, though, was the exodus from rural Wales, which was to remain an enduring feature of the second half of the nineteenth century. For a number of reasons the period from repeal of the Corn Laws to the mid 1870s were years of relative prosperity for agriculture, but underlying grievances and problems remained. In particular, overpopulation and underemployment stimulated an exodus from rural Wales. Many people headed for the major cities of England, others headed abroad (principally to the United States), but the great majority remained within Wales itself and migrated to the rapidly expanding industrial areas of the south. After 1850 the number of agricultural wage-earners fell steadily, there was increasing rural depopulation and Wales became overwhelmingly an industrial country.

Internal migration was greatly facilitated by the railways, most of which were built in the three decades from 1840 to 1870. Some linked the industrial heartland of south Wales to the coast, and accordingly, the ports of Cardiff, Newport, Penarth, Barry, Swansea, Llanelli and Port Talbot developed extensively with the boom in the coal trade. Above all, Cardiff grew into an important world port. From a small market town with a population of 1,870 in 1801, it had expanded to 18,351 by 1851; over the next twenty years it more than doubled in population to 39,356 and would more than quadruple again by the end of the century. Similarly, by 1871 Swansea had all but overtaken Merthyr as the largest town in Wales, with just under 52,000 people.

Industrial Wales, therefore, shared to a large extent in the economic growth and increased prosperity that characterized much of Britain in the 1850s and 1860s. Periodic interruptions occurred, most notably in the mid sixties, and some workers remained unemployed, or very poorly paid, but many others enjoyed a rise in real wages. In particular, the standard of living of the skilled workers, of whom there were large numbers in the Welsh iron, tinplate and copper industries, rose faster than that of the semi-skilled and unskilled. In this climate, working-class protest was fragmentary and localized, and discontent was far more muted than in the 1830s and 1840s when economic hardship had fuelled so much political agitation and militancy. Religious Dissent, however, offered a very different avenue of protest and a critical feature of these decades in Wales was the rise of Nonconformist radicalism, led by a politically and socially conscious middle class.

The middle classes of mid-Victorian Britain were also prominent in recommending self-improvement as the best way of tackling social evils and extolling the virtues of hard work, thrift and respectability as embodied in Samuel Smiles's highly successful *Self-Help*, published in 1859. How far the working classes subscribed to this philosophy is unclear, but this was certainly a time when amenities and organizations such as reading rooms, mechanics institutes, literary institutes, benefit societies, mutual improvement societies, and elementary and Sunday schools sprang up all over the country. By encouraging and actively participating in such initiatives, the enlightened middle classes sought to raise working-class living standards and to instil disciplined, respectable, and responsible attitudes. The petition of the Aberdare Non-Electors' Association to John Bright in February 1859 demanding separate parliamentary representation for Aberdare stressed, among other points, the town's worthiness in terms of its educational facilities (7 public schools, several private schools, and 45 to 50 Sunday schools) and its more than 100 benefit societies, contributing £812 to the sick in 1858.[1]

In education, the fifties and sixties were indeed years of progress in Wales. In reaction to the disdainful indictment of the 1847 Education Report, Nonconformists were particularly active. Elementary schools were founded both by voluntaryists and by the state-aided British and Foreign Schools Society. In 1853 the latter appointed Revd William Roberts ('Nefydd'), Baptist minister at Blaina, as its south Wales agent and during his eleven-year tenure the number of British schools in the region increased from 14 to 164. At the same time, a reawakening in the established Church brought the opening of many National schools. In south Wales, works schools associated with ironworks, collieries and tinplate works also helped in the provision of education.

[1] *Merthyr Telegraph*, 12 Feb. 1859.

Above all, the great expansion of the press in these decades was a powerful educational force, particularly in terms of politics. The repeal of the 'taxes on knowledge' (the stamp duty) in 1855 and of the duties on paper in 1861 ushered in a new kind of newspaper—cheap, respectable, and popular. Places like Merthyr, Aberdare, Swansea, Caernarfon and Denbigh became important centres for newspaper publishing in the English and Welsh languages.[2] By the late sixties almost every town and district of Wales had at least one local newspaper; a market town like Brecon could boast three. Representing a variety of political persuasions, these invariably reported parliamentary, national and international affairs, carried detailed verbatim accounts of local meetings, delivered forceful editorials and had lively correspondence columns. The latter often served to sustain interest in an issue at grass-roots level; '... prolonged local controversies, carried on by means of the newspaper press, have kept alive a feeling which might otherwise have been evanescent', acknowledged the Liberation Society executive in 1868.[3] The circulation of increasing numbers of denominational journals, pamphlet literature, and radical papers like the *People's Paper*, the *Commonwealth* and the *Beehive* added to the ferment. The press continued to prosper over subsequent decades and by 1886 it was calculated that there were 83 newspapers in Wales as compared with 18 in 1856,[4] leading the Welsh correspondent of *The Times*, the barrister, J. E. Vincent, to observe:

> The growth of journalism, and of vernacular journalism in particular, in the Principality has of late years been little short of phenomenal. My impression, indeed, is that Wales supports more journals in proportion to its population than any other part of the civilised world.[5]

In the 1830s and 1840s editors of the Nonconformist periodicals, such as David Rees, Samuel Roberts and William Rees, had firmly established the connection between the Welsh press and radical campaigns, publicizing and encouraging a variety of agitations. Men like Thomas Gee of Denbigh, proprietor-editor of the influential *Baner ac Amserau Cymru*, established in 1859,

[2] See I. G. Jones, *Explorations and Explanations*, pp. 294–5.
[3] Lib. Soc. Mins., 4 Dec. 1868; quoted by J. Vincent, *The Formation of the British Liberal Party, 1857–1868* (1966), p. 96.
[4] H. Whorlow, *The Provincial Newspaper Society, 1836–1886* (1886), p. 37.
[5] J. E. Vincent, *Letters from Wales* (1889), p. 118.

J. W. James, founder of the *Merthyr Star* in the same year, and Josiah Thomas Jones, Independent minister and publisher of a number of periodicals in Aberdare in the fifties and sixties, performed a similar role, while in the following decade *Tarian y Gweithiwr* and J. T. Morgan's *Workman's Advocate* and *Amddiffynydd y Gweithiwr* were notable as weekly organs of the workers' movement. Many others proffered more moderate Liberalism or Conservatism in these decades. The new local press thus amounted to a potent opinion-forming agency and, above all, bred political awareness. Reform movements, from the 1860s in particular, had a new and potentially great source of strength to tap for their agitations.

VI

'A HOST OF LOST ENTERPRISES'

'To the organization, the efforts, and the funds of the Anti-Corn Law League, the public would be adduced to ascribe in a great measure the commercial revolution which this House was now called upon to sanction.'[1] The apprehension of the Radnorshire MP, Sir John Walsh, about the precedent created by the League was shared by a number of political commentators of the day. Thus, responding to the Home Secretary's optimism of an abatement in 'the din of this odious and endless topic of democratic agitation', J. W. Croker, the Tory publicist, insisted that 'repeal of the Corn Laws will *feed* nothing but agitation'.[2] And indeed, the A.C.L.L. did act as a monument and an inspiration to pressure on Parliament from without.

In its heartland the League immediately generated two off-shoots, the Lancashire Public School Association in 1847 and the Liverpool Financial Reform Association in the following year. The former, striving for a free, national, rate-aided and secular education system, developed in 1850 into the National Public School Association, while the latter, advocating government retrenchment, inspired the National Parliamentary and Financial Reform Association in London. The demand for parliamentary reform and political Dissent formed the core of mid-century reforming activity, but pressure groups espousing a wide spectrum of causes operated. Essentially, through propaganda and agitation, they sought to drum up public opinion in support of a minority interest and then make an impression on the legislature.

Some campaigns, most obviously the anti-slavery and peace movements, were of course long-established. Indeed, the Anti-Slavery Society, founded in 1823, with branch associations throughout the country co-ordinated by a large central committee,

---

[1] *Hansard*, LXXXIII, col. 591, 9 Feb. 1846.
[2] L. J. Jennings (ed.), *The Croker Papers: The Correspondence and Diaries of the Late Rt. Hon. John Wilson Croker* (1885), III, p. 63.

organizing meetings, distributing literature, and preparing petitions, had introduced a level of proficiency which subsequent pressure groups like the Catholic Association and the Birmingham Political Union sought to emulate.[3] In Wales it appealed to humanitarians and Nonconformist radicals. The Quakers, Joseph Tregelles Price, the Neath industrialist, and his brother-in-law Revd Elijah Waring, were active campaigners and established the only Welsh organization of permanence, the Swansea and Neath Auxiliary Anti-Slavery Society, which functioned in the 1820s and 1830s. Another prominent member was the Baptist minister then serving in Swansea, Revd David Rhys Stephen, who undertook several south Wales lecture tours. In mid Wales, the Independent ministers, Revds Samuel Roberts ('S.R.') and William Williams ('o'r Wern'), addressed meetings in Merioneth and Montgomeryshire. Speakers from England made occasional incursions into Wales but generally the Anti-Slavery Society and other similar bodies remained distant. Thomas Clarkson, the prominent abolitionist, toured the Principality only once, in 1824.[4] Though he formed committees in a number of towns, all proved transitory, the influence of Tory landlords apparently making it difficult for groups to operate effectively. Thus, while from time to time meetings were held, propaganda was circulated, and petitions were assembled, over the years the movement relied heavily on the leadership of the press, especially the Welsh-language periodicals.

Activity did not cease with the emancipation of slaves in the British Empire in 1833, for attention soon focused on the ill-treatment of West Indian negroes via the apprenticeship system (which was abolished in 1838) and on the continued existence of slavery in other countries, particularly in the USA. Nevertheless, by mid century anti-slavery was neither the popular cause nor the potent political force it had been in earlier decades, though at times it was still capable of arousing considerable sentiment, as was apparent in the 1860s. Then, in Wales, as elsewhere, pro-Unionist sympathies were expressed during the American Civil

[3] For the anti-slavery movement, see Howard Temperley, 'Anti-Slavery', in P. Hollis (ed.), *Pressure from Without in Early Victorian England*, pp. 27–51; G. E. Owen, 'Welsh anti-slavery sentiment 1795–1865: a survey of public opinion' (University of Wales MA thesis, 1964).

[4] See NLW, MS 14984 A, Diary of Clarkson's Tour on Behalf of the Anti-Slavery Society, 1824.

War, and anti-slavery societies were operating in, for example, Merthyr and Aberdare.[5]

The peace movement was another radical campaign evoking a Nonconformist appeal, if on a narrower scale. Joseph Tregelles Price and another Neath Quaker, Evan Rees, were leading figures in the formation of the Society for the Promotion of Permanent and Universal Peace (generally known as the Peace Society) in London in 1816, the former serving as its first president and the latter as secretary as well as editing its monthly organ, the *Herald of Peace*, in the early years. The Society adopted an uncompromising pacifist position, arguing the inhumanity, anti-christian aspect and sinfulness of all war, whether defensive or aggressive. Despite efforts to publicize the movement in the columns of Welsh periodicals and by the distribution of tracts, the only auxiliary society established in the Principality in the 1820s and 1830s was the Quaker-dominated one in the Swansea and Neath area. Greater impact was, however, made in the following decade when Peace Society agents visited south Wales, with branch associations resulting in a number of towns, and prominent radicals like 'S.R.', 'Caledfryn', and William Rees ('Gwilym Hiraethog') giving support to the cause both in print and in public lectures. During the forties the Society also sought to dissuade the Rebeccaites of west Wales from violence and benefited from association with the A.C.L.L. (which contended that free trade would make for international harmony) and from the protest in 1846 against the proposed revival of the militia.[6]

It was at this time, too, that the influential London Welshman, Henry Richard, began his long tenure (1848–85) of the secretaryship of the Society, thereby greatly strengthening the link between Welsh Nonconformist radicalism and the peace movement. Richard became particularly identified with the promotion of arbitration between nations through international congresses. In the mid fifties he and other Welsh radicals denounced the Crimean War and again, two decades later, when the Eastern Question flared up once more, Wales protested strongly against the 'Bulgarian Atrocities' and the Government's pro-Turkish foreign policy with its attendant threat of war with Russia. On the other hand,

[5] *Merthyr Star*, 7 Feb., 6 June, 10 Dec. 1863.
[6] This paragraph is based largely on Goronwy J. Jones, *Wales and the Quest for Peace* (Cardiff, 1969), pp. 1–15.

it is clear that the bulk of opinion in Wales was ranged loyally behind the state in these crises and in other military ventures and, despite increasing support during the century, the Peace Society made only a limited impression, even in Welsh Nonconformist circles.[7]

Instinctively attractive to Nonconformists was the temperance movement.[8] Moderation and teetotal societies sprang up in many Welsh localities in the thirties and forties, with the latter gaining popular ascendancy. The common aim was to tackle the drink problem by reclaiming the individual to sobriety through 'moral suasion'. Nevertheless, relations between moderationists and teetotallers were far from harmonious in these years, with men like 'Caledfryn', an outspoken critic of the compulsion of total abstinence, at the centre of a fierce controversy. Mid century saw a significant new departure in the movement with the formation of the United Kingdom Alliance in 1853. 'The question is now changed,' observed the *Cardiff and Merthyr Guardian*; 'total abstinence is held in abeyance, and the agitation henceforth is to be political rather than moral, legislative rather than social.'[9] Claiming that moral persuasion, as advocated by such bodies as the Band of Hope, was slow-moving and ineffective, the Alliance sought state intervention to suppress intemperance, in particular some measure of 'local option' on the closing down or limitation of public houses. Rapid progress was made in Wales where, by the spring of 1857, 45 of the 64 Alliance auxiliaries were located. Lecturers and the distribution of publications, some in the Welsh language, were the inevitable vehicles for disseminating the cause. It fell largely to district agents and auxiliaries effectively to translate favourable public opinion into agitation and pressure, which essentially took the form of petitioning, local plebiscites, and electoral activity at a municipal and parliamentary level. With local supporters seeking to implement Alliance policy, temperance was a prominent factor in Welsh political life throughout much of the second half of the nineteenth century.

---

[7] See Kenneth O. Morgan, 'Peace movements in Wales 1899–1945', *Welsh History Review*, 10, No. 3 (June 1981), pp. 398–400.

[8] For the temperance movement, see W. R. Lambert, *Drink and Sobriety in Victorian Wales c. 1820–c. 1895* (Cardiff, 1983); B. Harrison, *Drink and the Victorians* (1971); D. A. Hamer, *The Politics of Electoral Pressure* (1977), Chs. IX–XIII.

[9] *Cardiff and Merthyr Guardian*, 4 Aug. 1855; quoted in W. R. Lambert, op. cit., p. 166.

Other campaigns, often of a more local significance, added to the complexity of the mid-century scene. Though hardly 'popular', the public health movement was, of course, of central importance to the mass of the population enduring a thoroughly squalid and frequently diseased environment. The agitation was not marked among the working class—indeed many looked to Chartism for substantial amelioration in living and working conditions—but in towns like Merthyr Tydfil in the 1840s and 1850s small groups of middle-class reformers emerged as vociferous· and effective forces.[10] The improving drive of such elements extended to housing, hospitals, schools, libraries, and other civic amenities too. At the same time, of course, the working class, or more accurately the skilled or semi-skilled workers, sought their own advancement through trade unionism. Inevitably, the principal concern was wages and conditions of work but gradually unions took on the role of political pressure groups, a theme discussed in a subsequent chapter.

In part energized by the apparent success of the A.C.L.L., mid nineteenth-century Britain therefore exhibited a plurality of agitations. Yet these yielded only limited success in the decades after repeal in 1846. Pressure groups had to adjust to certain realities. Agitations, however vigorously conducted, did not readily rouse public sentiment or influence parliamentary opinion, and reform campaigns frequently meant a lengthy, laborious and frustrating process with no guarantee of achieving the desired objective.

Certainly, in the 1850s and early 1860s initiatives failed to rouse widespread public interest. A period of economic prosperity, bringing rising wages and a better standard of living for many, acted as a sedative on agitation among the lower orders. But absolutely basic and inherent was the reality that politics simply did not enter the lives of a sizeable portion of the population. 'We leave aside the beer-besotted and unthinking of the working classes', wrote the Chartist leader, Ernest Jones, while the *Cardiff and Merthyr Guardian* contended in 1859 that:

> a penny an ounce abatement in the price of tobacco would give greater satisfaction to the bulk of the working class than any unsaleable vote. They have not even the curiosity to inquire about the matter. We find that

[10] See I. G. Jones, *Communities: Essays in the Social History of Victorian Wales* (Llandysul, 1987), Chs., 11, 13; idem, *Health, Wealth and Politics in Victorian Wales* (Swansea, 1979).

the present crisis [parliamentary reform proposals] has not caused the sale of an additional 1*d.* paper, and if any question is ever asked by a working man it is inevitably one of 'peace or war'. That he knows by sad experience to be a bread and cheese question.[11]

There was, indeed, a deep-seated ignorance of politics, not confined to the remote and inaccessible rural areas but pervading manufacturing districts too. At root lay the excessive labour demanded of the masses which drained the vitality necessary for political, and indeed social and cultural, activity. '. . . It is very difficult', observed Edward Miall, 'to interest them [the working classes] deeply in any political opinions or movements, even when their own positions and prospects are thought to be involved—as everyone who has had much experience in public agitation can testify.'[12]

Thus pressure groups sought the allegiance of the 'thinking and intelligent' elements of society. Such was the proliferation of movements from the 1830s that reformers' attentions, certainly at a local level, were often much dissipated and activity spasmodic and inconclusive. A correspondent to the *Monmouthshire Merlin* wrote:

> The scene is constantly changing, and ever showing the many weaknesses and instability of mankind; old ideas, without any real cause, are given up and fresh ones are grasped at. A few short months since saw teetotalism engraven on the thoughts of the inhabitants of Abergavenny. The subject burst forth at first like a thunder-clap ... Now, none but a meagre few deign to advocate the cause.[13]

The observation is surely applicable to other movements and other localities; activity was often ephemeral. Local reform societies frequently burst into life on a wave of enthusiasm for a new enterprise only to lapse quickly into stagnation. The stimulus was commonly the appearance of a visiting speaker. Thus the C.S.U. lecturer, Revd Thomas Spencer, was said to have done 'more to advance the cause in one evening, than had ever been achieved before

[11] *People's Paper,* 4 Sept. 1858; *Cardiff and Merthyr Guardian,* 26 Mar. 1859.
[12] A. Miall, *Life of Edward Miall,* p. 240.
[13] *Monmouthshire Merlin,* 18 Dec. 1841. Cf. the complete suffrage movement at Stockport: 'We heard the other day of something like an *organised movement* for effecting "complete suffrage" being begun in this town, but we have heard no more of it latterly. We wonder if, with a *host of other lost enterprises,* it too has sunk to the "tomb of the Capulets".' *Stockport Chronicle,* 13 May 1842: quoted by J. W. Croker, 'The anti-Corn Law agitation', *Quarterly Review,* LXXI, No. CXLI, Dec. 1842–Mar. 1843, p. 276.

in Newport by months of turbid agitation'.[14] Once the external influence was removed, the dedication of local advocates was critical. When their fervour cooled, management committees became smaller, membership fell, and activity dwindled. While an organization might technically be in existence, in reality it had folded. Sometimes local reform leaders withdrew by shifting their energies to an equally attractive campaign. In the same way, many who might have rallied to one movement looked instead to another. Reflecting on 'the true secret' of the A.C.L.L. success, the south Wales agent, John Jenkins, emphasized that it 'zealously excluded other, even cognate subjects, on which most of its leading members thought and felt strongly ...'[15]

The various commitments of local radicals are clear from the overlap of personnel involved in different movements. They agreed that a number of reforms were desirable and that public pressure was necessary for their attainment. The dilemma for many was to decide which campaign should be pre-eminent. The uncertainty was mirrored in local reformers turning from one campaign to another, though Chartists, perceiving their programme as the universal remedy, tended to be more loyal and single-minded. Many pressure groups, after all, contained a strong ideological link, the common enemy frequently being monopoly or inequality, be it political, religious, or economic. The battle was therefore against the privileged orders—government, Established Church, or aristocracy.

Invariably, it was the Nonconformist leaders in the localities, ministers, journalists, shopkeepers, professional men, businessmen, and independent farmers, representatives of an emergent middle-class consciousness, who were the key figures in a succession of reform agitations in the early Victorian period. David Rhys Stephen, Baptist minister in Swansea and Newport in the 1830s and early 1840s, provides a good illustration, since he actively supported the Anti-Slavery Society, the Peace Society, the A.C.L.L., the C.S.U., the Religious Freedom Society, and the A.S.C.A. While in Newport he also helped set up a Mechanics Institute and a British School, and in 1841 launched a short-lived, radical, weekly newspaper, entitled *Morgan Llewelyn's Journal*, which

---

[14] *Monmouthshire Merlin*, 24 Feb. 1844.
[15] J. Jenkins, *The Ballot and Ministerial Reform*, p. 10.

campaigned in particular for the three central issues of pressure-group activity at this time, parliamentary reform, repeal of the Corn Laws, and political Dissent. Similarly, Thomas Davies, Baptist minister in Merthyr (1836–56) and subsequently first principal of Haverfordwest Baptist College, had links with the A.C.L.L., Chartism, the C.S.U., the Administrative Reform Association, temperance, and the A.S.C.A. In north Wales, William Williams ('Caledfryn'), Independent minister at Caernarfon (1832–48), was prominent in the anti-Corn Law, peace and anti-state-church agitations, while also supporting temperance, anti-slavery, and complete suffrage. Samuel Roberts ('S.R.'), the Independent minister from Llanbrynmair, was likewise an ardent campaigner for peace, anti-slavery, temperance, free trade, disestablishment and parliamentary reform (including votes for women but arguing against the secret ballot), vigorously promulgating his views on the public platform and in his writings, especially in his popular monthly periodical, *Y Cronicl*, founded in 1843. Others, too, men like Thomas Thomas, Baptist minister and first College principal at Pontypool, David Rees, the Llanelli Independent and editor of the influential *Diwygiwr* (from 1835 to 1865), and more, participated in a similar spectrum of reform campaigns and testify to the major role played by ministers of religion in the broad movement for civil and religious liberty.

A large number had a journalistic side to their activities. The outstanding example of the preacher-publicist was Thomas Gee of Denbigh, owner and editor of the highly political *Baner ac Amserau Cymru* and an ordained Calvinistic Methodist minister even though he never undertook a pastorate. From the 1860s until almost the end of the century Gee was a pillar of Welsh Nonconformist radicalism, active in the United Kingdom Alliance, the Liberation Society and the Reform League pressure groups, and in other campaigns such as those relating to education, tithes and land, as well as being influential in Liberal Party circles.

Besides ministers, other leading Nonconformists in the local community were frequently at the forefront of reform initiatives. At Abergavenny, for example, a strong Baptist element centring on the forceful Revd Micah Thomas's Frogmore Street Chapel and including men like the merchant, John Daniel, and the grocer, John Harris Conway, both deacons and lay preachers, inaugurated temperance, anti-Corn Law, complete suffrage, and freehold land movements in the town in the 1840s. In isolated Merioneth the striking figure is Griffith Evans of Maes-y-pandy Farm, who energetically promoted the Religious Freedom Society, the A.C.L.L., the C.S.U., and the A.S.C.A., as well as the Plymouth Brethren movement during this same decade. Throughout Wales, individuals of that breed, men like Dr O. O. Roberts, the Caernarfonshire physician, Joseph Roberts, the Aberystwyth draper, and Thomas Griffiths, the Abergavenny schoolmaster, supported a range of radical campaigns in their localities. Griffiths was a Chartist and, in places like Merthyr, former Chartist leaders took up a variety of causes in the fifties and sixties. Increasingly, too, enlightened industrialists like the Darby brothers (W. H. and C. E.) of Brymbo, and the Cory brothers (John and Richard) of Cardiff, appear as supporters, often in a substantial financial capacity, of organizations such as the Liberation Society, the United Kingdom Alliance, the Peace Society and the Reform League, in addition to undertaking a considerable local philanthropic role. Another excellent example of the radical Nonconformist entrepreneur in the second half of nineteenth-century Wales is Thomas Williams of Gwaelod-y-garth House, Merthyr Tydfil.[16]

Nonconformity, then, so often provided the driving force for Victorian reform movements, both in ideology and personnel, its leaders appearing with regularity at the forefront of local initiatives. Their efforts reflected their passionately held view that the common good demanded an array of reforms and also the widespread contemporary belief that change was dependent on fervent public agitations. Radicals, in particular, seized every opportunity to reinforce this belief. Thus, for example, abolition of the property qualification for MPs in 1858 was, to the Chartist *London News*, 'striking proof how popular pressure can alone effect Reforms'.[17]

---

[16] W. R. Lambert, op. cit., pp. 181–3, 252.
[17] *London News*, 8 May 1858.

VII
PARLIAMENTARY REFORM

I 'FLOGGING A DEAD HORSE'

The period between the abrupt revival of Chartism in 1848 and the reform crisis of 1866–7 was not uneventful in the campaign for further parliamentary reform, even if it displayed no great drama. Bills and resolutions were placed before Parliament and various schemes were propounded in the country. Inexhaustible speculation in pamphlets, books, the press and on the public platform also ensured that parliamentary reform was a recurrent theme in British politics during the 1850s.

Another facet of the activity was the survival of Chartism, which persisted throughout the 1850s in organizational terms and, more broadly, on an ideological level. It did so, however, with a greater complexity, palpably expressed in the fragmentations of 1849–50 when several rival organizations sprang up. Within the N.C.A. there was a rift between the now more conciliatory but mentally declining Feargus O'Connor and those led by Ernest Jones and George Julian Harney, who advocated a strongly socialist programme. By late 1851 Jones had assumed control of the N.C.A. which remained the largest Chartist organization. The N.C.A., along with Jones and his *People's Paper*, gave the cause its tenuous unity during the decade. Wales was very much part of this survival right until the demise of the N.C.A. in 1860.

Subscription lists indicate knots of Chartist supporters in a large number of areas in the 1850s.[1] Organizationally, the Welsh survival was a fitful one, mirroring the N.C.A.'s own experience of revival and quiescence. 'For a long time passed', wrote a Llanidloes correspondent in July 1852, 'the good old cause of democracy has been dormant in our town, but the visit of Mr Gammage ... has awakened us to life once more.'[2] Missionaries like R. G. Gammage, James Finlen and Ernest Jones himself were frequently the spark to light or relight Chartist fires. Obviously

[1] See A. V. John, 'The Chartist endurance', p. 34.
[2] *People's Paper*, 24 July 1852.

much depended on individual resolution. Stalwarts like Thomas C. Ingram of Abergavenny, Thomas Clayton of Newtown, John Lewis and John James of Llanidloes, and William Croose of Buckley were the life-blood of their local societies. By the same token, loss of leadership could prove fatal. Death and emigration were instrumental in this regard, while others, often in disillusionment, turned away from Chartism.

The societies were clearly minority groups. In 1851 N.C.A. enrolments on Ernest Jones's tour were 48, 32, and 50 at Merthyr, Llanidloes, and Newtown, respectively.[3] In 1856 the Merthyr branch began with 10, hoping to treble the number.[4] There was a clear distinction, too, between 'members' and 'good paying members', the latter being the faithful few upon whom the work fell. Everywhere there was a very much larger 'adherence', visiting lecturers frequently addressing meetings of several hundreds. With revival, however impermanent, the normal wheels swung into motion. Officers were elected, the first task of the secretary being to communicate with the central executive for cards and tracts. Regular meetings began, often at a member's house. Sometimes a special room was acquired; at Newtown in 1856 the old Chartist schoolroom was reopened, four evenings for lessons and two for branch business.[5] Local activity concentrated on the basics of propaganda and education. At times of euphoria ambitions soared—for example, the proposed parliamentary candidatures put forward by mid-Wales and Merthyr Chartists of Gammage and John Frost respectively.[6] More rationally, Chartists looked upon elections as occasions to question candidates and air their own views, a regular feature at Merthyr.

Much Chartist preoccupation in these years, as in the past, centred on the question of middle-class alliance. Organizations like the People's League and the People's Charter Union sought to promote this object. There were also middle-class initiatives, the most important of which was the National Parliamentary and Financial Reform Association (N.R.A.), formed in March 1849 and supporting Hume's 'Little Charter'. Chartists were divided on such enterprises and, as we have seen, the Welsh response

---

[3] *Northern Star*, 23 Aug. 1851.
[4] *People's Paper*, 5 Apr. 1856.
[5] Ibid., 12 Apr. 1856.
[6] Ibid., 30 July, 6 Aug. 1853, 20 Dec. 1856; *Shrewsbury Chronicle*, 29 July 1853.

reflected this divergence. At Merthyr, despite the acquiescence of the 'respectable and moral Chartists', a public meeting supporting Hume's proposals was not convened for fear of disturbance by the extremists.[7] It was this sort of dissension which made middle-class leaders understandably sceptical. 'What proportion of the Chartists are become rational?', queried John Bright.[8]

The spirit of collaboration evinced by some Chartists was manifested in other campaigns. In late 1849 a number of Merthyr Chartist leaders were 'actively engaged in carrying out the arrangements' after a local A.S.C.A. meeting.[9] This same group—men like William Gould, Henry Thomas, Matthew John, and Morgan Williams—were also prominent in the administrative reform movement, which, amidst the clamour over the conduct of the Crimean War in the mid fifties, demanded civil service reform. A branch of the Administrative Reform Association (A.R.A.) functioned in the town in the summer of 1855.[10] Other Chartists clung instinctively to 'old enmities, old suspicions and old revenges' and, indeed, hostility to middle-class organizations was at this time essentially N.C.A. policy, under the direction of Ernest Jones. Thus the A.R.A. was trifling in importance; only with the Charter 'shall we be in a position to compel our government to put the right men in the right places'.[11] Jones was by now firmly established as the mentor of Chartist die-hards in Wales. After a tour in 1851, denouncing compromise and 'half measures of Reform', he reported: 'The spirit and temper of the men of Wales and the West cannot be too highly eulogized.'[12] In reciprocation, the Newtown N.C.A. branch resolved that the *People's Paper* was 'the sole organ of Chartism'.[13]

By the later 1850s Jones's attitude had noticeably softened on the basis that 'under the present social system the capitalists are the social enemies of the small shopkeeper and of the working man—and that the two latter classes are marked by that same

---

[7] *Principality*, 23 June 1848; see above p. 56.
[8] Wilson Papers, Box 17, Bright to Wilson, 28 Mar. 1851.
[9] *Nonconformist*, 28 Nov. 1849; *Principality*, 30 Nov. 1849.
[10] *Cambrian*, 25 May, 8 June, 13 July 1855; *Merthyr Telegraph*, 11 Aug. 1855; see also O. Anderson, 'The Administrative Reform Association, 1855-7', in P. Hollis (ed.), op. cit., pp. 262-88.
[11] *People's Paper*, 30 June 1855.
[12] Ibid., 23 Aug. 1851.
[13] Ibid., 12 June 1852.

system, as allies and friends'.[14] Accordingly, in 1858 he was one of the leading sponsors of the Political Reform League (P.R.L.), which, under the presidency of Joseph Sturge, advocated manhood suffrage, the secret ballot, abolition of the property qualification for MPs, triennial parliaments, and equalization of electoral districts. 'We wish to bury in oblivion the faults of the past on both sides,' declared Jones; 'the want of faith shown by the middle classes in not making the Reform Bill the fulcrum to enfranchise the masses, and the deadly hatred of the working men to that great middle class movement—the Repeal of the Corn Laws.'[15] Inevitably, rival Chartists responded with the National Political Union for the Obtainment of the People's Charter (N.P.U.) and denounced the P.R.L. and its programme 'trimmed to suit the middle classes'.[16] Both societies launched journals and tried to stimulate provincial branches.

No N.P.U. organizations seem to have been formed in Wales though there were reservations about middle-class alliance. John Lewis, the Llanidloes Chartist, counselled 'great caution in adopting the terms of agreement, guarantees of faith, and relative nature of union',[17] while the repatriated John Frost, refusing the invitation to represent Nottingham Chartists at the inaugural conference of the P.R.L., was sharply condemnatory: 'I can see no good from its assembling but much evil ... there are at present no Chartists and no Chartist agitation.'[18] Generally, though, Welsh Chartists remained faithful to Ernest Jones who, as Llanidloes Chartists put it, 'deserved their unlimited confidence'.[19] From Newtown, the local leader Thomas Clayton gave 'the kind assurance of the faithful few', while the Llanidloes N.C.A. appointed officers to visit factory-workers and several gentlemen in the locality to solicit views on the enterprise and was answered with both moral and pecuniary support.[20] Accordingly, Chartist delegates from Montgomeryshire and Merthyr attended the P.R.L. conference of February 1858.[21] A branch was certainly formed

[14] Ibid., 6 June 1857.
[15] London News, 8 May 1858.
[16] National Union, May 1858.
[17] People's Paper, 26 Dec. 1857.
[18] Ibid., 14 Nov. 1857.
[19] Ibid., 20 June 1857.
[20] Ibid., 12, 26 Dec. 1857.
[21] Ibid., 14 Nov. 1857.

at Llanidloes and ordered a dozen weekly copies of the League's mouthpiece, the *London News*, for circulation. It also provided middle-class and Chartist representatives on the General Committee of the League, supporting a degree of class co-operation.[22] A P.R.L. committee was set up in Aberdare, though this seems to have been entirely working-class. Members adopted the Charter 'in its entirety' but declared themselves 'willing to suspend minor points for a while'. One of the committee's first acts was to vote ten shillings 'to support the *People's Paper* in the Editor's present difficulties', indicating that loyalty to Ernest Jones was the main motivation.[23] But nationally, the movement failed to generate widespread support. Within a short time Jones was concerned that the middle classes were displaying 'no great alacrity in the cause'.[24] By the end of 1858 the P.R.L. was obsolete.

Ernest Jones consistently expounded Chartism in socialist terms, an interpretation which the Convention of March 1851 endorsed. Inevitably, such doctrines had some currency in Wales during the decade. 'We have no dislike for the word chartism in itself', argued a Merthyr columnist, 'but as it was practically expressed in former years, and as it is understood at the present day in this neighbourhood, we have a decided objection. We do not want to level society. That would be unscriptural, unphilosophical, unjust, inexpedient, impossible ...'[25] Similarly, the *Cardiff and Merthyr Guardian* spoke of the widespread, deep-rooted 'Welsh Chartist' idea that 'the moneyed classes are their bitterest enemies, and that the national wealth would be a fine thing if it were equally divided'.[26] In mid Wales, too, socialist journals like the *Red Republican*, the *Democratic Review*, and the *Friend of the People* found an eager audience, and local Chartists called for social as well as political emancipation. On their visits to Wales in the early 1850s Jones and Gammage lectured on topics like land nationalization, currency reform and redistribution of wealth.

Foreign affairs also assumed a prominent role in Chartist discussions, particularly after the stirring European events of 1848. Affinity between British and Continental radicals was fostered and

[22] Ibid., 2 Jan., 3 Apr., 24 July 1858.
[23] Ibid., 13 Mar. 1858.
[24] Ibid.
[25] *Merthyr Telegraph*, 15 Jan. 1859.
[26] *Cardiff and Merthyr Guardian*, 26 Mar. 1859.

sustained by a large number of committees and societies, the most famous of which were the Fraternal Democrats, founded in 1845. This society attracted support from Welsh Chartists in centres like Merthyr and Newtown.[27] In 1849–50 Welsh Chartists were prominent in the public sympathy for Hungarian independence, dispatching honorary addresses to the movement's leader, Louis Kossuth, and contributing to the refugee fund.[28] During the fifties and early sixties Italy, Poland, India and the United States roused emotions, particularly in Merthyr, where local sympathies for the north during the American Civil War gave birth to an anti-slavery association in 1863.[29]

In organizational terms, the Chartist survival in Wales was limited, centring primarily on mid Wales and the Merthyr area. Immeasurably more widespread was its survival at a less formal level as a body of opinion. It was the reservoir of uncoordinated sympathy which struck Ernest Jones most forcibly on his 1851 tour: 'Not withstanding the apparent inactivity, the neglect in subscribing funds and organising, it is evident that a democratic undercurrent is at work beneath the surface, waiting ... to roll its waves ...'[30] The continued circulation of 'infidel and Chartist publications' was substantial enough to concern politicians like H. A. Bruce (MP for Merthyr 1852–68),[31] while lectures by old campaigners such as Henry Vincent in various parts of Wales in the 1850s invariably attracted a good attendance.

The survival of Chartist ideology was also visible at parliamentary elections where working-class representatives rose to demand democratic principles. Non-electors became an increasing force at elections as the years progressed; by the end of the fifties they had formed their own political organizations in places like Aberdare, Merthyr and Wrexham. Radicals could vehemently voice opinions and disconcert candidates but affecting the outcome was another matter altogether, and indeed difficult to assess. Victory for the popular choice on a show of hands and subsequent defeat at the poll, as was the fate of G. M. Whalley in Montgomery

[27] *Red Republican*, 27 July, 28 Sept. 1850.
[28] *Northern Star*, 11 Aug. 1849, 19 Oct. 1850, 1 Nov. 1851; *Nonconformist*, 8 Aug. 1849; A. V. John, op. cit., p. 34.
[29] *Merthyr Star*, 7 Feb., 6 June, 3, 10 Dec. 1863.
[30] *Northern Star*, 20 Sept. 1851.
[31] H. A. Bruce, *Merthyr Tydfil in 1852* (Cardiff, 1852), pp. 8–9.

District in 1852 and James Maurice in Denbigh District in 1857, was not uncommon.[32]

At a national level, the last years of the decade saw the collapse of Ernest Jones's journalistic enterprises and with them the termination of organized Chartism, into which he had breathed life for almost a decade. The N.C.A. was finally wound up in 1860. The ideology was, of course, by no means dead and was most visibly to re-emerge in the parliamentary reform debates of 1866-7.

In some communities Chartist activists are recognizable as a cohesive, significant influence in local political and social affairs for many years and were certainly ever ready to initiate or revive reform agitations and popular protest. Nowhere was this more striking than in Merthyr where, in the early 1870s, veteran Chartists, at a series of public meetings 'with the object of promoting a political agitation favourable to the masses' on such issues as the secret ballot, land reform, fairer and reduced taxation, and international peace, lamented the popular apathy compared with the enthusiasm of thirty years earlier.[33] These Merthyr stalwarts, who had consistently counselled constitutional rather than direct action, are also illustrative of the natural gravitation of many Chartist activists into mid-Victorian Liberalism, a path which often coincided with self-improvement.[34] William Gould (1811-75) is a case in point. Beginning working life as an errand boy and servant at Cyfarthfa Castle, he was subsequently transferred to the ironworks as a puddler. From the late thirties he was active in the Chartist movement, 'coming fresh from work, leathern apron around him to address a meeting', activities which brought him into conflict with William Crawshay. By 1848, aged thirty-seven, Gould was in a position to take up a grocery business in Brecon Road. Here he lived comfortably, retiring in 1873, two years before his death, upon which he left £100. Over the years Gould continued his advocacy of radical principles. Customers

---

[32] *Shrewsbury Chronicle*, 9, 16 July 1852; Jane Morgan, 'Denbighshire's annus mirabilis: the borough and county elections of 1868', *Welsh History Review*, 7, No. 2 (June 1974), p. 76.

[33] *Merthyr Star*, 29 Jan., 14 May, 6 Aug., 10, 24 Sept. 1870.

[34] See A. V. John, op. cit., pp. 36-44; D. J. V. Jones, 'Chartism in Welsh communities' p. 252; B. Harrison and P. Hollis, 'Chartism, Liberalism and the life of Robert Lowery', *English Historical Review*, LXXXII (1967), pp. 503-55.

at his shop were regularly subjected to a political sermon while in 1872, as a Board of Health candidate, he was still being disparagingly designated 'the Chartist lip'. Yet his interests and energies had long been much broader. Late in his life he served as a member of the Burial Board and the Board of Health and as a Poor Law Guardian. He died a respected local figure, 'an immense concourse' attending his funeral.[35]

Following repeal of the Corn Laws in 1846 and especially after the Continental excitements of 1848, a number of middle-class radicals concurred with the Chartist appeal for 'a hearty and determined agitation out of doors' to secure democratic advance. Others, most eminently Richard Cobden, considered such an agitation inopportune and alternatively sought an extension of the franchise through the creation of forty-shilling freeholds, a strategy attempted by the A.C.L.L. and by Chartists. Accordingly, the National Freehold Land Society (F.L.S.) came into being in mid 1849, developing from an original Birmingham organization, formed some eighteen months earlier. Basically, estates were to be purchased through funds raised by the regular subscriptions of members and then divided into plots of sufficient value to confer voting rights on the owners. Two large conferences, the launch of a monthly journal, the *Freeholder*, and ambitions for a £50,000 fund, all within the national movement's first year, bore the unmistakable A.C.L.L. stamp. By 1850, 80 land associations were in existence with 30,000 members; by 1852 there were 130 with 85,000 members.[36] The F.L.S. remained the most important body of its kind, though similar organizations came into being.

Besides the creation of votes, supporters claimed social and moral benefits. To the *Principality* the movement was edifying in 'reforming the drunkard, teaching the spendthrift to save, and the poor man to aim at independence'.[37] In this way the project was attractive to the more conservative elements of society, for

[35] *Merthyr Express*, 31 July 1875; *Aberdare Times*, 31 July 1875; *Merthyr Telegraph*, 30 July 1875. In 1875 William Gould bequeathed £20 each to the 'old guard', Morgan Williams, Matthew John, Henry Thomas and David Ellis, with whom he had been associated in political movements at Merthyr from the late 1830s. The remaining £20 was to go to 'the constructor of a perfect ballot box'. *Merthyr Express*, 31 July 1875.
[36] J. E. Ritchie, *Freehold Land Societies, Their History, Present Position and Claims* (1853), p. 5; *The Reformer's Almanack and Political Year Book* (1850), p. 34; D. Read, *Cobden and Bright: A Victorian Political Partnership* (1967), pp. 157–8; D. Martin, 'Land Reform', in P. Hollis (ed.), *Pressure from Without in Early Victorian England*, p. 150.
[37] *Principality*, 22 Feb. 1850.

it conformed to their belief that men should show by self-improvement that they were worthy of the privilege of voting and that franchise reform should be cautious. Thus, to the Tory *Monmouthshire Merlin*, the scheme represented 'a real extension, and that of the safest and most unobjectionable kind'.[38] Indeed, Society promoters were often at pains to emphasize they belonged to no party; accordingly, the Cardiff branch secretary applauded the formation of a Midland organization by protectionists.[39]

A spate of freehold land societies sprang up in south Wales in 1850.[40] In the north, a Welsh Freehold Land Society was formed at Wrexham in February 1853, followed by branch associations in the main towns of the region.[41] Promoters looked principally, of course, to the unenfranchised, though electors were also encouraged to acquire a second vote.

Most Welsh societies began modestly with 20–30 subscribers, as at Rhyl and Denbigh, and grew steadily; the Pontypool branch started in early March 1850 with 38 members and by mid May had 150. Others increased more rapidly; at Abergavenny the number of shares rose from 65 to 195 in just a few weeks in the summer of 1850 while, at the same time, the Newport society was progressing even better—with 320 names holding 520 shares, weekly receipts of £32 and a bank balance of £600, it was looking for suitable property in the area. At Abergavenny it was reported that of the 135 shareholders in June 1850 'above a hundred of them were really working men, men who gain their livelihood by their daily labours'.[42] Despite such allusions, the estimated saving of around £50 emphatically precluded the vast majority of the workers.[43] And most conspicuous in the localities were middle-class radicals, frequently progressive employers—men like W. H. Darby of Wrexham and John Cory of Cardiff—stalwarts of mid-Victorian Liberalism who were active in a number of campaigns for social and political progress. Old A.C.L.L. supporters were attracted to the movement. So, too, were temperance advocates

---

[38] Quoted in *The League*, 14 Dec. 1844.
[39] *Principality*, 2 Aug. 1850.
[40] Ibid., 1, 22 Feb., 8 Mar., 3 May, 28 June, 19 July 1850.
[41] *Carnarvon and Denbigh Herald*, 14 Aug. 1852, 5 Feb., 6, 13, 20 Aug., 1 Oct. 1853, 17 June 1854.
[42] *Principality*, 1 Feb., 8 Mar., 17 May, 7, 21 June 1850.
[43] D. Read, op. cit., p. 157.

and militant Dissenters; the Merthyr society originated among A.S.C.A. supporters led by Revd Abraham Jones.[44]

Significantly, within a few years the nature of the freehold land movement changed fundamentally. As the Fourth Annual Report of the F.L.S. recognized, 'the primary motive ... was the extension of the County Franchise by means of freeholds, but experience has shown that other and equally important benefits follow ... The Land Society has solved the problem of the savings banks; traders and capitalists found in it a new and profitable investment for surplus funds.'[45] Noticeably in the foundation of societies at Connah's Quay and Holywell in June 1854 the prime consideration was the provision of improved houses; similarly others, as in Swansea, became in time little more than building societies.[46] The shift confirmed that original aspirations went unrealized and, despite the Birmingham society's claim of 195 new electors in its first year,[47] most societies could claim very little success in increasing the electorate. By the mid fifties, Cobden, the movement's most revered patron, was turning away from the idea. For a time, however, Welshmen had supported the enterprise with enthusiasm and much of the motivation for this had been political—the resort to an unobtrusive means of franchise extension when the prospects of a parliamentary measure seemed unpromising. Indeed, the scheme retained an appeal. In 1865 an abortive attempt was made by Revd James Rhys ('Kilsby') Jones to create a Welsh Freehold Land Society at Aberystwyth, again a political organization in genesis.[48]

Middle-class radicalism was also manifested in direct pressure for parliamentary reform. In the late forties and early fifties Joseph Hume's programme of household suffrage, secret ballot, equal electoral districts, and triennial parliaments generated largely short-lived enthusiasm in the country. In Wales, public meetings in such places as Newport, Cardiff, Haverfordwest, Sirhowy and Llangefni endorsed the 'Little Charter' and adopted petitions.[49]

[44] *Principality*, 30 Nov. 1859.
[45] *Carnarvon and Denbigh Herald*, 14 Feb. 1854.
[46] Ibid., 17 June 1854; *Swansea Journal*, 16 Apr. 1859.
[47] D. Read, op. cit., p.158.
[48] I. G. Jones, *Explorations and Explanations*, p. 183.
[49] *Principality*, 16, 23 June, 14 July 1848; *Welshman*, 16 June 1848; David A. Pretty, 'Richard Davies and Nonconformist radicalism in Anglesey, 1837–68: a study of sectarian and middle-class politics', *Welsh History Review*, 9, No. 4 (Dec. 1979), p. 437.

The Nonconformist press also renewed its democratic campaign, while in the columns of the *Principality* 'Ieuan Gwynedd' eulogized the new French Republic based on universal male suffrage and the secret ballot and exhorted the people of Wales to 'a powerful but determined agitation' for similar rights.[50] Seeking to promote Hume's proposals, as well as the reduction and equalization of tax burdens, was the N.R.A, which, despite its nation-wide aspirations and its propaganda efforts in the early 1850s, remained essentially metropolitan. Certainly, it made little impact in Wales. A committee existed at Merthyr in mid 1850 and a handful of Welsh representatives attended its reform conference of that year.[51] But John Bright's overtures towards Dissenting ministers and middle-class radicals in the Principality and hopes of engaging lecturers there, as the A.C.L.L. had done, came to nothing, while the Welsh liberal press, far more interested in the secret ballot, gave the N.R.A. little attention.[52]

Hume's 'Little Charter' was defeated in the Commons in 1848, 1849 and 1850. At the same time, motions for suffrage extension met a similar fate. There were government-sponsored bills in 1852 and 1854, reflecting Lord John Russell's commitment to further parliamentary reform, but they aroused little enthusiasm in Parliament or in the country and failed ingloriously. Middle-class radicals condemned their moderation, while Chartists were predictably disdainful; on his visit to Wales in 1852 Gammage denounced 'the miserable tricksters who are seeking to palm their delusive scheme upon the public'.[53] Parliamentary reform re-emerged as an issue following the Crimean War (1854-6) but not on any significant scale until the end of the decade. Late 1858 and early 1859 saw increased activity, with Disraeli presenting a bill on behalf of the Conservative Government and John Bright drafting a rival scheme. In Wales, as elsewhere, reform meetings were held, petitions adopted, and organizations formed. Welsh

[50] *Principality*, 14 Mar. 1848.
[51] Ibid., 12 Apr., 3 May 1850.
[52] Wilson Papers, Box 18, Bright to Wilson, 31 May 1850. A particularly eager ballot campaigner throughout the 1850s was the ex-A.C.L.L. agent and subsequent editor of the *Swansea and Glamorgan Herald* (1847 57), John Jenkins. He was the moving spirit behind the formation of a South Wales Ballot Society and on several occasions urged Cobden's leadership of a great popular movement similar to the League. WSRO, Cobden Papers 42 and Add. MS 2761, Cobden to Jenkins, 23 Oct. 1852, 4, 29 Dec. 1857; J. Jenkins, *The Ballot and Ministerial Reform*, pp. 13-15.
[53] *People's Paper*, 16 Oct. 1852.

reformers expressed disappointment with some aspects of Bright's proposals, particularly its advocacy of household suffrage only, which antagonized working-class activists. Nevertheless, there were enough attractive points, especially the secret ballot, to win much sympathy, and meetings in various parts of the Principality expressed support for the proposals. By contrast, Wales greeted Disraeli's very modest Reform Bill with antipathy. Liberal organs like the *Merthyr Telegraph* and the *Carnarvon and Denbigh Herald* rejected it out of hand as 'a miserable sham' and worse than no reform at all. At a public meeting arranged by the Merthyr Reform Association speeches 'teeming with denunciation' were the order of the day. Other meetings, at places like Flint, Mold, Pontypridd and Swansea, were similarly condemnatory. Reformers were critical of the nature of the suffrage extension, especially the 'fancy franchises' relating to specific social groups which gave the working classes 'no hope for the future', but as ever the sharpest words concerned the omission of the secret ballot.[54] The bill was summarily dismissed as a blatant political manoeuvre by Parliament, which was then dissolved before John Bright had presented his scheme.

Merthyr reformers were particularly active in the ensuing general election, vainly championing E. M. Elderton, a London barrister, against the incumbent, H. A. Bruce. More dramatic were the events in Merioneth. Originating as an agitation to gain borough representation, the local reform movement developed into a challenge, in the person of David Williams, the Castell Deudraeth landowner, to the Wynne dominance of the county seat. Bala, where the 'Merioneth Progressive Reform Society' had been formed in 1852, once more assumed the leadership through a distinct group, composed of Nonconformist ministers, professional men, shopkeepers, and tradesmen. These formed the nucleus of the election committee campaigning for Williams, who above all was calling for redress of Dissenters' grievances and for parliamentary reform. Opinion was certainly effectively mobilized in Bala, but the overall result was a victory for the sitting Tory, W. W. E. Wynne, by a margin of thirty-eight votes. The Bala reformers subsequently sought to build on their efforts by

[54] *Merthyr Telegraph*, 19 Feb., 5 Mar. 1859; *Merthyr and Aberdare Times*, 12 Mar. 1859; *Swansea Journal*, 12 Mar. 1859; *Carnarvon and Denbigh Herald*, 26 Mar. 1859.

founding the Merioneth Reform Association in 1859 for 'the
revision of the Register of Voters, the promotion of Liberal principles ... and also taking all necessary steps for the return of a
Liberal member at the next vacancy in the representation'. One
of its first concerns, though, was organizing protest against the
political evictions following the 1859 election and providing aid
for the victims. The Association proved to be more than a registration body; it was also a propaganda agency, providing an
important basis for the intervention of the Liberation Society and
eventually for David Williams's triumph in 1868.[55]

Nationally, the 1859 election saw the return of Palmerston's
'Liberal' coalition with Lord John Russell again ready to take
up the question of parliamentary reform. However, his modest
bill of 1860 received short shrift in the Commons, being withdrawn
without a second reading. Nor did it find enthusiastic favour in
the country. Radical and even moderate reformers were critical
of its deficiencies but often emphasized its value as an instalment.
They were therefore scathing of the failure of such an insubstantial
measure; Thomas Gee, for example, denounced the many professed reformers in Parliament as 'unprincipled hypocrites'.[56]

To the *Merthyr Telegraph*, the bill had 'nothing in it to raise
up the nation in wrath, or to elicit vociferous outbursts of appro-
bation',[57] and, indeed, indifference was the most prevalent emotion. Russell himself acknowledged this fact: 'The apathy of the
country is undeniable. Nor is it a transient humour, it seems rather
a confirmed habit of mind.' He now prescribed that 'the best
course which can now be taken is to wait till the country itself
shows a manifest desire for an amendment of the representation'.[58]
This is effectively what happened and for the next five
years or so the question of parliamentary reform was largely in
abeyance.

Indeed, the feature which struck contemporaries most forcibly
about reform movements during the whole of the 1850s and early
1860s was the lack of popular participation. 'Flogging a dead horse'
was Bright's reflection on his efforts to raise agitation in the years

[55] NLW, MS 787, Minute Book of the Merioneth Reform Association; I. G. Jones,
Explorations and Explanations, Ch. 3.
[56] *Baner ac Amserau Cymru*, 20 June 1860.
[57] *Merthyr Telegraph*, 18 Mar. 1860.
[58] S. Walpole, *Lord John Russell*, II (1889), pp. 341-2, quoting Russell to Palmerston,
13 Nov. 1860.

1858–61.[59] Often, reform leaders seemed to lack vigour too: 'We are certainly become a very tame set of politicians compared to the striving days of the "League"!', wrote Cobden to John Jenkins of Swansea.[60] Successive parliamentary reform proposals engendered neither enthusiasm nor protest on any large scale, and opponents could consistently argue that the people manifestly did not want such a measure. Yet the schemes served to spotlight the issue, if with no great durability. Moreover, this was a period when much of the suspicion and bitterness generated in earlier years was being buried. Although in the mid 1860s the middle and working classes had distinct organizations pressing for parliamentary reform, the co-operation was considerable and effective.

II THE REFORM MOVEMENT, 1866–1868

Parliamentary reform was not prominent in the general election of July 1865, the majority of candidates of both parties ignoring it. The election was conducted on the basis of a vote of confidence in the Liberal Government, and Palmerston, Prime Minister for most of the previous decade and the shield against progressive forces, remained firmly in control. Within a few months, however, Palmerston's death in October had significantly changed the situation. Russell, his successor, was less secure politically, having to court radical support in Parliament, a course requiring prompt action on parliamentary reform. Gladstone was already committed to it. At the same time, organized pressure outside Parliament increased dramatically.

The history of the passage of the Second Reform Act in 1867 is a particularly curious one. In 1866 a very moderate Liberal bill, extending the vote to only about 400,000 people, was rejected by the Conservatives and a section of the Liberal Party. The Conservative leaders, Derby and Disraeli, were intent on using reform to divide the Liberals, to enable their party to govern on its own and be established as a party of government. They were anxious that the Conservatives should gain the credit for reform. It was thus a Conservative bill which eventually became law and in the process became more radical than was originally intended. In purely material terms, the Act almost doubled the

[59] Quoted in *N.E.L. Monthly Paper*, Mar. 1874.
[60] WSRO, Cobden Papers 42, Cobden to Jenkins, 19 May 1858.

old electorate of just over one million and redistributed a large number of seats. But its importance must also be seen in the broader context of the extension of democracy, rendering further reform inevitable in a way the Reform Act of 1832 had not.[61]

In 1866, out of a total population in Wales of around 1,313,000, there were just over 62,000 voters. The Act of 1867 gave the vote to about another 59,000 Welshmen, thereby raising the percentage of the population eligible to vote from 4.5 per cent in 1866 to about 9.1 per cent in 1868. The Act perpetuated the differences between the borough and county franchise. The latter was extended principally by the substitution of a £12 rating for a £50 rental qualification, a much less spectacular concession than in the boroughs where household suffrage was brought in; henceforth every adult male householder who had paid his rates, had not been in receipt of parochial aid during the twelve months prior to registration, and who was properly registered, was to have the vote. The major changes in the size of the electorate occurred in the borough constituencies, especially the industrial ones, although the growth of the county electorates was also substantial.[62] The Act gave Wales one additional MP, thereby making its total thirty-three: on population grounds Merthyr became a two-member constituency.

The final passage of the measure was the result of an intense struggle within Parliament. Outside Parliament, too, there was enthusiastic activity, though its precise importance has been disputed. Opinions vary in shades from Royden Harrison's view that the Act represented 'a capitulation by government to the Reform League', to Maurice Cowling's that the outcome was entirely determined by party complexities at Westminster.[63] Most scholars

[61] G. Himmelfarb, 'The politics of democracy: the English Reform Act of 1867', *Journal of British Studies*, VI, No. 1 (1966), p. 97.

[62] *Return of the Number of Electors on the Register in each of the Parliamentary Cities and Boroughs* ..., PP 1868–9, L, p. 109. The rise in the Welsh electorate was about 50 per cent in the counties and about 250 per cent in the boroughs. I. G. Jones, *Explorations and Explanations*, p. 296.

[63] For varying interpretations, see R. Harrison, *Before the Socialists* (1965); R. Blake, *Disraeli* (1966); M. Cowling, *Disraeli, Gladstone and Revolution* (1967); F. E. Gillespie, *Labour and Politics in England, 1850–67* (Durham, North Carolina, 1927); F. M. Leventhal, *Respectable Radical: George Howell and Victorian Working-Class Politics* (1971); G. Himmelfarb, op. cit.; F. B. Smith, *The Making of the Second Reform Bill* (1966). For Professor Himmelfarb's criticisms of Dr F. B. Smith, see 'Commitment and ideology: the case of the Second Reform Act', *Journal of British Studies*, IX, No. 1 (1969). The same number of this Journal contains Dr Smith's reply: 'The "dependence of license upon faith": Miss Gertrude Himmelfarb on the Second Reform Act'.

place some emphasis on the influence of public agitation, central to which were the Reform League (R.L.) and the National Reform Union (N.R.U.), the two national organizations involved in urging an extension of the suffrage. The N.R.U. was middle-class in character. Founded in April 1864 and based in Manchester in the old offices of the A.C.L.L., it was essentially an association of Lancashire merchants and manufacturers. It was a household suffrage association which carefully avoided the phrase 'manhood suffrage' in order not to offend the middle classes. The programme of the N.R.U. also included triennial parliaments, the ballot, and equal distribution of seats. It was most powerful in the vicinity of its headquarters, although, like most national reform bodies, it encouraged the formation of branch societies throughout the country; in February 1867, it claimed 192.[64] Their location is difficult to establish for no list has survived. More information is available on individual support. At most, N.R.U. vice-presidents totalled over 500, 8 of whom were resident in Wales,[65] while several other Welsh representatives attended delegate conferences.[66] For the most part, these individual supporters do not seem to have worked for the formation of branches. Rarely do they seem to have gone beyond participation in local reform meetings. Only at Brymbo, near Wrexham, was N.R.U. support translated into a branch association. This operated for several months in the early part of 1867 and was dominated by middle-class reformers, including the industrialists, W. H. and C. E. Darby, a number of Dissenting ministers and William Griffiths, overseer of the poor. Few working men were involved; indeed, its inaugural meeting consisted of 'the electors of Brymbo and Broughton'.[67] The Union paid little attention to the Principality. One agent spoke at Wrexham in April 1866;[68]

---

[64] *Manchester Examiner and Times*, 20 Feb. 1867.

[65] These were Revd Dr Price, Aberdare; Revd Thomas Gee and Dr H. Sandwith, Denbigh; Revd A. J. Parry and Richard C. Rawlins, Ruabon; Revd J. Jones, Brymbo; George Bradley, Wrexham; and Robert Platt, Anglesey. George Howell Collection (HC), Miscellany, 'Political Parties and Associations', 53a NRU Circular 1867.

[66] A number of the above vice-presidents attended delegate conferences. Other Welsh representatives included Revd Benjamin Williams of Denbigh, Revd Thomas Levi of Swansea, E. J. Williams of Brymbo, and Thomas Law of Conwy. *Manchester Examiner and Times*, 20 Feb. 1867; HC, National Reform Conference Pamphlet, 324.42.

[67] *Wrexham Weekly Advertiser*, 26 Jan. 1867, 23 Feb. 1867, 2 Mar. 1867.

[68] *Denbighshire and Flintshire Telegraph*, 7 Apr. 1866; *Carnarvon and Denbigh Herald*, 7 Apr. 1866.

meetings 'under the auspices of the N.R.U.' were held at Caerleon in April 1866 and Rhosllannerchrugog in January 1867.[69] But this was the sum of its Welsh activity. Its limited impact was largely confined to north-east Wales, the area nearest its Manchester headquarters. Thus, although reform meetings all over Wales passed resolutions broadly in line with the Union's programme, this potential support remained unharnessed.

More effective than the N.R.U. as an organization for political pressure was the R.L. which was founded in February 1865. Based in London, it was poor in comparison with the wealth of the Union and proclaimed the radical principles of manhood suffrage and the secret ballot. It was also essentially working-class, attracting large numbers of working men, including trade unionists. At its zenith it claimed nearly 600 branches in London and the provinces. Wales's contribution was a modest one. League archives list thirteen branches: at Aberdare, Aberystwyth, Brecon, Cardiff, Cwmbrân, Denbigh, Llandudno, Llanidloes, Newtown, Swansea and two at Merthyr.[70] There is also evidence of interest in the movement at Neath, Milford Haven, and Caernarfon, but no formal organizations were established there.[71] Provincial branches of the R.L. sprang up all over the country. Many, however, did not remain as separate entities, for provincial departments were formed, centred on large towns. There were moves towards a Welsh provincial department but they were not successful.[72]

Essentially, little cohesion existed among the Welsh R.L. branches; they were separate units of political activity. Most were located in industrial towns, which was characteristic of nineteenth-century Wales. National reform bodies evidently achieved least response in largely rural areas, where even the most intense efforts, like those of the A.C.L.L., produced only short-lived enthusiasm.

As far as the R.L.'s impact on Wales was concerned, the most striking exception to the direct relationship between reform activity and industrial communities was Brecon, an important market centre. The town facilitated the establishment of the first League

---

[69] *Baner ac Amserau Cymru*, 14 Apr. 1866; *Wrexham Weekly Advertiser*, 22 Dec. 1866.
[70] HC, Miscellany, List of Departments and Branches.
[71] HC, Executive Council Minutes, 11, 18, 25 Aug. 1865; HC, Letter Books (L.B.), Vol. 3, pp. 166, 256, 629.
[72] HC, L.B., 2, p. 149; *Merthyr Express*, 12 Jan. 1867; *Beehive*, 9 Feb. 1867; *Baner ac Amserau Cymru*, 19 Jan. 1867.

society in Wales in the autumn of 1865. It continued to exist over the next three years, holding regular and enthusiastic meetings, before petering out in the latter months of 1868, the last of the League societies in Wales. The surprising degree and durability of this activity in Brecon were primarily due to the inspiration of Alfred Walton, who resided in the town from 1861 to 1875, and who had been prominent in London radical circles for a number of years. He had originally been a stonemason in Newcastle before employment as an architect brought him to Brecon, where he established his own business as a builder. Inevitably, controversy surrounds the relative importance of personality in such a movement. Although it would clearly be wrong to attribute the R.L.'s appeal totally to the presence of particularly active individuals, there is no doubt that in this instance Walton's personal influence had unusual significance. Indeed, the success of all reform societies owed a good deal to those people who were prepared to devote time, effort, and even money to their activities and were ready to act as hard-working officers. Nowhere, however, can personal influence account for the whole story. Even at Brecon, Walton met with favourable circumstances. In particular, political activity in the town benefited from two by-elections in the borough constituency in 1866. Both were enthusiastic affairs, in which the question of parliamentary reform was an issue. Similarly, both involved controversy over electoral corruption which, in turn, stimulated a demand for the ballot. The candidature of Dr Thomas Price of Aberdare in the first of these elections was particularly advantageous for the cause of franchise reform. According to one newspaper, Price's intervention had 'fanned the slumbering embers of Liberalism into a brisk flame throughout the length and breadth of the constituency'.[73]

The Brecon R.L. branch was established in late 1865 but the majority of Welsh branches appeared in the late summer and autumn of 1866. This represented a period of quickening public temper and League activity following the defeat of the Liberal Reform Bill in June and the excitements of the Hyde Park demonstration of July. Two Welsh branches originated through local trade unions. The initiative for one of the Merthyr societies came

[73] *Aberdare Times*, 8 Feb. 1866.

from the Shoemakers' Union, while at Cardiff it came from the Trades Council.[74] But most Welsh branches sprang from a nucleus of local reformers. 'The plan for forming a branch is very simple and easy. Call together a few earnest men and form a committee as you may require.'[75] Thus George Howell, the League secretary, explained the procedure to Thomas Richards of Newport. Each branch had its own elected officials and an established meeting-place, usually a schoolroom, public house, or local hall. Frequency of meetings varied according to enthusiasm. At these meetings, discussion most often revolved around policy, local activities and the present position of reform in the county. A good deal of time was spent on the day-to-day running of the branch. Inevitably, finance was a leading consideration and most societies struggled to meet a variety of costs.

An immediate preoccupation was to awaken public interest and this meant a thorough canvass of the town and neighbourhood to gain membership and support. The first objective of the Cardiff Reform Committee was 'to wait on the working men in the different factories, foundries and workshops'.[76] Meanwhile, Newport reformers promptly sought the co-operation of other local societies and organizations.[77] Most branches burst into life with great enthusiasm. On its foundation the Newport association was sent 200 membership cards. Three weeks later, more were requested.[78] Within three months of its inception, the Cardiff R.L. branch had enrolled 300 members and a series of meetings in the districts of the city increased this number.[79] A vigorous agitation on the outskirts of Merthyr resulted not only in increased membership but also in the formation of auxiliary associations.[80] Auxiliaries may have been established, too, in Montgomeryshire.[81] However, local support fluctuated markedly. When attendance settled down after the initial excitement, one suspects that numbers attending rarely exceeded thirty or forty. On the other hand, when passions ran high, local halls were often packed. On such

[74] HC, L.B., 2, p. 489; and L.B., 1, p. 426.
[75] Ibid., L.B., 1, p. 339.
[76] *Cardiff Times*, 16 Nov. 1866.
[77] HC, L.B., 1, p. 438.
[78] Ibid., L.B., 1, p. 349 and p. 429.
[79] *Cardiff Chronicle*, 7 Dec. 1866.
[80] *Merthyr Star*, 29 May, 5 June 1867.
[81] *Shrewsbury Chronicle*, 2, 24 Nov. 1866; *Baner ac Amserau Cymru*, 1 Dec. 1866.

occasions attendance would far exceed the number of regularly paid-up members. Some were simply interested observers, but many were unregistered sympathizers. Public meetings and demonstrations were important in publicizing the movement. The largest were reserved for special occasions—to inaugurate the local association, to greet a League agent, or possibly as a response to national events. Large demonstrations were costly and bit deeply into the branch's coffers; the one at Merthyr in November 1866 cost £17, and accordingly an admission fee had to be charged the next time. They also required considerable organization, involving much committee work. The Merthyr Reform Association spent weeks preparing for its demonstration on Easter Monday 1867. Much time was devoted to discussion and decision-making. Committee members met delegates from local benefit and friendly societies to discuss co-operation. A subcommittee was appointed to draw up resolutions. Chairmen and speakers were selected. Invitations were sent to influential local gentlemen. There was a host of other arrangements—hire of hall, admission tickets, publicity, bands, processions, and seating.[82]

Such demonstrations were a very important way of publicizing the movement. Their processions of bands and banners made them occasions of great ceremony, attracting crowds of onlookers, as illustrated by this report of a demonstration at Newport on 24 September 1866:

> It is a long time since Newport has witnessed a political demonstration but on Monday night there was one that showed the hearts of the working classes to be in the right place. It was at first intended that the meeting should be at the Town-hall, but, short as the notice was, the feeling became so evident that the large Drill-hall of the Rifle Corps was secured. At seven o'clock upwards of 2,000 persons assembled in front of the Queen's hotel to escort the local President of the Reform Association, Mr James Brown, and the deputation from the London League, Mr W. Harper, formerly of Newport, and Mr Alfred A. Walton, of Brecon, to the Drill-hall. A procession was formed, headed by those gentlemen and the local committee, followed by a brass band, and comprising about 2,000 persons, who marched through the principal streets . . .

[82] *Merthyr Star*, 9, 17 Apr. 1867.

On arriving at the hall the doors were thrown open and in a few minutes the large area was densely packed with about 3,000 persons while hundreds were unable to gain admission.[83]

The amount of central control over branches varied considerably, largely depending on the degree of subordination which the local societies were prepared to accept. Some, like the Merthyr Reform Association, proudly asserted their independence. As one member insisted: 'If they had adopted the same principles as the Reform League, it did not follow that they were a branch of the League ... they were entirely independent ...'[84] The Denbigh reformers were prepared to be described as a League branch but in no way did they regard themselves as subordinate to the London organization.[85] Wisely, the League avoided undue interference. George Howell told Aberdare reformers: 'If you form a branch of the League, the entire management, financial and otherwise, will be in your hands, and it will be much stronger than a mere local association.'[86]

Almost everywhere there was much discussion as to whether to affiliate or not. Sometimes finance was an important consideration. Each branch was supposed to send one-third of its membership subscriptions to the executive. A few Welsh societies did so; most did not. Welsh contributions came from a handful of middle-class supporters rather than out of branch payments. Welsh reluctance to support the League financially was a feature emphasized by the lecturer, George Mantle. Reviewing his experiences in Wales, he wrote:

> I have not received one Donation since I started out. I experience the same difficulty in that respect in every town I visit. Namely, an objection by the Branches to any attempt to raise money except for the Branch itself ... In money matters I am flogging a dead horse with a vengeance ...

Mantle found himself in a dilemma. Efforts to exact money could harm the cause:

> ... I am afraid that any attempt in that direction would be regarded as an act of open hostility ... If I were to do anything to offend the Branches

[83] *Hereford Times,* 29 Sept. 1866.
[84] *Merthyr Telegraph,* 27 Oct. 1866.
[85] *Llandudno Register and Herald,* 1 Dec. 1866.
[86] HC, L.B., 1, p. 330.

should I be serving the League? If I fail to obtain a profit from my tour will my mission be considered a failure?[87]

Each local society was, of course, struggling financially. Beyond this, however, was a suspicion of contributing to a distant organization; one-third of subscriptions, according to a Newport working man, were being 'spent in the London places of amusement'.[88]

Most often the question of affiliation centred on policy. All branches, to some degree, experienced a division between moderates and radicals, between those who stood for a limited extension of the franchise and those who were prepared to embrace manhood suffrage and the ballot. Relations between the groups were amicable in some places, such as Newtown and Cardiff. In Newtown it was decided not to hold a county demonstration under the auspices of the R.L.; rather, 'in order that all grades of reformers can act together harmoniously ... a purely local meeting should be convened'.[89] In Cardiff, household suffragists worked with radicals on the basis that the League was 'a necessary and ... useful instrumentality in the promotion of Parliamentary Reform'.[90] No such co-operation was possible at Merthyr, where there was bitter disagreement between ex-Chartists and the moderates. Indeed, the latter withdrew 'when the more radical members succeeded in committing the committee to "manhood suffrage and the ballot"'.[91]

If some Welsh branches insisted on self-determination, others bound themselves closely to the national organization and adopted League rules to the letter. Executive control was in part exercised by George Howell through correspondence. Another means lay with delegate conferences. Some of these were attended by a few Welsh representatives, but most branches never sent delegates. Lecture tours also helped to co-ordinate local and national activity. One such tour incorporated parts of Wales; the lecturer was George Mantle, a member of the League's executive in London. He addressed only six meetings in four Welsh towns in November 1866 and, despite requests for speakers, neither he nor any other League agent again toured Wales. Thus, societies were very much

[87] HC, Mantle's Letter Book, Mantle to Howell, 22, 29 Nov. 1866.
[88] *Monmouthshire Merlin*, 22 Sept. 1866.
[89] *Shrewsbury Free Press*, 5 Jan. 1867.
[90] *Cardiff Times*, 16 Nov. 1866.
[91] *Swansea and Glamorgan Herald*, 24 Nov. 1866.

dependent on local speakers like William Gould and J. W. James of Merthyr, James Brown of Newport, and Alfred Walton of Brecon. Tracts and newspapers also had to be relied upon to disseminate principles and information. On request, the League sent circulars, addresses, speeches, and pamphlets to local secretaries and individual supporters. Working-class newspapers, such as the *Beehive*, *Reynolds's Newspaper*, the *Commonwealth*, and the *National Reformer*, also circulated in the industrial towns of north and south Wales. Everywhere, however, these radical journals attained but a limited readership. Clearly the role of the local press was more influential. By the mid sixties, virtually the whole of the Welsh press, including its more conservative elements, accepted that some measure of reform was necessary. A minority, including Thomas Gee's *Baner ac Amserau Cymru*, the *Merthyr Star*, the *Cardiff Chronicle*, and the *Star of Gwent*, strongly advocated R.L. principles and gave powerful backing to local branches. More often, newspapers expressed a preference for moderate change rather than for the radical demands of the R.L. A section of the Welsh press spoke out vehemently against the League. The *Merthyr Telegraph* conducted a vigorous campaign against the local radicals, whom it regarded as 'unconstitutional and revolutionary in their tendencies'.[92] The *Cambrian*, too, whole-heartedly condemned the League and its affiliated branches. In Monmouthshire, the arch-enemy of the movement was the *Merlin*, and local branches frequently complained about the 'bosh' written by 'our slanderers'.[93] When local activity was belittled and defamed, this bred resentment which could act as a stimulus, as the Cwmbrân branch experienced: 'The articles in the *Merlin* of the last two weeks have done more good to our cause in Cwmbrân than six months local agitation.'[94]

A common accusation made against Welsh R.L. branches was that they were associated with Chartism. Leading members were often anxious to refute any such connection since they feared that its violent and revolutionary implications would be detrimental to their cause. The Newtown Reform Committee discussed the image of the movement at length in November 1866. 'Some people actually thought it had a Chartist tendency which was

[92] *Merthyr Telegraph*, 27 Apr. 1867.
[93] *Star of Gwent*, 29 Sept. 1866.
[94] Ibid.

rubbish and something ought to be done to dispel the idea', insisted one member.[95] The *Shrewsbury Free Press* rallied to the Committee's defence: it was not about 'to inaugurate a reign of terror ... they are genuine, honest Reformers'.[96] Similarly, Merthyr moderates argued that advocacy of 'a wide extension of the franchise' rather than 'manhood suffrage' was the best way of making the local Reform Association 'free of being classed among the Chartists'.[97] Official League representatives spoke in the same vein. At the Newport demonstration of November 1866, which in some minds evoked memories of the 1839 march, William Harper was adamant that 'this movement was totally distinct from the old-fashioned Chartist movement' and its participants 'did not hold a single disloyal thought, did not mean anything wrong or destructive to the upper classes of society'.[98]

Despite these denials, there were definite links between them in terms of personnel and ideology. At the top, ex-Chartists served on the R.L. executive; George Mantle, for example, had been imprisoned in 1839 for seditious speech. At a provincial level, Alfred Walton had once been a supporter of the Chartist leader, Bronterre O'Brien, while in mid Wales Mantle noted that 'one or two old Chartists' were concerned in the Newtown reform movement.[99] In Merthyr, ex-Chartists like William Gould, J. W. James and Matthew John dominated the agitation. At meetings these and others proudly proclaimed the old Chartist doctrines and when the question of inviting a lecturer arose their preference was for Ernest Jones.[100] Their public meeting in September 1867 to celebrate the Reform Bill's passage was the occasion to point out that the Charter, 'the most simple, just and honest points ... a free country could possess', was still a far cry away.[101]

The Chartist legacy did not extend to violent tactics. Nevertheless, it was useful for opponents seeking to diminish League support to imply direct action. This opposition was usually vented in the press and in public debate, although in Denbigh adversaries went

---

[95] *Shrewsbury Chronicle*, 23 Nov. 1866.
[96] *Shrewsbury Free Press*, 8 Dec. 1866.
[97] *Merthyr Telegraph*, 29 Sept. 1866.
[98] *Newport Gazette*, 29 Nov. 1866.
[99] *Commonwealth*, 22 Dec. 1866.
[100] *Merthyr Star*, 29 Oct., 3 Dec. 1867.
[101] *Merthyr Telegraph*, 21 Sept. 1867.

as far as printing a series of ballads, 'full of obscene expressions', abusing the members of the local R.L. branch.[102] In reality, R.L. activists demonstrated noticeable restraint and discipline. Working-class radicals were also more disposed than formerly to a middle-class alliance. This was partly a matter of expediency. Earlier events had convinced many Chartists both of governmental power and of their own weaknesses. Energies also found new directions and the alternatives, such as the disestablishment campaign, often involved joint action with middle-class liberals.

About the social composition of the societies it is difficult to be precise. Although ordinary workers—miners, colliers, dockers and factory workers—must have formed the bulk of supporters, it was the shopkeepers, tradesmen and professional people who dominated the leadership. In Wales an important element was provided by Nonconformist ministers, particularly of the Baptist and Independent denominations. George Mantle wrote to the executive thus: 'At both Merthyr and Brecon the Nonconformist ministers afforded most hearty, unqualified and valuable support, no less than Eleven Ministers having supported me in those two towns.'[103] Elsewhere, too, they were prominent. No doubt many such ministers, and ordinary people, saw political reform as the precursor of religious reform. Manhood suffrage and the secret ballot would enable the election of MPs who were sympathetic to Dissenters' grievances. Thus, in Wales, a bond between the R.L. and the Liberation Society was inevitable. The basic aim of the latter was disestablishment of the Church, but it had long had political aspirations as a means to this end. It had stressed the need for 'an enlarged and amended representative system ... for helping on the cause of religious equality'.[104]

Almost everywhere in Wales the link between the R.L. and the Liberation Society was apparent. At meetings of the Denbigh R.L. branch, Thomas Gee and others regularly called for a 'Liberal Nonconformist representation for Wales'. These same men were active in Liberationist circles in the county. Revd Benjamin Williams, an Independent, was secretary of both the R.L. branch

[102] *Wrexham Weekly Advertiser,* 9 Nov. 1866.
[103] HC, Mantle's Letter Book, Mantle to Howell, 22 Nov. 1866.
[104] Minute Book of the Liberation Society Council, Jan. 1862–Dec. 1867, p. 328, quoted by A. D. Bell, 'The Reform League from its origins to the Reform Act of 1867' (University of Oxford D.Phil. thesis, 1961), p. 411, App. 2.

and the Liberation Society committee.[105] At Newtown, the school-master, William Cooke, and the manufacturer, Richard Spoonley, served on the committees of both organizations.[106] Professors Morris and Roberts of Brecon Independent College were also active Leaguers and Liberationists.[107] The Brymbo N.R.U. branch provides a good illustration of the religious aspect of the Welsh reform movement. Meetings were held in chapels, Nonconformist ministers were prominent and there was a definite religious motive behind the agitation. Branch leaders were active Liberationists; the two Baptist ministers, Revd A. J. Parry of Cefn-mawr and Revd John Jones of Brymbo, served as Liberation Society agents. The two movements were linked, as Revd John Jones, also presi-dent of the N.R.U. branch, explained at a local Liberation Society meeting:

> ... although the liberation of the church from state control was not at present the question of the day, in public opinion, it was second only to the all-absorbing question of Reform, and that there existed a certain rela-tionship between the two questions: that the success of the one depended in a great measure on the success of the other. Reform was the harbinger of the liberation of the church ...[108]

Apart from the religious motive, Wales heard the usual political and moralistic arguments for suffrage extension. The vote was a man's right, for 'each was of the same flesh and blood ...'[109] Of greater interest were the wider implications of reform. Alfred Walton of Brecon was doubtless speaking for many Leaguers when he declared that the main reason for seeking the enfranchisement of the people was 'as a means to an end, and that end must be the political, social, industrial, educational advancement and improvement of the whole community'.[110] Many reformers indulged in less sober analysis. Parliamentary reform, according to a Newport enthusiast, would solve 'high and heavy taxation on the one side, pauperism and crime on the other'.[111] Some romantically harked back to the First Reform Act; at a meeting in Newtown, for example, it was asserted that before 1832 'great

[105] *Nonconformist*, 5 Sept. 1866.
[106] Ibid.; *Aberystwyth Observer*, 29 Sept. 1866.
[107] *Liberator*, 1 June 1866, p. 107.
[108] *Wrexham Weekly Advertiser*, 27 Apr. 1867.
[109] Ibid., 23 Nov. 1866.
[110] *Commonwealth*, 25 May 1867.
[111] *Star of Gwent*, 11 May 1867.

poverty, wretchedness and misery prevailed among the masses
... Food was scarce, but since then how great have been the
changes'.[112] Fanciful arguments, outlining the improvements that
reform was expected to bring, were an integral part of the agitation.
The R.L.'s agitation was wholly constitutional in approach. The
mere existence of a central body with 600 branches spread over
the country was itself an influential force. Public meetings, demonstrations, conferences and widespread press coverage were obvious
forms of pressure. So, too, was petitioning, which remained a
favourite device. Communities all over Wales held public meetings
and adopted petitions in favour of some measure of reform. Those
organized by League branches usually called for manhood suffrage
and the secret ballot. R.L. activity in this direction reached a
peak prior to the parliamentary session of 1867. At this juncture,
supporters were urged to send individual petitions to Parliament
and some Welsh branches actively supported this plan.[113] Petitioning also revealed the local concerns of many reformers. How might
the reform proposals benefit their particular community? Merthyr,
Swansea and Cardiff each pressed their claims for a second
member. Aberdare petitioned for separate representation from
Merthyr. In this local context, branches kept a watchful eye on
the behaviour of their own MPs. The reform societies at Brecon,
Merthyr, Newtown, and Denbigh were clearly dissatisfied with
their representation. To the Brymbo N.R.U. branch the three
local MPs were mere 'political dummies'; the main target, though,
was the Tory member for Denbigh District, Townshend
Mainwaring, the subject of bitter criticism, ridicule and even satiri-
cal poetry.[114] Future electoral pressure afforded one reason for
the continuance of reform society activity after the passage of
the Second Reform Act.

In particular, the defeat of the Liberal Reform Bill had led
to scathing criticisms of those members who had voted against
the measure: '... let us pay them back the next time that they
ask for our votes', urged *Y Diwygiwr*, which had a long tradition
of campaigning for radical reform.[115] The most bitter feelings were
directed against the 'Adullamites', those Liberals who had voted

[112] *Shrewsbury Chronicle*, 20 Apr. 1886.
[113] *Cardiff Chronicle*, 11 Jan. 1867.
[114] *Wrexham Weekly Advertiser*, 23 Feb., 2 Mar. 1867.
[115] *Y Diwygiwr*, July 1866, p. 223.

against their own party's Reform Bill in 1866. Among these were Colonel R. M. Biddulph (Denbighshire), Sir Richard Williams Bulkeley (Anglesey), Lord Richard Grosvenor (Flintshire), and C. D. R. Hanbury-Tracy (Montgomery District). Threatened reprisals did not always materialize. In Denbighshire, however, where Colonel Biddulph's 'Adullamite' association had but affirmed existing misgivings, a vigorous campaign led to his rejection in favour of George Osborne Morgan in the 1868 election. The local R.L. branch was now dead, but ex-members, notably Thomas Gee, who wielded tremendous influence through his editorship of *Baner ac Amserau Cymru*, played a significant role in Morgan's success.[116]

The extension of the reform agitation to electioneering was strongly apparent at Cardiff. Here, the Trades Council had formed the League branch in 1866 and dominated the movement throughout. In the 1868 election the trade unions exerted their influence in the Liberal cause. As at Cardiff, the R.L. branch at Newport had lapsed by the 1868 election, but the newly formed Working Men's Liberal Association actively supported the Liberal candidature in the borough election. Prominent in the foundation and the functioning of this Association were middle-class radicals like Councillor James Brown, Revd Henry Oliver, Thomas Richards and T. B. Batchelor, all of whom had been leading members of the old reform society.

In Merthyr, the continued operation of a League branch throughout 1867 inevitably meant electoral involvement. Branch meetings were dominated by the old Chartist stalwarts, men like William Gould, Matthew John, J. W. James and Henry Thomas, who demanded the completion of the Chartist programme. After thoroughly scrutinizing Henry Richard's suitability, branch members worked assiduously for his return.[117] Their staunch support, expressed by 1868 through the official canvassing committees rather than the League branch, helped present Richard as the working-class candidate, and that was an important ingredient of his success. It was in Brecon, however, that the connection

[116] See Jane Morgan, 'Denbighshire's annus mirabilis: the borough and county elections of 1868'.
[117] HC, L.B., 3, pp. 470, 828; L.B., 4, p. 40; see also, I. G. Jones, 'The election of 1868 in Merthyr: a study in the politics of an industrial borough in the mid-nineteenth century', in *Explorations and Explanations*, Ch. 5; A. V. John, 'The Chartist endurance'.

between the R.L. and the 1868 election was most direct. Here, Alfred Walton, the president of the local branch, which was apparently still in existence, presented himself as a candidate in the borough election, though he withdrew before the poll, once the weight of traditional political power was exerted:

> the moment I issued my address ... I speedily found that the two great landlords who own the town of Brecon—the houses of Tredegar and Camden—were united against me, and the screw put upon the tradesmen and working men in all directions ... [118]

Throughout the reform agitation period, references were made to the inactivity of Wales and these were substantially true. There was no shortage of reform meetings in Wales, and they occurred in some rather remote locations—at Newquay, Llechryd, Pwllheli, and Dyserth, for instance. However, passionate enthusiasm was often wanting, as a comparison with Chartist days indicates. Working men, commented Morgan Williams, the former Chartist leader at Merthyr, 'did not have the political feelings they had thirty years ago'.[119] What was missing was a continuity of agitation, which would have been best afforded by an active reform society. There were relatively few of these in Wales. There was only one N.R.U. branch. The R.L. claimed thirteen, but clearly a number of them were ephemeral, and there was no Welsh provincial department of this organization.

An obvious reason for the lack of impact of the N.R.U. and, more especially, of the R.L. since the N.R.U. was not truly 'national', was their short period of life. The R.L. existed from 1865 to 1869, but within this period it was active for quite a short period. Its relatively brief life heightened difficulties which otherwise could have been surmounted. In particular, there was the language barrier which the R.L. failed to overcome. In March 1866 a League executive meeting approved the translation of the 'Principles and Objects of the League' into Welsh, but there is no evidence that a translation materialized.[120] Furthermore, although a radical and influential Welsh Nonconformist press had grown up in Wales, only a few publications, notably Thomas Gee's

[118] *Beehive*, 22 May 1869.
[119] *Merthyr Telegraph*, 22 Sept. 1866.
[120] HC, Exec. Council Mins., 9 Mar. 1866; *Beehive*, 17 Mar. 1866.

Baner ac Amserau Cymru, came out decisively and fervently in advocacy of the R.L.

Wales also suffered from geographical remoteness, of course. Much of the country remained rural. In October 1866, Alfred Walton, in a letter to the *Commonwealth,* urged the League to extend its organization and agitation into the agricultural districts.[121] Wales would, of course, have benefited greatly from such a policy; understandably, however, the R.L. continued to concentrate on the populous industrial regions.

A further obstacle to political agitation was the industrial configuration of south Wales. The area comprised deep valleys, between which mobility and collaboration were difficult. Although industrialized, south Wales was not yet urbanized. Its industrial communities were scattered, lacking a focal point, and that militated against unified political activity. As the *Merthyr Star* observed '... it takes double the time to leaven the population, and that is easily accounted for by the straggling form of the town ...'[122] Although the Merthyr area was well advanced industrially, it was very different from towns like Birmingham and Glasgow.

Not surprisingly, neither the League nor the Union paid any great attention to Wales. Despite passing a resolution 'to bring the principles of the R.L. under the electors and non-electors of the Principality', only one League lecturer visited Wales and he spoke at only four towns.[123] Some Welsh branches complained of neglect. At Merthyr, on the other hand, the lack of response to political meetings was blamed on the R.L.'s influence: its programme was too extreme and supporters ran the risk of being stigmatized as 'Chartists' or 'Revolutionaries' and possibly of suffering 'in their trade, business or profession, and perhaps have to break "caste" and lose their "social status"'.[124]

Local newspapers also had an influential role; in Merthyr, they were accused of doing 'all they could to damn the cause of Reform by faint praise'.[125] There were other interpretations. C. H. James, the Merthyr solicitor and future MP, attributed the local indifference to the Liberal Reform Bill to the fact that it 'did not exactly

[121] *Commonwealth,* 20 Oct. 1866.
[122] *Merthyr Star,* 25 Oct. 1862.
[123] *Brecon County Times,* 24 Nov. 1866.
[124] *Merthyr Telegraph,* 1 Dec. 1866.
[125] Ibid.

reach Merthyr', meaning that the town would have been little affected by the measure.[126] The important factor for Morgan Williams was 'that those men who had influence on the working class had to a great extent gone'.[127] Their successors, whether of equal calibre or not, certainly acted with similar fervour, so much so that they were often involved in several organizations at the same time. This detracted from the cause everywhere. Thus, in November 1866, the R.L. branch secretary at Cardiff was urging 'reconstituting the committee, as the present members had a great deal of work in connection with various other societies, under which they held office. Their duties to those societies prevented their meeting so frequently, or in such numbers as was necessary to promote the cause of Reform.'[128]

More importantly, perhaps, the success of the R.L. and N.R.U. in Wales was impaired by the presence of the Liberation Society. Although initially an English movement, the Society became a national organization in Wales. Liberationist cells had been formed in the Principality in the 1840s and 1850s, but it was not until the mid 1860s that the Society became particularly active in Wales—at precisely the time when the R.L. was trying to make an impact. Moreover, one aspect of the Society's policy was a demand for parliamentary reform.

---

[126] Ibid., 22 Sept. 1866.
[127] Ibid.
[128] *Cardiff Chronicle*, 16 Nov. 1866.

VIII
RADICAL DISSENT

'The society', claimed the *Nonconformist* in 1858, 'has transplanted the greatest question of modern times from the unfruitful region of theological controversy to the more congenial soil of political debate ... from the chapel to the senate.'[1] Indeed, building on foundations laid in its early years, the A.S.C.A., or rather the Society for the Liberation of Religion from State Patronage and Control as it was renamed in 1853, made considerable progress in the 1850s. Organizational deficiencies were remedied with the creation of parliamentary, electoral and publishing subcommittees, the employment of more lecturers and a travelling agent, the initiation of a system of district agents, and the foundation in 1855 of the Society's own journal, the *Liberator*. The result was a decade of increasing success in the country, expressed in a larger annual income from an increased number of subscribers, together with a greater impact on public opinion. Moreover, these were years of intensive parliamentary activity, the Society co-operating with other pressure groups and also initiating its own legislation, especially on the perennial issue of Church rates, and achieving several notable successes in the alleviation of minor practical grievances.[2]

The A.S.C.A. had launched no intensive propaganda campaign in Wales in the 1840s, though the periodic appearances of emissaries, a measure of sympathetic press coverage, and the fluctuating enthusiasm of local supporters ensured some important groundwork was carried out. South Wales received increased attention from late in the decade, being visited by Association lecturers at least annually in the years 1847–56 and again in 1859, reflecting a policy of concentrating efforts 'on the most influential and productive districts'.[3] North Wales, covered in 1850, 1851, 1854, and 1860, attracted less attention. Here, the problems of language

---

[1] *Nonconformist*, 6 May 1858.
[2] See David M. Thompson, 'The Liberation Society, 1844–1868', in P. Hollis (ed.), *Pressure from Without in Early Victorian England*, pp. 218–22.
[3] *Nonconformist*, 9 Nov. 1853. Of the 102 A.S.C.A. meetings recorded in the paper in 1851 and 1852, for example, 23 were in Wales.

and geographical remoteness were most acute. Moreover, the rural regions were frequently subject to overwhelming aristocratic dominance; in the words of one Liberationist: 'It is a fearfully unequal fight that we, in these small country towns, have to sustain. The bulk of the wealth and influence is on the side of the Church.'[4] But, as yet, lecturers encountered little organized opposition, though occasionally there were difficulties in gaining the use of town halls, meeting-rooms and even chapels, and lectures had to be cancelled. Normally, however, missionaries in Wales delivered addresses and distributed tracts without hostility, finding local Nonconformist ministers a ready source of support and having chapels placed at their disposal.

Yet lecturers inevitably performed only a limited role. 'They were', impressed John Kingsley at Cardiff, 'birds of passage: the burden of the contest rested with the committee.'[5] And clearly this was the key to the creation of an organized public opinion in the localities. Committees in each town were vital 'in order to make Welsh dissent stronger politically and aid executive resources ... without some such provision for permanent effort, public meetings lose half their permanent value'.[6] During the late forties and fifties committees were established, and often re-established, in a large number of Welsh towns, frequently on the visit of a Society agent.[7] But few achieved much permanence, and local agitation was usually confined to flurries of enthusiasm engendered by the committed handful and frequently centring on the collection of funds or some sort of propaganda activity. At Haverfordwest in 1860, for instance, a thousand copies of one of Edward Miall's articles were reproduced and distributed while, elsewhere, activists like Revd William Morgan of Carmarthen sometimes visited other towns to lecture.[8]

The introduction of a scheme of district agents in 1857 was designed to address some of the shortcomings of local support. Revd Elijah Short of Swansea was appointed for south Wales late in 1858. As yet, no agent was assigned to north Wales, though

[4] Ibid., 1 Apr. 1857.
[5] *Principality*, 30 Nov. 1849.
[6] Ibid., 16 Nov. 1849.
[7] Cardiff, Merthyr, Newport, Aberdare, Hirwaun, Pontypool, Tredegar, Neath, Llanelli, Carmarthen, Monmouth, Cardigan, Narberth, St David's, Pembroke Dock, Milford Haven, Rhyl, Denbigh, and possibly elsewhere.
[8] *Nonconformist*, 24 Oct. 1858, 14 Mar. 1860.

the region was periodically visited by deputations from London and by Callaway, the Midland Counties' appointee.[9] Though appointed primarily to raise funds, district agents were expected to carry out a range of propaganda duties similar to the lecturers. At the same time, they often sought to gather electoral statistics and information on the various constituencies. Indeed, the Society had placed much greater emphasis on electoral and parliamentary work, on activity 'of a less demonstrative kind but more likely to issue in important practical results', since the Triennial Conference of 1853, and the following year a deputation led by Carvell Williams had attended a series of private meetings with leading supporters in south Wales 'for the purpose of bringing the society, in its new form, under the notice of the Dissenters of the Principality'.[10]

Some Welsh elections of the 1850s certainly did signify increased political consciousness on the part of Nonconformists. At the 1852 general election, Richard Davies, a Calvinistic Methodist ship-owner and businessman, unsuccessfully contested the Caernarfon Boroughs, standing as a 'Liberal Dissenter' and backed by a substantial body of Nonconformists, including, most significantly, the traditionally apolitical Calvinistic Methodists.[11] In the same election, the return of the Unitarian, Walter Coffin, for Cardiff District contributed to the Nonconformist political awakening that affected Wales in the fifties and sixties, even though his success was essentially a triumph for local middle-class commercial interests.[12] In Bala the 1852 election brought the formation of a 'Progressive Reform Society', an organization which was to re-emerge and expand later in the decade, sponsoring the candidature of David Williams for the Merioneth seat in 1859.[13] The Liberation Society did nothing directly towards these particular campaigns but was at the forefront of the shaping of radical Nonconformist political attitudes, a steady process in these decades. Its executive regularly exhorted Dissenters to question candidates, insist on pledges and return sympathizers of the movement but, as yet, the Society's

[9]*Liberator*, Dec. 1858, Mar. 1860.
[10]*Nonconformist*, 26 July, 2 Aug. 1854.
[11] See David A. Pretty, 'Richard Davies and Nonconformist radicalism in Anglesey, 1837–68: a study of sectarian and middle-class politics', *WHR*, 9, No. 4 (1979).
[12] I. G. Jones, 'Franchise reform and Glamorgan politics in the mid-nineteenth century', *Morgannwg*, II (1958), p. 58.
[13] See above, pp. 102–3.

electoral influence was minimal in Wales. It did claim two gains at the general election of 1857—Colonel E. L. Pryse in Cardigan District and W. O. Stanley in Beaumaris District—but in fact neither was a Liberationist, a Nonconformist, nor returned principally by organized Nonconformity.[14]

Subscriptions from Wales increased, at variable rates, during the 1850s, the industrial towns of south Wales providing the bulk of memberships, though a large number of rural communities, had their individuals who regularly subscribed. The pattern was a growing number of Liberationist cells dotted around the country. During the decade the most consistent contributors were groups at Cardiff, Swansea, Neath, Llanelli, Pontypool, Carmarthen, Haverfordwest and Wrexham, towns where Liberationists were well organized. But the most conspicuous financial support came from Hirwaun and Aberdare where local organization and activity had a marked continuity at this time. Much was due to the enthusiasm of Thomas Williams of Gwaelod-y-garth, Merthyr Tydfil, a self-made businessman in the iron trade, local reformer, and philanthropist.[15] He had been busy collecting subscriptions for the A.S.C.A. in Hirwaun in 1848, over a year before the first official deputation visited the town, and was no doubt instrumental in forming the committee there, which in 1854 amalgamated with that at Aberdare. Later, as the Aberdare Branch Association of the Liberation Society, it had its own executive, finances for local expenses, and a healthy membership, regular meetings being held in a local chapel. Cash was raised by chapel collections and occasionally through social events like concerts. Local membership increased considerably in the late fifties, from 16 in 1857 to 59 in 1859, though the annual total contribution to the central body remained fairly constant, at between £10 and £14.[16] At Aberdare and elsewhere middle-class liberals were prominent, though there seems to have been some working-class appeal in places like Aberdare and Merthyr.

The 1850s were essentially years of consolidation for the Liberation Society in Wales. Most significantly, the headway made,

[14] *Nonconformist*, 1 Apr. 1857.
[15] See W. R. Lambert, 'Thomas Williams, JP, Gwaelod-y-garth (1823–1903): a study in Nonconformist attitudes and actions', *Glamorgan Historian*, II (1975).
[16] A.S.C.A., A/LIB/89, Secretary's Cash Book, 8 Mar. 1848, 5 May 1851; *Nonconformist*, 2 Jan. 1850, 2 Aug. 1854; *Liberator*, 1856–61.

at least in the industrial south, ensured a favourable response
to the executive committee's resolution in September 1861 to
afford unprecedented attention to the Principality: 'Looking to
the great preponderance of Nonconformity in Wales, and to the
fact that it is at present scarcely represented in Parliament, we
think it important that a special and decided Electoral effort should
be made in that part of the Kingdom.'[17] The initiative was timely.
The year 1862 marked the bicentenary of the Puritan ejections
of 1662, when 2,000 incumbents were removed from the Church.
Welsh Nonconformists busily celebrated the anniversary. Books
and pamphlets were published and memorial chapels built. Mass
commemorative meetings were held and ministerial conferences
convened.[18] These were not only religious observances but
occasions of political discussion too. While not initiating the cele-
bratory movement in Wales the Liberation Society certainly
sought to take advantage of it. Its South Wales Conference at
Swansea in September 1862, a landmark in the Society's operations in the Principality, was testimony to this (the proposed North
Wales Conference the same year was postponed on the advice
of leading supporters in the area).[19] Hitherto, Liberationist activity
in Wales had been 'fitful, desultory and partial'. Elaborating, the
Nonconformist observed: 'She [Wales] has at all times extended a
welcome to the representatives of the Liberation Society who have
visited her—she has always sent able and active delegates to its
Triennial Conferences—she has always contributed a respectable
quota to its funds—and she has actively assisted in some of the
special enterprises in which we have been engaged. But Welsh
Nonconformity has never yet organised its great comparative
strength on the question of political churchism.' The chief cause,
continued the columnist, was that 'no adequate effort had been
made to enlighten its judgement, enlist its conscience, interest
its sympathies, and arouse its enthusiasm on the subjects sought
by the Liberation Society'.[20]

The Swansea Conference spanned two days and was attended
by over 200 delegates, comprising leading Nonconformists, laymen

---

[17] Lib. Soc. Mins., Vol. III, A/LIB/2, Min. 1207 (27 Sept. 1861); see also, ibid., Vol.
IV, A/LIB/3, Min. 23 (14 Feb. 1862).
[18] *Baner ac Amserau Cymru*, 8 Jan., 23, 30 Apr., 30 Aug. 1862.
[19] Lib. Soc. Mins., Vol. IV, A/LIB/3, Min. 64 (5 Sept. 1862).
[20] *Nonconformist*, 1 Oct. 1862.

and ministers, principally from south Wales but with a few from the north. Edward Miall, Carvell Williams and Henry Richard formed a powerful deputation from the parent body. Attention inevitably focused on the absurdity of the parliamentary representation of an overwhelmingly Nonconformist nation and on the action needed to remedy the situation. Liberationist candidatures were urged but, as speakers pointed out, factors like landlord and industrialist influence and lack of finance often rendered this impractical. Alternatively, as Carvell Williams insisted, concerted pressure could force MPs to vote in a certain way; hitherto, 'abstinence from out-door agitation' had allowed Welsh members complete freedom of action.[21] The Conference had immediate tangible results, most significantly the establishment of a South Wales Committee with headquarters at Cardiff. Acting in cooperation with the London executive, of which Henry Richard now became a leading member and expert adviser on Welsh political affairs, the Committee became the cornerstone of the Liberation Society's operations in Wales. Its activities began with the circulation of a report on the recent conference, available as a pamphlet in English and Welsh, the issue of Welsh-language tracts, and overtures to the periodical press. A blueprint for local agitation was also published. Emphasis was placed on organization through committees or individual correspondents, though denominational associations could fulfil the role. Partisans should then concentrate on 'the systematic inculcation of Nonconformist principles by means of addresses, sermons and Bible-class instruction . . . especially among the younger portion of the community'. Reports and letters should be sent to the press, and the *Liberator* and other Society publications circulated. Further recommendations included the scrutinizing, questioning and pressurizing of MPs, attending to the register and taking action at the next election. At a parochial level, agitation should aim at the extinction of Church rates 'as a fulcrum for the large and loftier purposes of the Liberation Society'.[22]

How well did Liberationists in the localities respond to such exhortations? Committees were formed or reconstituted in places

---

[21] Ibid., *Liberator*, Nov. 1862; Lib. Soc. Mins., Vol. IV, A/LIB/3, Min. 45 (30 May 1862), Min. 63 (5 Sept. 1862), Min. 119 (3 Oct. 1862); I. G. Jones, *Explorations and Explanations*, pp. 260–1.
[22] *Nonconformist*, 21 Jan., 27 May 1863.

like Merthyr, Swansea, Cardiff and Denbigh. However, it was the support received from the denominational press and the religious bodies which afforded the South Wales Committee most satisfaction. Within a year, all the Independent associations of south Wales and most of the Baptist ones had adopted resolutions commending the Swansea Conference, and a number of these associations were represented at the 1865 Triennial Conference.[23] Nevertheless, there was no striking display of a heightened Liberationist campaign around Wales in these years. The new south Wales agent, Revd John Rees of Swansea, and local enthusiasts, like Revd Evan Griffiths of Bala College, undertook some public speaking engagements, while English representatives made fleeting appearances. But generally there was a paucity of public meetings and lectures, something of concern to the South Wales Committee. Indeed, at the general election of 1865, when the Liberation Society hoped to see the fruits of its new campaign in Wales, the results proved most disappointing.

The focus of the Society's involvement in Wales in 1865 was the Cardiganshire seat, where Henry Richard, albeit briefly, was a candidate. For some time, electoral registration activity in the constituency had been carried out by Thomas Harries of Llechryd, a member of the South Wales Committee. It was reported in November 1863 that the Liberals had recently gained a majority of 247 on the county's new register, chiefly as a result of his efforts and he had purportedly visited every parish in the constituency urging Nonconformists to send in claims.[24] Henry Richard's candidature (along with that of David Davies, the Nonconformist railway contractor) came at a time when it appeared as if there would be no Liberal challenge to the Conservative incumbent, W. T. R. Powell of Nanteos. The renewed aspirations of Sir Thomas David Lloyd of Bronwydd, the local Liberals' choice, prefaced Richard's swift withdrawal.[25] Though brief, Henry Richard's experience in Cardiganshire gives some insight into the Liberation Society's reception and difficulties in rural Wales. Its Parliamentary and Electoral Committee subsequently explained the retirement thus:

[23] Ibid., 11 Nov. 1863, 19 Apr. 1865.
[24] Ibid., 11 Nov. 1863.
[25] For a detailed examination of the election, see I. G. Jones, *Explorations and Explanations*, Ch. 4.

Influenced by the fact that some of the Nonconformists, whose support had been looked for, regarded Mr Richard's proposed candidature with coldness, instead of with warmth, and having but a few hours to decide on the course to be pursued, those who were on the spot, and with whom the decision rested, were of opinion that Mr Richard should not incur the risk of dividing the liberal party, and that Nonconformists be content with the return of Sir Thomas Lloyd, who had pledged himself to vote for some of their practical measures.[26]

Evidently, political Dissent, of which the Liberation Society was the most potent and radical exponent, had not sufficiently penetrated the county. Thus over the next few years the Society intensified its propaganda efforts in the area, aiming at breaking down apathy, ignorance and antipathy, and creating a well-organized, independent body of opinion; with an eye on the next contest, further attention was given to the electoral register.[27] In the past, official deputations had been irregular and insubstantial, although there had been a modest increase in the 1860s. A committee had been formed at Cardigan in 1849 but was apparently short-lived. Canvassing for Henry Richard in Aberystwyth in July 1865, J. M. Hare, the Liberation Society's electoral agent, and Revd John Rees, district agent for south Wales, were reportedly unable to gain one prominent supporter.[28]

In the aftermath of the election, the *Nonconformist* depicted landlord intimidation as the crucial reason for the Society's disappointment in Cardiganshire and other Welsh constituencies: 'Never were negroes driven afield in the Southern States of America under terror of the white overseer's lash more deeply to be commiserated than are the tenant farmers of Merionethshire, Denbighshire, Montgomeryshire and ... more places than we like to enumerate.'[29] Such emotive language was widely adopted by Nonconformist publicists. Certainly, on his intrusion into Cardiganshire electoral politics, Henry Richard was made sharply aware of the extent of local aristocratic power. This influence was not necessarily coercive though such methods could be oppressively

---

[26] Lib. Soc. Mins., Vol. IV, A/LIB/3, Min. 563 (21 July 1865). For Henry Richard's own account, see *Baner ac Amserau Cymru*, 19 July 1865.
[27] Lib. Soc. Mins., Vol. IV, A/LIB/3, Min. 729 (22 June 1866).
[28] NLW, MS 8321 E, John Matthews to his son, 22 July 1865.
[29] *Nonconformist*, 12 July, 2 Aug. 1865.

applied—witness the Merioneth evictions of 1859. But, at the same time, there was the powerful and inherent influence deriving from the natural extension into politics of the deferential and reciprocal order of rural society.

Gentry and Nonconformist activity were again prominent themes early the following year in the Brecon Boroughs by-election, where Dr Thomas Price, the influential Aberdare Baptist minister, was a candidate. Price was an active supporter of the Liberation Society, a member of the South Wales Committee from its inception in 1862. At Brecon in February 1866 he came forward as a 'Welsh Nonconformist Liberal', essentially seeking representation for 'eight-ninths of Welshmen'.[30] The intervention caused the Liberal candidate, the Earl of Brecknock (eldest son of the Marquis of Camden), to issue a second, more advanced programme, thereby satisfying local Liberals, and shortly afterwards Price felt compelled to withdraw. He did so acrimoniously, deploring the powerful aristocratic influences at work, and, most acidly, the response of Brecon Nonconformists to his candidature. Again, these were clearly not ready to display the spirit of independence necessary to challenge the established order. As in Cardiganshire, the Liberation Society had made little impact locally, attracting only isolated subscribers over the years.

The elections of the fifties and sixties brought home certain convictions to Nonconformist radicals in Wales, one of which was the necessity of a much extended franchise to overcome influence, traditionalism, and indifference in the constituencies. Thus, as we have seen, Welsh Liberationists participated enthusiastically in the reform agitation of 1866–7 and were active in R.L. branches, helping to give the movement a religious flavour. The Society itself was anxious to avoid any action which might undermine the effectiveness of the parliamentary reform campaign.[31] In Wales the Reform Bill agitation coincided with invigorated Liberationist efforts, once again electoral in emphasis but giving greater attention to the northern counties on the premise that 'South Wales was pretty well indoctrinated'.[32] Accordingly, the South

[30] NLW, MS 3317 B, Election Address of Dr T. Price, Baptist minister, Aberdare, to the Electors of Brecknock Boroughs, 1866.
[31] *Liberator*, Dec. 1865.
[32] *Nonconformist*, 4 May 1865.

Wales Committee, which was very much at the heart of the drive, resolved first that the Society's agency in Wales should be extended. Revd John Rees of Swansea, who for the past three years had been employed on a part-time basis in the south, briefly became full-time for the whole of the Principality.[33] However, on Rees's resignation in the summer of 1866, a replacement could be found for south Wales only—Revd Watkin Williams, Calvinistic Methodist minister of Pen-coed, near Bridgend.[34] The first north Wales agent, Revd D. Milton Davies, Independent minister of Llanfyllin, was not engaged until August 1867, on a part-time basis.[35] The South Wales Committee itself became more business-like at this time with the setting up of various subcommittees.

The central plank of the Liberationist campaign in Wales in 1866 was a series of county conferences. Four were eventually held in September and early October, at Newtown, Denbigh, Bala and Aberaeron, accompanied by large public meetings in these and other towns. Each conference was attended by delegates from throughout the respective counties and Edward Miall, Carvell Williams and Henry Richard again represented the central body. Predictably, the dominant theme was the chronic and iniquitous misrepresentation of Nonconformist Wales and steps were immediately taken to translate the enthusiastic response of delegates into tangible success. Four county committees and seven local committees were established, to propagate the principles of the Society and organize the constituencies electorally. Moreover, the executive now formed its own Welsh Subcommittee, comprising Miall, Williams, Richard and H. S. Skeats, editor of the *Liberator*, 'to take charge of all matters relating to organisation and electoral action in Wales and generally to the Society's operation in that part of the kingdom'.[36]

The Welsh Subcommittee promptly concerned itself with registration activity which hitherto in the Principality had relied on the initiative of local sympathizers, though Thomas Harries of Llechryd was being paid for such work in Cardiganshire.[37] The Subcommittee, in collaboration with influential local enthusiasts,

---

[33] *Liberator*, Jan. 1866; Lib. Soc. Mins., Vol. IV, A/LIB/3, Min. 650 (2 Feb. 1865).
[34] Lib. Soc. Mins., Vol. IV, A/LIB/3, Min. 764 (5 Oct. 1866).
[35] Ibid., Min. 521A (2 Aug. 1867).
[36] Lib. Soc. Mins., Vol. IV, A/LIB/3, Min. 772 (19 Oct. 1866).
[37] Ibid., Min. 773 (19 Oct. 1866).

was involved in the formation of the South Wales Liberal Registration Society, launched at a conference held in Carmarthen
in July 1867.[38] In north Wales, a similar function was performed
by the Liverpool-based Welsh Reform Association after its rebirth
in June 1868. A number of Welsh Liberationists were involved
in its operations and the Liberation Society gave it, and the South
Wales Society, financial support.[39]

Accordingly, Liberationist activity in Wales reached a new peak
in 1867, the efforts of the agents and the county committees resulting in more meetings being held than in any previous year.
Increased support was reflected in the subscription lists with about
750 contributors in 1867.[40] After years of fitful activity, Welsh
Liberationism found its strength in the mid sixties. By 1867, the
Society had two paid agents in the Principality and, in addition
to the South Wales Committee which had existed since 1862,
there were now four county ones, in Cardiganshire, Denbighshire,
Montgomeryshire and Merioneth, and a network of local organizations. Designed primarily for electoral purposes, these bodies
eagerly sought to enlist the newly enfranchised; one of the earliest
acts of the Denbighshire and Montgomeryshire committees was
'to institute a canvass of the counties to ascertain the possible
effect of the Reform Bill in regard to the electoral strength of
the voluntaries'.[41] Of considerable importance, at a time when
the national parties had few constituency organizations in Wales,
was the Liberationist hold on the recently formed South Wales
Liberal Registration Society and the Welsh Reform Association.

Thus, the *Liberator* could look forward optimistically to the next
general election: 'The time is favourable, attention is excited, and
men's minds in Wales are open to receive right impressions ...
some electoral victories at least should reward the Liberation Society
for its recent labours in the Principality. And there should be
protest and resistance, even when there cannot be success at

---

[38] Samuel Morley, the wealthy English radical, agreed to contribute £500 to the Society's
first year's expenses. Ibid., Min. 495a (7 June 1867), Min. 502a (21 June 1867), Min.
508a (5 July 1867).
[39] Ibid., Min. 520 (2 Aug. 1867), £200 to the South Wales Liberal Registration Society;
ibid., Vol. V, A/LIB/4, Min. 131 (26 June 1868), £50 to the Welsh Reform Association.
[40] 10 subscribers—1844; 50—1849; 154—1856; 269—1859; 353—1861; 421—1862;
585—1863; 673—1866; 750—1867. Figures compiled from Secretary's Cash Book 1844–
53 and monthly lists in the *Liberator*. For a geographical analysis, see I. G. Jones, *Explorations
and Explanations*, pp. 248–50.
[41] Lib. Soc. Mins., Vol. IV, A/LIB/3, Min. 515a (19 July 1867).

once.'[42] Suffrage extension in 1867 was crucial to the hopes of Nonconformist radicals, putting 'within their reach the realization of results which under the existing political system, they have not ventured to contemplate'.[43] Accordingly, in the Liberal triumph of 1868 four members of its executive were returned in addition to twenty supporters of the movement and a number of other Nonconformists.[44] Particular pride was taken in the Welsh results 'in as much as it is believed they are, in no small degree, distinctly traceable to the conferences and meetings held in the Principality at the instance of the Society, and to other efforts to induce the Nonconformists of Wales to improve the representations of their country'.[45]

The Liberation Society was most directly involved at Merthyr Tydfil, where Henry Richard successfully challenged traditional influence as represented by Henry Austin Bruce and Richard Fothergill. As a member of the London executive and a frequent emissary to Wales, his Liberationist affiliations were well known. In the year or so preceding the election, Society activities in the Merthyr area were stepped up, with the south Wales agent at work and other representatives addressing public meetings. Increased membership and financial contributions reflected the growing success of the movement locally; between May 1867 and April 1868 eighty to ninety individuals from the constituency contributed to central funds.[46] Local supporters of the Society were prominent in Henry Richard's campaign, particularly through the Welsh Representation Society formed at Aberdare in May 1867 'to sow the seeds of political Nonconformity, and labour to improve the representation' of Wales in the House of Commons'.[47] The return of 'the apostle of peace' was certainly an emphatic victory for organized Nonconformity in the Merthyr constituency and for the Liberation Society, though other factors, particularly relating to working-class industrial issues, were present to a significant degree.[48]

[42] *Liberator*, Nov. 1866.
[43] Lib. Soc. Mins., Vol. IV, A/LIB/3, Min. 563a (30 Apr. 1867).
[44] D. M. Thompson, op. cit., pp. 225–6; P. M. H. Bell, *Disestablishment in England and Wales* (1969), pp. 225–6; *Liberator*, July 1868.
[45] Lib. Soc. Mins., Vol. V, A/LIB/4, Min. 202 (4 Dec. 1868).
[46] A/LIB/388, Report of the Proceedings of the Eighth Triennial Conference, 1868, pp. 92–100.
[47] *Cardiff Times*, 11 May 1867.
[48] For a detailed analysis, see I. G. Jones, *Explorations and Explanations*, Ch. 5.

Henry Richard had, of course, transferred his parliamentary aspirations from the Cardiganshire seat. His replacement was the Swansea industrialist, E. M. Richards, who similarly came forward as a Welsh Nonconformist Liberal and was a supporter of the Liberation Society, having recently co-operated with its Welsh Subcommittee in the creation of the South Wales Liberal Registration Society. The Liberation Society had, for some time, been grooming Cardiganshire for a suitable candidate and clearly approved of the choice of E. M. Richards; indeed, Henry Richard recommended him to the county's Liberals.[49] Nevertheless, though the Society probably played a role in arousing local Nonconformist opinion, its influence was not decisive in Richards's triumph, which was actually founded on the backing of the Pryse family of Gogerddan. Significantly, Richards was at pains to disclaim Liberationism, considering its radical connotations detrimental and in this respect he was clearly responding to the strength of traditional Liberal opinion in the county.[50]

The role of the Society was more weighty in the two Denbighshire contests, although once again other factors were essential to the outcome.[51] George Osborne Morgan, who was returned as one of the two county members, voiced Liberationist principles, while another barrister, Watkin Williams, victor in the Boroughs, had strong sympathies with disestablishment even though he was not a Nonconformist himself. Thomas Gee, an executive member, brought his powerful mouthpiece, *Baner ac Amserau Cymru*, into support of both. Other middle-class Liberals were also active. At Wrexham, W. H. Darby, Charles Hughes, George Bradley and R. C. Rawlins campaigned for Watkin Williams. All had been contributors to the Liberation Society for some years and were members of the county committee set up at the conference of September 1866. This now had two years' work behind it and, indeed, Gee had approached the two candidates as long ago as its establishment. Local committees too, like the one at Wrexham, had been concerning themselves with registration.[52] In addition,

[49] NLW, MS 8308C (Gee 4), Henry Richard to Thomas Gee, 8 July 1868.
[50] For a thorough examination, see I. G. Jones, *Explorations and Explanations*, Ch. 4; idem, 'The elections of 1865 and 1868 in Wales, with special reference to Cardiganshire and Merthyr Tydfil', *Transactions of the Honourable Society of Cymmrodorion* (1964).
[51] For analysis of the two contests, see Jane Morgan, 'Denbighshire's annus mirabilis'.
[52] Lib. Soc. Mins., Vol. IV, A/LIB/3, Min. 515a (19 July 1867).

the recently formed Welsh Reform Association was probably at its most telling in this area; certainly a number of Denbighshire Liberationists were involved in its inception in Liverpool in June 1868.[53]

Another illustration of the kind of role the Society played at this time was Merioneth, where David Williams, unsuccessful in the two previous contests, was triumphant in 1868.[54] Growing support for Liberationism in the county in the sixties was reinforced by the disappointments of 1859 and 1865 and represented a shift by the leaders of the new political movement towards the adoption of more radical views and methods. For it was Williams's main promoters, members of the Merioneth Reform Association, who were the most regular and generous contributors to the funds of the Liberation Society in these years, and when the latter held a county conference at Bala in September 1866 it was Michael D. Jones, Dr Owen Richards, Lewis Edwards and other leading reformers who rallied to the call. As elsewhere, anger at misrepresentation of the local constituency was closely bound up with the general principles of Liberationism. In Anglesey, too, the Society generated and harnessed Nonconformist enthusiasm, sparking off the necessary organizational activity prior to the 1868 election with the formation of branch associations in all the major population centres on the island, though the uncontested return of the Nonconformist Richard Davies is again explained by circumstances in addition to organized Dissent.[55]

The Liberation Society exerted some electoral influence through its control of the South Wales Liberal Registration Society, which claimed registration gains as a chief factor in the Liberal victories in Cardiganshire, Carmarthenshire and in the Monmouth Boroughs.[56] In some areas, activists busily put forward voting claims; in north Monmouthshire, for instance, Revd David Evans, Calvinistic Methodist and 'the most active agent of the Liberation Society' in the area, aroused the concern of Revd D. Morgan, a local Churchman, who urged the Tory MP, Octavius

[53] *Liverpool Mercury*, 4 June 1868; NLW MS 8311D (Gee 7), J. Lloyd Jones to Thomas Gee, 8 June 1868.

[54] For a detailed study, see I. G. Jones, *Explorations and Explanations*, Ch. 3.

[55] See David A. Pretty, op. cit. Branches at Holyhead, Amlwch, Beaumaris, Llannerch-y-medd, Llangefni, and Menai Bridge—six branches and 105 subscribers. Ibid., p. 457.

[56] *Liberator*, Mar. 1869.

Morgan, to use his agents to scrutinize all claims put forward by 'the Preachers and the Liberation Society'.[57]

Thus, virtually everywhere in Wales, the role of the Liberation Society was essentially supportive and it could be accredited with no conclusive victory, save perhaps at Merthyr. In 1868 the break with the old order of parliamentary representation was far from complete but religious Dissent unmistakably showed its political strength in a number of improbable, indeed dramatic, election results and this manifestation of a new public opinion was the most significant phenomenon of the year. In no small measure the Liberation Society was instrumental in this development.

[57] NLW, Tredegar Park MSS, 71/420, Revd D. Morgan, Aberystruth, to Octavius Morgan, 3 Aug. 1868.

Part 3

1868–1886
'New and Important Circles'

IX

ECONOMIC AND SOCIAL CHANGE IN THE SEVENTIES AND EIGHTIES

As the century progressed the economic and demographic trends noted earlier for the fifties and sixties continued and intensified, sharpening the contrast between industrial and rural Wales. In common with Britain as a whole, the population of Wales continued to grow rapidly, from 1,412,583 people in 1871 to 1,771,071 in 1891, an increase of 25.4 per cent. The move from the land to the industrial areas accelerated, with people pouring into the south Wales coalfield. Above all, the growth came in Glamorgan, whose population rose from 397,859 to 687,218 in the two decades 1871 to 1891, an increase of 72.7 per cent. In 1891 the county contained 38.8 per cent of the population of Wales; by 1911 it was 46.3 per cent. In essence, these statistics reflected the remarkable growth of the coal-mining valleys and the urban areas around the ports. Most dramatically, the population of the Rhondda valleys grew from 16,914 to 88,351 in the period 1871–91 while Cardiff, expanding from 39,526 to 128,915, became the first Welsh town to pass the figure of 100,000 inhabitants and emerged as the world's greatest coal exporter; almost as strikingly, Swansea rose from 51,702 people to 90,349.

On the peripheries of the south Wales coalfield, too, the advance of the coal industry brought substantial population increases. As in central and eastern Glamorgan, the exploitation of the steam and bituminous seams of the Rhymney, Sirhowy, Ebbw and Llwyd valleys of west Monmouthshire was well developed by the eighties and, largely as a result, the population of Newport doubled to 54,707 in the years 1871–91. Large-scale extraction of the anthracite resources of the west, however, did not get under way until the eighties, whereupon a host of new industrial communities sprang up, especially in the Gwendraeth, Amman, Tawe and Neath valleys in east Carmarthenshire and west Glamorgan. By 1890 the output of the south Wales coalfield had doubled that of twenty years earlier and now stood at 29.4 million tons a year, almost a quarter of which came from the two Rhondda valleys; at the same time, almost 110,000 men were employed in the industry. Coal was now absolutely unrivalled in south Wales and wholly dictated life in many valleys.

Indeed, falling population in many of the districts along the upland heads of the valleys testified to the decline of the once paramount iron industry in those parts, in the face of European and American competition. Moreover, the dependence of the new steel-making processes on substantial capital investment and imported non-phosphoric iron ore meant that only the larger concerns were able to make the transition from iron; smaller companies perished. At the same time, the transfer of much of the Dowlais plant to Cardiff in 1891 was spectacular acknowledgement that the industry's future lay along the coast and no longer on the north-eastern rim of the coalfield; Merthyr's population in 1891 was 58,080, far behind that of Cardiff and Swansea. Other branches of the metallurgical industry in south Wales were more prosperous. Copper-smelting, which had long flourished in the area between Kidwelly and Neath in east Carmarthenshire and west Glamorgan, and now monopolized the British production, reached peak output in the 1880s. Similarly, tinplate manufacture thrived in the same region and also came to dominate the British stage; output quadrupled to 586,000 tons between 1871 and 1891, much of which supplied the United States market.

Elsewhere in Wales, too, industrial expansion significantly affected the population figures. Thus, the population of Denbighshire increased by 12.2 per cent in the years 1871–91 and that of Wrexham by 46.3 per cent, largely due to developments on the north-east coalfield; for the same reason, the Flintshire trend was also upward though in these decades somewhat erratically. At the same time, slate-quarrying continued to have a profound influence on the remote north-west, the heartland of the British slate industry. Peak output was reached in the 1870s, when some 14,000 men were employed in the region, though reduced demand throughout the following decade brought a contraction. Population levels reflected these fortunes, both Caernarfonshire and Merioneth experiencing large increases of 12.4 per cent and 11.6 per cent respectively in the years 1871–81, followed by decreases of 0.9 per cent and 5.4 per cent over the next ten years. Caernarfonshire at this time boasted the two largest slate quarries in the world, Penrhyn near Bethesda and Dinorwic near Llanberis, owned respectively by the Penrhyn and Assheton-Smith families. The other main slate-producing area in the county was in the Nantlle valley. The industry was less widespread in neighbouring Merioneth, though it was particularly important in the north around Blaenau Ffestiniog and in the south around Corris. Accordingly, considerable industrial centres like Blaenau Ffestiniog, whose population increased from 8,055 in 1871 to 11,073 in 1891, a rise of 37.5 per cent, developed, though far more prevalent were the small, often isolated, but distinctive quarrying villages. The construction of rail links to the coast and the demands of a huge export market also turned small towns like Portmadoc and Aberdyfi into bustling ports, though their importance diminished as the slate industry fell into decline in late century.

Thus economic growth was paralleled by population growth in seven of the counties of Wales in the 1870s and 1880s. Elsewhere, however, the census returns of the period 1871–91 showed a falling population—in Cardiganshire (by 14.7 per cent), Radnorshire (14.2 per cent), Montgomeryshire (14.2 per cent), Breconshire (4.8 per cent), Pembrokeshire (3.1 per cent) and Anglesey (1.8 per cent). Indeed, this was the pattern in the rural areas of the other counties, too, for industrialization and population increase were invariably highly localized. The figures registered the continued decay of industries like woollen production in Montgomeryshire, lead- and silver-mining in Cardiganshire, and copper-mining in Anglesey, and the demise of the small western ports dealing mainly in agricultural produce, casualties of the full development of the railway system in the eighties. Above all, though, the low wages and lack of work in the countryside, intensified by a general agricultural depression in the closing decades of the century in the face of intense foreign competition, caused the migration from rural Wales to gather momentum while the employment prospects and higher wages of the buoyant south Wales coal industry, in particular, acted as a powerful magnet.

Such was its expansion that, certainly from the 1880s, redistribution enabled Wales to retain most of her natural increase in population.

Not all Welsh migrants chose to remain within the Principality, of course. Significant numbers moved to England or, more dramatically, headed for the United States and other foreign parts. Serving to redress the balance, an increasing proportion of those flooding into industrial Wales in late century came from England. The percentage of the population of south Wales originating in English counties rose from 9.6 in 1871 to 16.5 in 1891. Large-scale English immigration was central to the demise of Welsh as the language of the coalfield. On a national scale, the 1891 census revealed that, though the total number of Welsh-speakers was still increasing, at only 54.4 per cent of the population it was declining in proportional terms, and successive censuses confirmed this downward spiral.

In time, demographic change also had a profound effect on Welsh Nonconformity, the industrial communities of the south Wales valleys presenting new social and economic issues for the denominations to address, giving birth to workmen's institutes as secular social centres and, especially through the influx of people from outside Wales, creating a population which identified less with the chapels. These factors challenged and ultimately helped undermine the influence of Nonconformity on Welsh life. This lay in the future, however. In the 1870s and 1880s the number of Nonconformist communicants continued to grow rapidly, reaching a peak in the Edwardian Age, though, given Anglican support and the number of non-worshippers, never attaining a majority of the Welsh people. In the late nineteenth century the construction of ornate, imposing chapel buildings in contrast with the simple structures of earlier years was a striking display of the position and strength of Nonconformity in the communities and bore witness to a more affluent membership, including many coal-owners and colliery officials in the mining valleys. The impact of the various denominations on Welsh society, therefore, continued to be far-reaching, though not the all-pervading force sometimes depicted.

Certainly, in local politics official Liberalism in the industrial areas, as in the countryside, was Nonconformist and middle-class, personified in ministers, shopkeepers, businessmen, and solicitors. By the end of the 1880s Nonconformist Liberalism stood triumphant at the Welsh polls, dominating parliamentary and local representation. This ascendancy was largely based on the traditional 'Welsh' concerns of Liberationist, education, land, and temperance reform; thus, reform agitations in Wales in the seventies and eighties continued to work in these directions. At the same time, the fundamental population shift towards the mining valleys of the south forged a society in which these issues gradually became more peripheral to a world of trade unionism and coal-owners' associations, wage rates and sliding scales, shift systems and working practices. Strikes and militancy were key features of the 1870s, re-emerging after the relative calm of the two preceding decades, and specifically labour politics came to the forefront. A lengthy period of conciliation followed, epitomized in the sliding scale and the Lib-Lab ethos, but open industrial and political confrontation was to return, with greater depth and permanence, by the end of the century.

X

PARLIAMENTARY REFORM

To many working-class radicals the Second Reform Act was palpably insufficient and pressure to secure remedy of the defects
was imperative. The R.L. executive circulated its branches to this
effect and the more flourishing responded. The Brecon society
agreed that 'progress had been made but more needed to be
done. The personal payment of rates must be got rid of, ballot
adopted, duration of Parliaments shortened and the redistribution
of seats properly adjusted.'[1] At Merthyr, the Reform Act celebration was simultaneously 'to inaugurate a new ... movement in
favour of the Ballot and equal electoral districts ...'[2] George
Maddocks, secretary of the Newport Working Men's Liberal Association, formed in mid 1868 expressly for further agitation, spoke
in similar vein: '... make no mistake about it the Reform Bill wants
a great deal of doing up'.[3]

Indeed, the electoral system remained undemocratic and anomalous. In 1868, out of a total population in Wales of 1,418,698,
there were 121,112 voters (9.1 per cent).[4] Women were, of
course, excluded while the Act also wholly disregarded agricultural
labourers. Moreover, thousands of industrial workers, living outside borough boundaries, were omitted. Workmen in unrepre-
sented towns like Tredegar and Ebbw Vale had exactly the same
claims to representation as their enfranchised counterparts in
Merthyr and Aberdare. The former were Monmouthshire constituents, but the nature of the county qualification, particularly in
such mountainous districts, meant that they were voteless: 'To
look for agricultural voters on this sterile surface is pure nonsense',
observed the *Merthyr Telegraph*.[5] Moreover, in industrial areas
many working-class electors lost their vote by changing residence
in search of work, while registration conditions effectively meant

---

[1] *Beehive*, 8 June 1867; *Baner ac Amserau Cymru*, 15 June 1867.
[2] *Merthyr Star*, 10 Sept. 1867.
[3] *Star of Gwent*, 17 Oct. 1868.
[4] *Report from the Select Committee on Parliamentary and Municipal Elections*. PP, 1868–89, VIII.
[5] *Merthyr Telegraph*, 19 Feb. 1859.

much disfranchisement. Thus, even in borough constituencies, adult male suffrage was still some way off. While demands for parliamentary reform were soothed in 1867, they were by no means satisfied. After the enactment of the Reform Bill, however, the fortunes of the national pressure groups declined. Finding 'there was a difficulty in keeping up an interest in the Union',[6] the N.R.U. fell dormant, while internal dissension rendered the R.L. inoperative in the aftermath of the 1868 general election, and it was formally dissolved in March 1869. In Northumberland and Durham, the Miners' Franchise Union represented a significant development,[7] but there was no national campaign for further suffrage extension in the early 1870s, bodies like the Labour Representation League and the Trades Union Congress offering it as just one point in a broad programme. Rather, democratic advance in these years centred on the successful ballot campaign, in which the Principality figured prominently. In a number of areas of Wales, Tory landowners had reacted to electoral defections in 1868 with recrimination, evicting tenant farmers. The popular outcry was given parliamentary voice by Henry Richard and other members and helped bring about the Hartington Committee, set up to investigate the conduct of elections. Witnesses from Wales recounted instances of political evictions and other forms of persecution; Thomas Harries of Llechryd, for example, spoke of custom being withdrawn from shopkeepers, parochial officers being removed, and two congregations being turned out of the rooms in which they worshipped.[8]

Within Wales, a delegate conference at Aberystwyth in November 1869 launched a £20,000 fund for the victims, and county committees were established to stir support and collect donations.[9] Sympathy for the evicted tenants was inevitably coupled with a passionate demand for the secret ballot. At the same time, there were protests from industrial areas against their own brand of coercion, threat of dismissal from work. At Newport, the Working Men's Liberal Association desired the ballot 'because

[6] Reform Gazette and Manchester Critic, 18 Oct. 1878.
[7] W. H. Maehl, 'The north-eastern miners' struggle for the franchise, 1872–74', International Review of Social History, 20 (1975), Part 2, pp. 198–219.
[8] Nonconformist, 23 June 1869, quoting evidence before the Committee; see also, I. G. Jones, Explorations and Explanations, p. 191; Kenneth O. Morgan, Wales in British Politics, 1868–1922 (Cardiff, 3rd edn., 1980), pp. 25–6.
[9] Newtown and Welshpool Express, 23 Nov. 1869.

many of their members were under landlord or company owner contracts'.[10] In the Merthyr area, the ballot, 'the panacea for a sea of political evils', was the main concern at a series of open-air demonstrations convened by veteran Chartists in 1870; the government, it was claimed, had not moved on the question 'because we have ceased to agitate on the point...we must jog their memories'.[11] Nationally, the Ballot Society was acting with greater zest in the late sixties and attracted some Welsh subscribers though it paid scant attention to the Principality.[12] In Wales, Nonconformity gave the campaign much of its drive. Its press had long championed the cause, while religious bodies such as the Pembrokeshire Baptist Association and the Congregational Union of Wales now petitioned strongly; Merioneth Independents urged Parliament 'either to take the vote away from the farmers or to give them the protection of the ballot'.[13]

A less widespread but nevertheless significant campaign of the early seventies was the republican movement, fuelled in particular by the birth of the Third French Republic and by the continued withdrawal from the public eye of the grieving Queen Victoria a decade after the loss of Prince Albert. Republican clubs certainly operated in Cardiff and Merthyr in 1872–3, while knots of supporters also existed in Aberdare, Beaumaris, Carmarthen, and probably elsewhere in Wales. They tended to be anonymous organizations; at Carmarthen, for example, republicans met 'in a private house in preference to a "public", as it will not only look better, but we shall thereby gain the good wishes and co-operation of the members' wives'.[14] Similarly obscure was the Magna Charta Association (M.C.A.). This originated with the claim to the Tichborne estates by a man professing to be Roger Tichborne, eldest son of the family, supposedly drowned in 1859. Opening in 1866,

---

[10] *Star of Gwent*, 17 Oct. 1868.

[11] *Merthyr Star*, 29 Jan., 14 May, 6 Aug., 10, 24 Sept. 1870; *Merthyr Telegraph*, 15 Mar. 1872.

[12] HC, Various Envelopes, Associations, Ballot Society leaflet, 6 May 1869.

[13] *Nonconformist*, 28 June, 25 Oct. 1871; *Report from the Select Committee on Parliamentary and Municipal Elections*, PP, 1868–9, VIII, Min. 6608.

[14] *Cardiff Times*, 23 Nov. 1872; *Merthyr Telegraph*, 15 Mar. 1872; *National Reformer*, 28 Jan., 27 Oct. 1872, 16 Mar., 13 Apr. 1873; *Republican Herald*, 6, 13 June 1874; see also R. Harrison, *Before the Socialists* (1965), Ch. V; R. J. Gossman, 'Republicanism in nineteenth-century England', *International Review of Social History*, 7 (1962), pp. 47–60; and, for a review of republican sentiments in Victorian Wales, John Davies, 'Victoria and Victorian Wales', in G. H. Jenkins and J. B. Smith (eds.), *Politics and Society in Wales, 1840–1922. Essays in Honour of Ieuan Gwynedd Jones* (Cardiff, 1988), pp. 25–7.

the case was not concluded until 1874, when the claimant was adjudged Arthur Orton and sentenced to fourteen years' imprisonment for perjury.[15] The verdict aroused widespread popular protest, which the claimant's counsel, Dr Kenealy, sought to channel through the M.C.A., founded early in 1875 with the *Englishman* as its mouthpiece. The main theme of the movement was justice for the underprivileged and its programme included payment of MPs, triennial parliaments, and the abolition of income tax. Working men were to unite as Magna Chartists and return to Parliament members of their own class, thereby forming 'a third party in the State'.[16]

In the years 1875-6, M.C.A. branches were formed at Merthyr, Aberdare, Hirwaun, Mountain Ash, Dowlais, Swansea and Ystalyfera. The Swansea society was run by 'two trustees, a president, a vice-president, a working committee of eleven and a secretary' and within five weeks had eighty-six members; as elsewhere, members paid a penny a week to the central body though the branch was permitted to 'deduct up to 1/4 of subscriptions to cover its own expenses', such as hire of their room and cost of literature.[17] For a while the movement certainly captured popular imagination, at times the enthusiasm, flavour and anti-establishment emotion being reminiscent of Chartist days; when Dr Kenealy visited Swansea and Merthyr a brass band accompanied his carriage from the railway station to the meeting-hall where several thousand turned up to hear him.[18] Merthyr produced a petition of 9,000 signatures and 300 feet in length calling for justice in the Tichborne case.[19] At the Stoke-on-Trent by-election of 1875, Kenealy, standing as an independent, emphatically defeated Liberal and Conservative opponents, while in the same year, the Merthyr M.C.A. was making preparations for a candidature when Richard Fothergill's resignation seemed likely.[20] Thereafter, however, popular interest subsided, though the M.C.A. was apparently still struggling

[15] See D. Woodruff, *The Tichborne Claimant* (1957).
[16] *Englishman*, 9, 16 Jan. 1875.
[17] Ibid., 12 June 1875.
[18] Ibid., 10 Apr. 1875, 2 Oct. 1876; *Swansea and Glamorgan Herald*, 7 Apr. 1875. The claimant himself had addressed a large meeting in Swansea in 1872, organized by the local Tichborne Defence Fund Committee. *Tichborne News and Anti-Oppression Journal*, 6 July 1872.
[19] *Workman's Advocate*, 16 Apr. 1875.
[20] Ibid., 18 June 1875; *Englishman*, 12 June 1875.

on in 1884;[21] there is no evidence of Welsh branches operating beyond 1876.

The mid seventies saw the return of agitation of a more familiar order with renewed impulse for further parliamentary reform coming from several directions. The N.R.U. was reorganized on a much enlarged programme in 1875,[22] while the National Agricultural Labourers' Union (N.A.L.U.), formed in 1872, now made franchise assimilation 'a front plank' in its platform.[23] The growth of organizations associated with the Liberal Party represented a third and increasingly influential force. Conservative and Whig-Liberal societies, supervising the registration of voters and sponsoring candidates, had of course sprung up in many areas over previous decades but were exclusive to those contributing financially to their operation. After the 1867 Reform Act traditional oligarchical control remained strong in many rural counties and small boroughs, but elsewhere new party organizations came into being and became linked to the National Union of Conservative and Constitutional Associations and the National Liberal Federation (N.L.F.). The initiative for the former came from above, from the party leadership, and the secretary, J. E. Gorst, Disraeli's nominee, provided vigorous direction. The Union was accredited with an important role in the electoral victory of 1874, by which time over 400 local Conservative associations had affiliated. These looked to the central body for the supply of propaganda and for guidance, the fundamental aim being simply to win votes; party policy was the preserve of the parliamentary leadership.

In stark contrast, the N.L.F. founded in 1877, a decade after the National Union, was essentially the product of constituency zeal and was specifically designed to induce party leaders to adopt certain policies. The inspiration came from Joseph Chamberlain and other radicals in Birmingham, where a Liberal Association had existed since 1865 and where the campaign for non-sectarian education through the National Education League (N.E.L.) was centred. By 1876, when he was elected as a Birmingham MP, Chamberlain was convinced that the Liberal Party needed to be

---

[21] *Tarian y Gweithiwr*, 18 Sept. 1884.
[22] HC, Miscellany, 'N.R.U. List of Executive, Vice Presidents ...' (n.d.); *Reform Gazette and Manchester Critic*, 18 Oct. 1878.
[23] J. G. O'Leary (ed.), *The Autobiography of Joseph Arch* (1966), p. 102.

revitalized on a radical programme of 'Free Church, Free Land, Free Schools and Free Labour' and on the Birmingham model of constituency organization. The N.E.L. was wound up early in 1877 and in May the N.L.F. was launched at a Birmingham conference attended by delegates from over a hundred places. In his speech Chamberlain distinguished two methods of attaining reform. Irish disestablishment and land reform had become 'burning questions at the suggestion of Mr Gladstone himself', and were thus examples of pressure from within. On the other hand, the Reform Act of 1867 was conceded 'when it became dangerous any longer to resist the demands of public opinion'. He went on: '... the time is coming when we must again trust to popular initiative', and the N.L.F. was to be the instrument, acting as a pressure group within the Liberal Party.[24] It was not that reformers had been inactive in recent years; rather, they suffered from sectionalism, each group 'advocating some favourite reform and producing little impression'.[25] The N.L.F. would be the umbrella for a variety of causes, as William Harris, another Birmingham radical, commented:

Why should those interested in education have to form a separate Education League, those interested in parliamentary reform have to form a separate Reform Union, those interested in religious equality have to form a Liberation Society, and those interested in land a separate Land Reform Association, especially as many of the same people were involved in each? Why should they not once and for all form a federation which, by collecting together the opinion of the majority of the people in all the great centres of political activity, should be able to speak on whatever questions arose with the full authority of a national voice?[26]

The N.L.F. proposed to operate through already existing Liberal associations and to assist in the formation of new ones, modelled on the Birmingham Association. Divided into wards, each with an elected committee, the city's Liberals were united in one structure through executive and general committees, the aim being

---

[24] *Proceedings Attending the Formation of the National Federation of Liberal Associations* (Birmingham, 1877), p. 17.
[25] J. Chamberlain, 'A new political organisation', *Fortnightly Review*, XXII (1877), quoted by D. Read, *The English Provinces, c. 1760–1960* (1964), p. 178.
[26] *Proceedings Attending the Formation of the National Federation of Liberal Associations*, pp. 21–2.

the creation of a democratic body. A council, comprising representatives of all affiliated societies, was to meet annually to determine N.L.F. policy with day-to-day management in the hands of an executive based in Birmingham.[27]

The inaugural conference was not an unmitigated triumph, only half the delegations agreeing to join the Federation; some clearly feared for their independence—an enduring suspicion. Moreover, the N.R.U., the Liberation Society, and the Land Reform Association rejected merger. Indeed, though the N.R.U. 'anticipated no clash with the Liberal Federation, whose work would doubtless refer rather to the Southern part of the country [and] if they ever infringed on each other's district it would be their common understanding that it was done for the common good',[28] there was rivalry between the two. Whilst agreeing with the N.L.F.'s assertion that Liberalism suffered from 'a plethora of organisations, and its resources need to be focused and concentrated...',[29] the N.R.U. claimed to be better equipped to do this.

Neither the N.R.U., the N.A.L.U., nor the N.L.F. made much impact in the Principality in the late 1870s and early 1880s. Apart from ephemeral combinations for shorter hours, agricultural labourers were unable to organize effective unions in nineteenth-century Wales, a phenomenon explained in the scattered nature of the work-force, which greatly reduced the influence of the press, and the close, often kindred, ties between employers and workers.[30] Thus, in Wales, no agitation for the suffrage came from this avenue, as happened in England.

Only one Welsh body, the Anglesey Liberal Registration Association, was represented at the N.R.U.'s reorganizational conference of December 1875, while four delegates, from Anglesey, Carmarthen, Llanelli and Rhayader, attended its annual gathering a year later.[31] Two Anglesey Liberals served on its General Council from 1876 to 1879, but at the first Triennial Conference in 1879, attended by about 150 delegates from 49 branches, there

---

[27] See H. J. Hanham, *Elections and Party Management, Politics in the Time of Disraeli and Gladstone* (1959), Ch. 7; F. H. Herrick, 'The origins of the National Liberal Federation', *Journal of Modern History*, XVII (1945).

[28] *The Times*, 25 Nov. 1880.

[29] *Reform Gazette and Manchester Critic*, 24 Jan. 1879.

[30] D. W. Howell, 'The agricultural labourer in nineteenth-century Wales', *Welsh History Review*, 6, No. 3 (June 1973), pp. 285–7.

[31] *Manchester Examiner and Times*, 15 Dec. 1875; HC, N.R.U. Conference 1876, 324.42.

were no Welsh representatives.[32] Despite extravagant claims of far-reaching influence—in 1882, for example, the number of affiliated and subscribing societies was said to be 284[33]—only a handful seem to have been located in Wales.

Similarly, only two Welsh Liberal associations—Cardiganshire and Newport—sent deputations to the founding conference of the N.L.F. in 1877; both were among the forty-seven which immediately affiliated to the Federation. Thereafter, the number of member associations from Wales increased slowly. By 1880 only the Aberystwyth Liberal Association had been added, but in 1881 the associations at Cardiff, Carmarthen and in the Rhondda joined. Between 1883 and 1886 eight more became linked—Denbighshire and Swansea (1883); Wrexham (1884); Anglesey, Merthyr, and West Denbighshire (1885); Abertillery and Flintshire Boroughs (1886).[34] The formation of the North and South Wales Liberal Federations, in December 1886 and January 1887 respectively, and their affiliation to the N.L.F. brought many more within the fold.[35]

Before 1886 the ties between Welsh Liberal associations and the N.L.F. were clearly not strong; by this year only fourteen had affiliated, though constituency organizations existed in every area. Separate borough and county associations were created. In the counties, focal bodies like the Montgomeryshire Central Liberal Association, formed in 1869, co-ordinated the activity of several local organizations. These associations were responsible for the selection of parliamentary candidates and the arrangement of electioneering work. The 1867 Reform Act brought one further development in some areas, the foundation of distinct working men's associations, as at Wrexham, Denbigh and Ruthin in 1868.[36] They demanded a say in the choice of candidate; at Newport in July 1868 four members of the Working Men's Liberal Association were included on the 24-man committee to do so.[37]

The Liberal associations in the different areas operated as separate entities and it was not until the creation of the two regional

[32] HC, Miscellany, 'N.R.U. List of Executives, Vice-Presidents ...', *Reform Gazette and Manchester Critic*, 14 Feb. 1879; *The Times*, 12 Feb. 1879.
[33] *The Times*, 24 Jan. 1883.
[34] N.L.F., *Annual Reports*, 1879–86.
[35] Ibid., *Annual Report*, 1887, p. 30.
[36] NLW MS 8309 E (Gee 5), Gee to Watkin Williams, 1 Dec. 1868.
[37] *Star of Gwent* 18 July 1868.

Federations in 1886–7 that Wales played any significant role in the development of party policy through the N.L.F.[38] The structure, composition and industry of local organizations varied considerably. The Cardiff Liberal Association was evidently formed upon the lines of the Birmingham model and based on popular election; it was organized in wards, each having its own officers and representatives on the general committee ('the three hundred').[39] The Carmarthenshire Liberal Association, founded in 1885, was also democratically structured, every 200 voters sending delegates to the central organization.[40] These were probably untypical, however, and most Welsh bodies were, or became, much less representative, particularly because of the financial dependence on the most wealthy. Some associations, like those at Newport and Cardiff, were clearly flourishing. The 1884 Annual Report of the Newport Liberal Association, as yet unaffiliated to the N.L.F., pronounced a gain of twenty-four votes in the local registration courts and referred to the year's educational work, including lectures in Newport, Usk and Monmouth and the setting up of a junior association as an auxiliary to the parent body.[41] This indicates unusual enterprise. There was the other extreme too: 'The Rhondda Liberal Association does nothing,' complained the *Cardiff Times*; 'it lives the strange existence of a political phantom.'[42]

In the late seventies and early eighties neither the N.L.F. nor the N.R.U. embarked upon a systematic lecturing and propaganda campaign throughout the country. One problem was financial weakness, the annual income of the N.L.F. being about £1,500, diminutive compared with the Liberation Society and the United Kingdom Alliance (around £10,000 and £13,000 per annum respectively at this time).[43] The N.R.U. was similarly encumbered. In any case, circumstances were not conducive to such a campaign. As the N.L.F. Annual Report of 1879 rightly acknowledged, the events in south-east Europe in recent years had concentrated the public mind on foreign policy. Liberal opinion in the country

[38] See G. V. Nelmes, 'Stuart Rendel and Welsh Liberal political organisation in the late-nineteenth century', *Welsh History Review*, 9, No. 4 (Dec. 1979) pp. 469–70.
[39] N.L.F., *Annual Reports*, 1879, p. 11, and 1881, p. 16.
[40] D. V. Evans, 'Some aspects of politics in Eastern Carmarthenshire 1868–85' (University of Wales MA thesis, 1972), p. 94.
[41] *Cardiff Times*, 16 Aug. 1884.
[42] Ibid., 23 Aug. 1884.
[43] H. J. Hanham, op. cit., p. 140.

focused on opposition to the Tory Government's pro-Turkish policy. In Wales, where sympathies 'could identify regional sentiment with a moral cause in politics', the total of thirty-one protests in late 1876 against the Turkish 'atrocities' in Bulgaria represented a disproportionately large participation in agitation in terms of population. This number consisted of not only local public meetings but also declarations from religious bodies like the Baptist Union of Wales and the South Wales Wesleyan Methodists. Again, the Welsh agitation owed much to the vitality of Nonconformity.[44]

Contesting the general election essentially as an anti-Beaconsfield crusade, Gladstone and the Liberal Party returned to office in 1880. But, absorbed with financial matters and beset with imperial and Irish troubles, the premier did not turn to parliamentary reform until 1883, when the Corrupt and Illegal Practices Act effectively limited election expenses. Since 1877 the Liberals had also been pledged to extend the franchise to rural householders and by 1883 reforming activity out of doors concentrated on this. The N.A.L.U. now agitated for the suffrage 'harder and louder than ever', while the N.L.F. and the N.R.U. entered into joint action, delegates from 500 Liberal associations at a Leeds conference in October calling for far-reaching reform and redistribution.[45] A Franchise Bill was indeed introduced in late February 1884. Passing safely through the Commons, it was thrown out by the Tory majority in the Lords in July. A previously lukewarm public was now stirred and three months of agitation and counter-agitation commenced.

Prior to the Lords' resistance, Wales had been largely undisturbed by the franchise question apart from the spasmodic enunciations of the press and local Liberal associations. The N.L.F. made few incursions into the Principality. In 1880 one of the Federation's provincial conferences was held in Gloucester where representatives from Glamorgan, Breconshire and Monmouthshire organizations attended.[46] Another, the following year, met in Cardiff, where south Wales delegates urged the government

[44] R. T. Shannon, *Gladstone and the Bulgarian Agitation* (1963), pp. 148–9, 157, 232.
[45] J. H. Rose, *The Rise of Democracy* (1897), p. 203; N.L.F., *Annual Report*, 1883, p. 15; *The Times*, 7 Sept., 16, 18 Oct. 1883.
[46] N.L.F. *Annual Report*, 1880, p. 8.

to introduce 'measures for the enfranchisement of the industrial population in the counties, and the more equitable distribution of political power, and for thorough reform of the land laws'.[47] In 1883 N.L.F. lecturers visited Monmouthshire. In July of the same year a rally of 12,000 miners in the Rhondda called for parliamentary reform.[48] But such expressions were as yet rarities. Even when the Franchise Bill was before Parliament there was little excitement, giving rise to Stuart Rendel's conjecture that 'the people don't yet believe that they have any serious battle to fight'.[49] The Lords' rejection significantly changed matters, shifting the controversy from Westminster to the country. As the *Annual Register* of 1884 recorded: 'The debates and divisions of the session had shown conclusively that if any agreement were to be arrived at, or any concessions to be given or extorted, it must be by means of pressure from outside. To stir up public opinion and to enlist it on their own side was therefore the task of the moment. and both parties [Liberals and Conservatives] accepted the duty without hesitation.'[50]

The Liberals were swiftly in the field. Protest meetings were now held in all parts of Wales. Unenfranchised mining towns like Abertillery, Abercarn, Tredegar and Pontypridd unequivocally denounced the Lords' action.[51] Such communities, dramatically transformed by rapid industrialization and population increase, were particularly fertile fields of agitation, for here the electoral system was most strikingly anomalous and indefensible. But deep rural areas were also vociferous. At meetings in places like Llandysul, Llanrhystud and Llangefni, scores of agricultural workers objected to the peers' denial of their claims.[52]

In some areas, like the Rhondda and in parts of Carmarthenshire, miners' organizations took charge of local demonstrations. For the most part, however, the Welsh agitation was directed by local Liberal associations. These summoned public meetings,

---

[47] Ibid., 1881, p. 16.
[48] *Cardiff Times*, 21 July 1883.
[49] NLW, MS 20572 D, Letters and Papers of Lord Rendel, Vol. III, Rendel to M. E. Grant-Duff, 7 Oct. 1884.
[50] *Annual Register*, 1884, p. 198.
[51] *The Times*, 20 Aug., 5 Sept. 1884; *Cardiff Times*, 23 Aug. 1884.
[52] *Cambrian News*, 17 Oct. 1884; *Aberystwyth Observer*, 9 Aug. 1884; *Baner ac Amserau Cymru*, 1 Oct. 1884.

planned processions, supplied the speakers, and drew up the resolutions. Some associations, such as Swansea, now awoke from
a period of torpor: 'Hitherto it was like creatures which hibernate;
but it now develops the right sort of spirit and energy.'[53] In the
main, Welsh people were content to champion Gladstone against
an unelected and privileged assembly thwarting the will of the
people. Demands for radical democratic principles were occasionally voiced, as at Pontypool in August 1884 when resolutions
in favour of manhood suffrage, equal electoral districts, and single-
member constituencies were carried,[54] but this was not the norm.
Generally, the agitation was notable for its moderation and,
indeed, its orderliness. In *The Times* the attitude and conduct of
the Welsh colliers were held up as exemplary.[55]

In the late summer and autumn of 1884 the 'peers versus the
people' battle-cry raised the political temperature and broadened
the agitation. At the forefront was Joseph Chamberlain, then a
Liberal cabinet minister, who did much to stir popular feeling
against the Lords; at the height of the protests he visited Wales.
In October, addressing rousing Liberal rallies at Newtown and
Denbigh, he pledged himself to Welsh disestablishment and land
reform and also took the opportunity of fiercely denouncing the
upper chamber: 'I have no spite against the House of Lords',
he told the Denbigh audience, 'but as a Dissenter I have an account
to settle with them...I share your hopes and your aspirations
and I resent the insults, the injuries and the injustice from which
you have suffered so long at the hands of a privileged assembly.'[56]
Elsewhere, too, the controversy was related to other issues. The
Anglesey Liberal Association condemned the Lords for 'the conse-
quent necessary postponement of the long promised measure of
intermediate education' and for 'depriving the nation of many
much-needed and long awaited for measures of social reform'.[57]

Critics everywhere recounted a century of opposition to progressive legislation. The Liberal press was emphatic, the *Cambrian*,
for instance, recalling the days of Catholic emancipation and the

---

[53] *Cambrian*, 29 Aug. 1884.
[54] *Cardiff Times*, 9 Aug. 1884.
[55] *The Times*, 26 July 1884.
[56] *Cambrian News*, 24 Oct. 1884.
[57] *North Wales Express*, 29 Aug. 1884.

First Reform Act, when the peers had brought the country 'to the brink of revolution and rebellion'.[58] Demands for reform or abolition of the second chamber were inevitable. Merthyr workers cheered a suggestion that it should be 'extinguished', while, at Denbigh, Chamberlain's tirade against 'an oligarchy which is the mere accident of birth' was rapturously applauded.[59] Thomas Gee, speaking at Bala, aired a widespread sentiment: 'It is not perhaps necessary to take very serious measures at first but if the House of Lords did not reform, then let it be abolished.'[60] Tories replied equally passionately, defending the Lords' role in an exemplary constitutional system. At a meeting of the Port Dinorwic branch of the Caernarfonshire Constitutional Association, whose walls were decorated with patriotic mottoes, the agitation against the Lords was depicted as 'the first step towards Republicanism'.[61]

As in 1866, the Conservative Party did not openly condemn the principle of reform but formulated its opposition along other lines. First, Tories argued that the Franchise Bill was the device of a discredited government to retain power. Addressing a demonstration at Bala, R. J. Ll. Price of Rhiwlas attacked the Liberal record in Egypt, the current agitation 'being designed to take eyes away from this'.[62] Meetings at Newtown, Bangor, Flint and elsewhere also protested against the deliberate distraction from foreign failures.[63] Secondly, it was asserted that there was no public demand for reform and the Lords' rejection of the Bill was therefore justified in affording an opportunity for expression of the popular will. Finally, the Tory Party maintained that franchise extension and redistribution were concomitant, and enactment of the former before the latter would be handing 'a blank cheque' to the government. Without exception, Welsh expressions of support for the Lords made this point. At such meetings, noticeably lacking in the industrial south, local landowners were frequently prominent, though sometimes bodies such as the Bangor

[58] *Cambrian*, 29 Aug. 1884.
[59] *The Times*, 29 July 1884; *Cambrian News*, 24 Oct. 1884.
[60] *Cambrian News*, 26 Sept. 1884.
[61] *North Wales Express*, 29 Aug. 1884.
[62] *Cambrian News*, 15 Aug. 1884.
[63] *The Times*, 29 July, 26 Aug., 18 Oct. 1884.

Conservative Working Men's Association and the Denbigh Workmen's Constitutional Association, initiated and organized demonstrations.[64]

Feelings certainly ran high in some communities. Rival Liberal and Conservative Associations were formed at Llanasa in Flintshire in August 1884.[65] At Bethesda in October, Tories arranged a demonstration, complete with torchlight procession and brass bands, on the very day William Rathbone, Liberal MP for Caernarfonshire, was to speak in the town; in anticipation of disturbance a large contingent of county police was brought into the district.[66] Bangor, Bala and Cardiff also saw impassioned contention.[67] The press, dividing strictly on party lines, both expressed and fed local arguments, Tory organs like the *North Wales Express* and the *Western Mail* confronting Liberal champions like the *Carnarvon and Denbigh Herald* and the *South Wales Daily News*.

The parliamentary stalemate was eventually resolved through negotiations between party leaders in late 1884, the 'Arlington Street Compact' sealing compromise on a redistribution scheme. The Franchise Bill, enacted in December, differed only marginally from Gladstone's original moderate proposals of February. Amendments introduced by Tories to limit the measure and by Radicals to democratize it (by such steps as the abolition of plural voting and the enfranchisement of women) were rejected by the Commons. Its chief feature was the reduction of the county qualification to the same level as that of the borough, that is, householders or lodgers of one year's residence; a £10 occupation franchise applied mainly to offices and shops (plural voting was not finally abolished until 1948). The United Kingdom electorate increased from two and a half million to almost five million. In Wales, thousands of miners, tinplaters and steelworkers previously outside borough boundaries became voters as well as agricultural labourers and tenant farmers. Thus, while rural areas were substantially affected, the industrial south experienced the most dramatic change. Glamorgan was transformed from a two-member constituency with 12,785 voters in 1880 into five new county divisions with a total electorate of 43,449, and Monmouthshire from a

[64] *North Wales Express*, 8, 15 Aug., 12 Sept. 1884.
[65] *Flintshire Observer*, 7, 28 Aug. 1884.
[66] *North Wales Express*, 17 Oct. 1844.
[67] Ibid., 1, 15 Aug. 1884; *Cardiff Times*, 2 Aug. 1884.

two-member constituency with just 7,609 voters into three constituencies comprising 31,541 voters. In all, the Welsh county electorate rose from 74,936 to 200,373.[68]

Equally significant was the redistribution of seats in 1885, which
aimed to create mostly single-member seats of roughly equal size.
Five Welsh boroughs, Beaumaris, Brecon, Cardigan, Haverfordwest and Radnor were disfranchised, and an additional member
given to Swansea. Wales received one member per 45,342 of
the population, while the ratio for England was approximately
one per 54,000. Welsh representation now consisted of 11 boroughs, or rather groups of boroughs, and 22 county constituencies.
All were single-member seats except Merthyr, which still returned
2 MPs, making a total of 34. The Representation of the People
Act, 1884, and the Redistribution of Seats Act, 1885, jointly known
as the Third Reform Act, had a profound effect on Welsh politics,
facilitating the repudiation of Conservatism at successive parliamentary elections and the great era of Liberal ascendancy in the
late Victorian and Edwardian decades.[69]

The two measures removed glaring anomalies in the electoral
system but certainly did not confer universal male suffrage or
equal electoral districts. In Britain, it has been estimated that only
63 per cent of adult males were on the electoral roll in 1911;[70]
Wales's large working-class population would mean a lower percentage. The 1884 Act disqualified certain categories of adult men,
most numerously those who had received poor relief, while the
complicated registration procedure excluded many eligible voters.
In 1911 Montgomeryshire had an electorate of 8,030 and a population of 36,332; in Montgomery District the ratio was 3,458 to
16,814. In industrial areas the position was more striking. The
five county constituencies of Glamorgan had a combined population of 631,989, of which 104,039 were on the electoral register;
at Merthyr there were 23,518 voters out of a population of
143,849.[71] Redistribution, too, left wide discrepancies in constituency size. Rural boroughs like Montgomery District with a population of less than 20,000 in the mid 1880s returned one member,

[68] See K. O. Morgan, *Wales in British Politics*, pp. 64–5; idem, *Rebirth of a Nation: Wales, 1880–1980* (Oxford and Cardiff, 1981), pp. 27–8.
[69] Idem, *Rebirth of a Nation*, pp. 27–33.
[70] N. Blewett, 'The franchise in the United Kingdom 1885–1918', *Past and Present*, 32 (1965).
[71] PP, 1911, LXII, pp. 679–700.

as did Cardiff with almost 100,000 inhabitants. Democracy made a significant advance in 1884–5; but anomalies survived and 'one man, one vote' was still some distance away, while women, of course, despite a substantial campaign from the 1860s, remained wholly unenfranchised.

XI
WOMEN'S RIGHTS

Though there had been a diffusion of feminist writings over the half century or so following the publication of Mary Wollstonecraft's *Vindication of the Rights of Women* in 1792, the women's movement in Britain with its spectrum of distinct elements did not really get under way until the second half of the nineteenth century. The various campaigns, in which men played a role too, were dominated by the middle class, certainly at national leadership level, if less so in the provinces.[1] Indeed, many such women had already gained experience in political agitation, particularly through largely supportive involvement in the causes of antislavery, temperance, and repeal of the Corn Laws.[2]

Working-class women had been similarly involved in political action. Welsh women had a long tradition of participation, even prominence, in public protest, certainly dating back to the food riots of the 1780s and 1790s.[3] Chartism presented the opportunity for more sustained political action and, as elsewhere in Britain, working-class women in Wales vigorously contributed to the movement. Although this field of enquiry was for long disregarded, historians now recognize the large number of female Chartist associations formed, estimates varying between 80 and 130.[4] Many of these were thriving in terms of both membership and dynamism.[5] Newspaper references indicate the existence of associations at Merthyr, Pontypool, Abersychan, Blackwood and Newport, and there were almost certainly more in the industrial south and in Montgomeryshire too. The largest and most active seems to have been in Merthyr, where a women's society operated for

[1] See J. Liddington and J. Norris, *One Hand Tied Behind Us: The Rise of the Women's Suffrage Movement* (1978), for the role of working-class women in the suffrage campaign in Lancashire.
[2] A women's Anti-Corn Law Committee was active in Wrexham, for example. *A.B.T.C.*, 24 Jan. 1843
[3] See D. J. V. Jones, *Before Rebecca*, pp. 33–4.
[4] See C. E. Martin, 'Female Chartism: a study in politics' (University of Wales MA thesis, 1974), Ch. 3; D. Jones, 'Women and Chartism', *History*, 68, No. 222 (Feb. 1983), pp. 10–11.
[5] See, for example, references to the Newport and Blackwood associations, *Silurian*, 13 Apr. 1839.

several years in the late 1830s and early 1840s. Members here attracted attention as productive fund-raisers;[6] they were also energetic petitioners, obtaining nearly 11,000 signatures for the reprieve of Frost, Williams and Jones.[7] Much activity was, of course, in co-operation with the menfolk, who sometimes initiated and served on the committees of female associations. Women were central to the implementation of the policy of exclusively dealing with tradesmen and shopkeepers who favoured Chartism and to the wide-ranging social life connected with the movement. At public meetings and demonstrations, and even in violent action, they stood shoulder to shoulder with their male counterparts. At the same time, women displayed a considerable amount of independent spirit and enterprise, setting up and running their own organizations, producing forceful leaders, arranging functions and 'diffusing political information'.[8]

Female suffrage had, from the first, proved a contentious issue among Chartists. It was incorporated in the original draft of the People's Charter but then dropped, much to the disapproval of a significant body of activists, who urged the inclusion of at least unmarried women and widows. The decision to drop the demand was essentially one of expedience, amid fears of impeding manhood suffrage and the other demands, though some Chartists certainly voiced traditional anti-suffragist arguments. Despite their heavy involvement, female Chartists did not, on any large scale, press their own franchise claims; their preoccupation was with the six-point programme as it stood. From the 1860s, however, female suffrage became an issue in British politics though it constituted only one demand of the disparate women's movement of the second half of the century, which included campaigns for legal rights, especially over property ownership and custody of children, repeal of the Contagious Diseases Acts, girls' education, employment opportunities, and birth control. These causes invariably found expression in reform organizations, propaganda and agitation. The Women's Education Union was formed in 1871 'to create a sounder public opinion with regard to . . . the

[6] C. E. Martin, op. cit., p. 92.
[7] D. Williams, *John Frost*, p. 296.
[8] For the activities of female Chartists, see D. Jones, op.cit., pp. 14–19; C. E. Martin, op. cit.; D. Thompson, 'Women and nineteenth century radical politics: a lost dimension', in A. Oakley and J. Mitchell (eds.), *The Rights and Wrongs of Women* (1976), pp. 124–6.

education of women, by means of meetings, of lectures and the press and to co-ordinate the efforts of scattered individuals and associations'.[9] Similarly, Emma Paterson founded the Women's Protective and Provident League in 1874 to promote women's trade unions, while Annie Besant and Charles Bradlaugh disseminated their views on birth control through their periodical, the *National Reformer*, and by conducting lecture tours. Two 'popular' agitations stand out, however—women's suffrage and the contagious diseases campaign.

I WOMEN'S SUFFRAGE

The suffrage lay at the heart of the movement for female emancipation. Its emergence as a central demand dates from the public agitation and parliamentary debates that led to the Second Reform Act in 1867. In June 1866 John Stuart Mill presented a petition to Parliament, signed by almost 1,500 women, calling for enfranchisement irrespective of sex, and the following May proposed such an amendment (which was defeated by 194 votes to 73) to the Conservative Reform Bill. Thereafter, a continuous campaign for women's suffrage was conducted. By the end of 1867 societies formed in Manchester, London and Edinburgh had federated into the National Society for Women's Suffrage, with societies at Bristol and Birmingham joining the following year. From 1870 the *Women's Suffrage Journal*, edited by Lydia Becker, the central figure of the movement in the seventies and eighties, performed a vital, unifying role while in 1872 a central committee was established specifically to co-ordinate activity. Over the following years itinerant lecturers toured the country addressing hundreds of public meetings, tracts were distributed, and petitions signed. In Parliament, women's suffrage bills were debated almost annually, but the high expectations of inclusion in the 1884 Reform Bill proved misplaced and, with Gladstone exerting his powerful influence in opposition, William Woodall's amendment in favour of women was rejected (271 votes to 135), ushering in two decades of relative impotence for the campaign.

The early 1870s saw vigorous propaganda activity through the dispatch of delegates to the provinces and, accordingly, suffragists

[9] Women's Education Union, quoted in P. Hollis, *Women in Public: The Women's Movement 1850–1900* (1979), pp. 150–1.

including Jessie Craigen, Lydia Becker, Caroline Biggs, Lilias Ash-
worth and others travelled extensively through Wales, addressing
many public meetings, extending the organization of the movement, and initiating petitions and other forms of agitation. In
the north, activity was often under the auspices of the Manchester
National Society, and in the south under the Bristol and West
of England Society, which had two committees and six corresponding secretaries in south Wales in 1875.[10] In the later seventies
and eighties speakers continued to visit Wales but there was less
systematic touring. Local supporters such as Revd Henry Chester
of Cardiff and the journalist John Griffiths ('*Y Gohebydd*') sometimes
accompanied the ladies on their itineraries and, where required,
gave translations of the addresses.

As elsewhere in Britain, the arguments voiced at women's suffrage meetings in Wales and in the local press were repeated
interminably over the many years of the campaign.[11] Suffragists
obviously had to reply to opponents' objections as well as make
their own case. In this respect a common anti-suffragist claim
was that most women did not want the vote. Thus J. H. Scourfield,
Conservative MP for Pembrokeshire and a regular contributor
to the early suffragist debates, 'did not see why, because a small
set of demonstrative women persisted in setting up what they
claimed as the rights of their sex, the House should force upon
the more numerous and more retiring section of the female community what they did not wish for, and would, if given to them,
probably repudiate. One of the nuisances of the present day was
the tyranny which was attempted to be exercised by societies who
professed to represent the opinion of the country.'[12] Similarly,
George Osborne Morgan, Liberal MP for Denbighshire, argued
that women's suffrage 'was advocated by only a small knot of
earnest women, who had been brooding over real or imaginary
wrongs'. Moreover, the effects, he believed, would be devastating:
'If the franchise were given to ... women, there would be a new
party in the House. There would be a women's party—a Home
Rule party in a new sense of the word and there would be ...

---

[10] N.S.W.S., *Fourth Annual Report* (1875). It also translated some of its leaflets into the
Welsh language.
[11] For detailed discussion of these, see C. Rover, *Women's Suffrage and Party Politics in
Britain, 1866–1914* (1967), Chs. IV, V; B. Harrison, *Separate Spheres: The Opposition to Women's
Suffrage in Britain* (1978).
[12] *Hansard*, CCVI, col. 87, 3 May 1871.

a war of sexes... He would not consent to make a revolution for the sake of a handful of fanatics.'[13] And certainly, not all women did want the vote, as the Appeal against Female Suffrage, a manifesto of distinguished women (or, rather, 'wives of distinguished men') published in 1889,[14] and the Women's Anti-Suffrage League of 1908 were to testify.

Opponents also frequently claimed that feminine interests were adequately cared for under the existing system; 'women were well represented by husbands, brothers and fathers, who were not indifferent to their welfare', Home Secretary and former member for Merthyr H. A. Bruce told the Commons in 1872.[15] Indeed, female suffrage would bring family dissension, 'disturbing one of the dearest domestic ties of the inhabitants of these isles'.[16] Women's essential role was marriage and child-rearing, and political functions, it was claimed, would mean the neglect of these. Anti-suffragists argued, as at Cardigan in 1881, that 'marriage was the best thing for women and... if the ladies who advocated the cause were to endeavour to make themselves good and loving wives, they would be labouring for better purposes than what they were doing now'.[17] Furthermore, it followed that as the nation's wealth and power was the product of men's efforts, then they should monopolize the franchise; 'it was men who built up and maintained this country, and were responsible for it', pronounced an opponent at an Aberystwyth lecture, 'and when women did the rough and perilous work done by men, let them have the vote.'[18]

Part of the resistance to female suffrage was founded on the supposed innate incapacity for political thought among women ('in point of brain inferior to men'), though this was gradually tempered as they assumed a role in local government from the 1870s. Indeed, anti-suffragists now faced a problematical anomaly. Some saw the incursion into municipal politics as undesirable,

[13] Ibid., CCXI, col. 56, 1 May 1872. While supporting the extension of married women's property rights the following year, he was anxious to assure fellow MPs that it would not lead to 'the development of "the women's rights" question, and looming behind that a Parliament in petticoats'. Ibid., CCXIV, cols. 676–7, 19 Feb. 1873.

[14] See P. Hollis, *Women in Public*, pp. 322–31. Mrs Osborne Morgan was one of the signatories.

[15] *Hansard*, CCXV, cols. 235–6, 30 Apr. 1873.

[16] *Cardiff and Merthyr Guardian*, 11 June 1870.

[17] *Women's Suffrage Journal*, 1 Oct. 1881; *South Wales Daily News*, 6 Sept. 1881.

[18] *Women's Suffrage Journal*, 1 Oct. 1881.

the thin end of the wedge; women, according to the *Cardiff Times* in 1872, sat 'with very questionable propriety and advantage on School Boards'.[19] Others acknowledged that they had a legitimate contribution to make to local affairs but stressed the distinction between that and national politics; 'school boards and municipal elections', insisted a Cardiganshire farmer, 'were minor things, not equal to that of the State, and should not be placed in the same category'.[20] The *Swansea Journal* enthused about the local election of Mrs Emily Higginson in 1879, 'an educated lady, and no school board should be without the presence of a lady experienced in the education of children ... she will bring to the school board debates much ripe wisdom and invaluable and long experience'.[21] Similarly, the *Star of Gwent* felt that 'the election of ladies to School Boards is a decided advantage. Here they have full scope for the exercise of talents peculiarly their own'. But parliamentary contests and the pandemonium of the poll were quite another proposition and wholly improper for women:

> The great mass of the sterner sex have far too much respect for the weaker one than to wish to see them embroiled in the tumult and the wild excitement of political strife ... it will be an evil day for the women of England when they are placed on a strict equality with men ... when they wish to take part and lot in proceedings frequently characterised by violence, uproar, and vulgar personalities, they must be protected from themselves.[22]

Thereby, political life would sully natural feminine virtues. Thus, the Mayor of Newport in 1881 'thought it quite right for women to take an interest in education but if they were to become too much involved in public matters, they would lose the sweetness which they now possessed'.[23] Or, as the *Cardiff and Merthyr Guardian* asserted:

> We would confine woman to her proper sphere. We would no more think of making her a politician or a surgeon than we should think of making her a soldier or a sailor. In the homes of Great Britain are many nameless graces which the political functions of women would scare away ... We

---

[19] *Cardiff Times*, 23 Nov. 1872. The same editorial spoke of 'the incompleteness of the average female mind'.

[20] *Women's Suffrage Journal*, 1 Oct. 1881.

[21] *Swansea Journal*, 29 Nov. 1879.

[22] *Star of Gwent*, 18 Mar. 1881.

[23] Ibid.

question if a woman would not lose immensely by stepping from the social or domestic circle into the political ring.[24]

Accordingly, the newspaper took Mrs Rose Crawshay, the Merthyr ironmaster's wife, to task for disturbing the peace of south Wales in respect of women's suffrage and urged her to 'reconsider before she sows the seeds of politics amongst the female population of her part of the country. By all means,' the editorial went on, 'let the education of women be improved, so that they may become better wives, mothers and neighbours. But assuredly their education will never be improved by giving them the franchise, by placing them on a political equality with their husbands.'[25]

Suffragists sought to refute their opponents' arguments. The vote, they contended, should not be denied to women who wanted it by those who did not and added that there was no compulsion actually to exercise the right anyway, points forcibly made by Mrs Crawshay to a Merthyr public meeting in 1873.[26] On the allegations of prospective family discord and neglect of responsibilities the rejoinder was that these fears were equally applicable to matters other than politics and in any case the campaign was mainly directed to spinsters and widows. At the same time, the argument that the country's economy was entirely dependent on men ignored the work of working-class women in industry, while the illogicality of the notion that women could usefully participate in local politics but were unsuited for national politics was increasingly difficult to sustain.

The positive side of the case for women's suffrage rested on three principal elements. First, advocates everywhere echoed John Stuart Mill's natural rights argument, that women's claims were legitimate on grounds of justice, equality and fitness to vote, and that there should be no taxation without representation. The second assertion was that women needed the vote to defend and to advance their interests, particularly in law, in education and at work. Miss Gertrude Jenner of Wenvoe, the most active campaigner in south Wales in the seventies and eighties, told fellow suffragists in Cardiff: 'Every-day life proved to many of them that

[24] *Cardiff and Merthyr Guardian*, 11 June 1870.
[25] Ibid.
[26] Ibid., 18 Oct. 1873; *Merthyr Telegraph*, 17 Oct. 1873.

widows and spinsters who contributed to the taxes and rates of
our country were all too often the victims of tyranny and
oppression and they were simply anxious to secure any protection
they could.'[27] In Merthyr, C. H. James 'enumerated several of
the laws as affecting women, which he characterised as barbarous',
while in Cardiff Revd Alfred Tilly blamed male monopoly of the
vote for 'some atrocious laws on the Statute Book'.[28] They certainly agreed with fellow activist Richard Cory on one such area
of legislation: '... if women had had votes they would never have
been disgraced by the present Contagious Diseases Acts'.[29] Law-
making was, of course, but one area in which Victorian society
discriminated against the interests of women. 'We desire', wrote
Mrs Rose Crawshay, 'all lucrative professions to be open to
women, and to the end we may embark in them, we want as
thorough an education for girls as is given to boys.' In short,
'female franchise is no more the end for which women are working
than church-going and prayer are religion. They are only means
to ends.'[30] Thirdly, women themselves and society as a whole,
it was claimed, would benefit. 'Possession of a vote', Rose Crawshay assured a Merthyr audience in 1870, 'will tend to ennoble
women's characters ... and a higher standard of morality [will
be] introduced throughout the world.'[31] At Cardiff the old Chartist, and now teetotal, campaigner, J. W. Manning, argued that
female suffrage would 'purify politics', while Revd Tilly, also 'a
temperance man', anticipated greater sobriety in society for
'women would favour those laws which tended to restrict the
temptation to drunkenness which exists now'.[32]

The novelty of female agitators no doubt helped swell local
attendances at early women's suffrage meetings and adversaries
readily seized on this point. 'Does anyone who was present at
the meeting believe that half a dozen persons besides the speaker
went there for any other purpose but that of being amused?',
asked one Merthyr observer in 1873.[33] Similarly, in a stinging

[27] *South Wales Daily News*, 26 Feb. 1881.
[28] *Cardiff and Merthyr Guardian*, 11 June 1870; *South Wales Daily News*, 10 Mar. 1881.
[29] *Cardiff Times*, 23 Nov. 1872.
[30] *Cardiff and Merthyr Guardian*, 11 June 1870.
[31] *Newtown and Welshpool Express*, 24 Dec. 1872.
[32] *South Wales Daily News*, 10 Mar. 1881.
[33] *Merthyr Express*, 18 Oct. 1873.

attack in 1881, the *Western Mail* commented thus on the movement in Cardiff:

> ... judging from the air of curiosity on the faces of a large number of those who entered the room, a considerable proportion came in anticipation of a little fun rather than genuine sympathy with the objects of that novel association of widows and old maids, which has earned for itself the sobriquet of 'the shrieking sisterhood' ... a fortnight ago ... only about fifteen attended, including half a dozen men who sat in back seats and had the bad taste to laugh at everything that was said.[34]

One wonders what species of woman audiences expected to encounter at meetings, but evidently some commentators were unexpectedly struck, even charmed, by the respectability, demeanour and skill of the 'petticoated politicians'. Thus, the *Star of Gwent*, reporting a Newport meeting in 1872, declared that 'the ladies who championed the cause advanced their arguments with a lucidity, a temperateness and withal an eloquence which were simply irresistible'.[35] Others, however, could not restrain their contempt for the agitation, as in the scurrilous concluding remarks of the *Brecon County Times*'s report on a Neath meeting in 1872: 'There is bitterness of truth in the irony which says, "Two places only are suitable for women, viz. the cradle and the grave!" Men will do well to weigh the probable future.'[36] On occasions, meetings became impassioned affairs, as at Cardigan in 1881, when there was 'bitter argument reminiscent of the late rowdy election meetings'.[37]

There was, of course, fierce personal condemnation too, most eminently from Queen Victoria herself, who in 1870 wrote in these trenchant terms:

> The Queen is most anxious to enlist everyone who can speak or write to join in checking this mad, wicked folly of 'Women's Rights', with all its attendant horrors, on which her poor feeble sex is bent, forgetting every sense of womanly feeling and propriety. Lady Amberley ought to get a GOOD WHIPPING.[38]

---

[34] *Western Mail*, 10 Mar. 1881.
[35] *Star of Gwent*, 23 Nov. 1872.
[36] *Women's Suffrage Journal*, 1 Oct. 1881.
[37] *Brecon County Times*, 23 Nov. 1872.
[38] Sir Theodore Martin, *Queen Victoria as I Knew Her* (1908), p. 69; R. Fulford, *Votes for Women* (1957), p. 75. Viscountess Amberley was the wife of a radical MP, the daughter-in-law of ex-premier Earl Russell and mother of the philosopher, Bertrand Russell. See Olive Banks, *The Biographical Dictionary of British Feminists* (1958), pp. 3–4.

Lady Amberley, active in London feminist circles and a notable women's suffrage pioneer, had recently delivered a much-publicized lecture at Stroud. From 1870 until an early death from diphtheria in 1874 she lived in rural Monmouthshire, near Chepstow, where she was instrumental in the formation of a county committee to promote the female suffrage cause early in 1871.[39]

Another early activist and friend of Lady Amberley was Mrs Rose Mary Crawshay, wife of Merthyr ironmaster, Robert Thompson Crawshay. Philanthropist and literary woman, she held advanced views on such subjects as cremation, euthanasia, corporal punishment in schools, domestic service for gentlewomen (lady-helps) and, of course, women's rights. Visits to London had drawn her into the feminist movement and among the many distinguished guests at Cyfarthfa Castle were leading suffragists Millicent Fawcett and her sister, Elizabeth Garrett Anderson, the first qualified female doctor. Rose Crawshay was especially prominent in Merthyr public life in the late sixties and seventies, during which time she frequently advocated women's suffrage on the platform and in the press. In March 1871 she was elected a member of the newly created Merthyr School Board, the first woman to take up such a position in Wales. The following month she headed the poll for the Vaynor School Board and subsequently occupied its chair for the next eight years; she lost her Merthyr seat in 1874. On her husband's death in 1879, she left Merthyr for the calm and beauty of neighbouring Breconshire and a cottage near the shores of Llangorse Lake.[40]

The pattern at the early women's suffrage meetings in Wales was the delivery of addresses by the visiting female deputation and then supporting speeches, proposing and seconding resolutions, from local male supporters—sometimes Churchmen, most often Nonconformist ministers, professional men and businessmen. Local women were invariably present in substantial numbers and became active in the cause—the Cardiff committee constituted in 1873 comprised five men and five women[41]—but, with the exception of Mrs Crawshay, did not yet chair or even speak at

[39] *Women's Suffrage Journal*, 1 Mar. 1871; *County Observer*, 18 Feb. 1871; *Star of Gwent*, 18 Feb. 1881.
[40] For Rose Crawshay, see M.S. Taylor, *The Crawshays of Cyfarthfa Castle* (1967); *The Queen*, 5 Mar. 1892; obituaries in *Merthyr Express*, 8 June 1907 and *Brecon County Times*, 7 June 1907.
[41] *Women's Suffrage Journal*, 1 Feb. 1873.

meetings; after all, they had no experience of public speaking, while the feeling persisted that it was not respectable. From the late seventies, however, meetings for women only were convened, as a supplement to mixed meetings, and local female activists became more conspicuous. In south Wales, Gertrude Jenner (1835–1904), middle-aged spinster and sister of the squire of Wenvoe Castle, emerged most strikingly. She sat on the General Committe of the Bristol and West of England Society from 1873 to 1888, was secretary of the Cardiff committee and organized meetings in Cardiff and elsewhere, some of which she chaired and addressed. As such she was a prime target for the ridicule of the hostile *Western Mail*:

> The 'savante' of Wenvoe who had donned her 'Sunday best' looked charming and ... on being elected to the chair, said more about the (Irish) Land League than the pertinent question of women's rights and wrongs![42]

Miss Jenner was one of an active group of suffragists in Cardiff, including the wives of the Dissenting ministers, Revds Tilly, Waite and Chester (plus the latter's daughter), Mrs Richard Cory and Christine Hollyer, a merchant's wife. In Swansea, Emily Higginson, wife of the Revd Edward Higginson, Unitarian minister and political radical, was the leading feminist and sat on the town's School Board from 1879 to 1882.[43] Indeed, in many Welsh localities, perhaps only for a short period, essentially middle-class women involved themselves in the campaign, acting as corresponding secretaries, subscribing to funds, organizing and speaking at meetings, getting up petitions and contacting local MPs.

Despite the inconstancy of commitment to the cause, the relatively few committees and societies formed, and the meagre financial

[42] *Western Mail*, 10 Mar. 1881. A life-long philanthropist, the eccentric Miss Jenner was especially proud of her efforts in support of young women facing capital punishment for infanticide, her boast being that she had saved some fourteen from the gallows. Obituaries in *Barry Dock News*, 22 Apr. 1904; *Penarth Observer*, 23 Apr. 1904; *Cardiff Times*, 23 Apr. 1904; *Western Mail*, 18 Apr. 1904; *South Wales Echo*, 18 Apr. 1904.

[43] Propertied women could vote for and serve on School Boards from 1870, Boards of Guardians from 1875 and Parish and District Councils from 1894. They could vote for County Councils from their inception in 1888 but could not be elected until 1907. Apart from Rose Crawshay and Emily Higginson, the only other woman to win local government office in Wales in the period up to 1886 was Miss Margaret Elizabeth Marsh of Tybrith, Carno, who sat on the Llandinam School Board from 1872 until 1877. Aged 28 when first elected, she was described by the census returns of 1881 as 'landowner'. *School Board Chronicle*, 16 Mar. 1872, 28 Feb. 1874; *Newtown and Welshpool Express*, 30 Jan. 1872; *Montgomeryshire Express*, 27 Feb. 1877. For a study of women in English local government, see P. Hollis, *Ladies Elect* (1987).

contribution, Welsh supporters certainly participated in the pressure for women's suffrage. Most obviously, there was heavy petitioning, upon which the early agitation placed great weight. Basically, resolutions and petitions repudiated the political distinction between male and female and urged the enfranchisement of women possessing the appropriate property qualifications. The Married Women's Property Acts of 1870–82 created a small number of married women with the requirements, but votes for married women were for some time a divisive issue among suffragists. The democratic demand for adult suffrage was avoided; the assumption that possession of the vote was a privilege remained fixed.

Pressurizing local MPs was a common tactic of activists too, either verbally during elections or by written memorial. One memorial elicited a very favourable response from Stuart Rendel to Newtown ladies in 1884.[44] In the early eighties Cardiff campaigners declared themselves well satisfied with the borough member, E. J. Reed, and one of the Glamorgan county members, C. R. M. Talbot, but the other county representative, H. H. Vivian, was 'a hopeless case'.[45] Others, such as W. Fuller-Maitland of Breconshire, were induced to give the subject full consideration for the first time.[46] At the time of the Third Reform Bill, Welsh MPs signed memorials to Gladstone urging the inclusion of female suffrage.[47] Suffragists also sought to win over town councils; Wrexham Town Council petitioned Parliament in 1872, 1873 and 1886.[48] By the mid eighties the cause was making an impression on other bodies too. Liberal associations such as those at Newport and Llandudno followed the lead of the N.L.F. and came out in support, as did some labour organizations like the Aberdare, Merthyr and Dowlais District Miners' Association, while female suffrage was also a favourite topic in debating societies around Wales.[49]

'The age of ridicule, in respect of Women's Suffrage, is past', observed the *South Wales Daily News* in 1881, the agitation in Cardiff affording 'unmistakable evidence of the growth of public opinion

[44] *Women's Suffrage Journal*, 2 June 1884.
[45] *Cardiff and Merthyr Guardian*, 18 Oct. 1873.
[46] *Women's Suffrage Journal*, 1 Apr. 1876.
[47] N.S.W.S., *Annual Reports*, 1883, 1884.
[48] *Women's Suffrage Journal*, 1 Apr. 1872, 1 Apr. 1873, 1 Mar. 1886.
[49] Ibid., 1 Jan., 2 Feb. 1885.

on the question... There is no doubt of the onward movement of the current.'[50] And certainly, the women's suffrage campaign did make its mark in Wales in the seventies and eighties and often brought women into the political arena for the first time. Yet enfranchisement lay more than thirty years away and only after the most ferocious struggle. In particular, political calculations increasingly affected the issue from the 1880s. Indeed, as early as 1870, explaining to Lydia Becker why he had voted against Jacob Bright's Women's Disabilities Bill having earlier promised support, Thomas Love Jones-Parry sounded a highly portentous note, for the argument that the Conservative Party would be the major beneficiaries of female suffrage proved the most enduring of all considerations:

> In the county I represent [Caernarfonshire] the women are all Liberal in politics and Nonconformists in religion—that is, the vast majority of them: and this may be said of all North Wales. On the other hand in England, and particularly in boroughs such as Bath, women are Conservative under great clerical influence, which always tends to fetter freedom of thought.
>
> I reluctantly, for these reasons, voted (against my own interests) to prevent women being made capable of doing what I consider politically wrong in many places, voting against the Liberal Party.[51]

II THE CONTAGIOUS DISEASES CAMPAIGN

Among the other aspects of the much dispersed Victorian women's movement, the most striking public agitation centred on prostitution and civil liberties in the campaign for the repeal of the Contagious Diseases Acts. The actual number of prostitutes operating in the country in mid century is impossible to determine. Contemporary estimates varied widely but certainly the total figure ran into many thousands. In the larger towns and seaports of Wales, as elsewhere in Britain, numerous women, actuated by poverty, upbringing, and other factors and supplying a demand from single and married men of all classes, practised prostitution, and places like Cardiff, Newport, Swansea, and Merthyr all had

---

[50] *South Wales Daily News*, 10 Mar. 1881.
[51] Quoted in R. Fulford, op. cit., p. 79.

their accepted streets and districts.[52] Of Cardiff in the 1870s the Chief Constable reported thus:

> ...prostitution is rampant in the lower parts of the town and...order is only maintained by the supervision of the police. We have in Cardiff about eighty brothels containing on an average two hundred women, known to the police...and I can add my testimony to the utterly abominable lives led by women who have given themselves over to prostitution.[53]

Similarly, Newport Town Council was told by the local police superintendent in 1872 that 'the present state of things was something alarming to contemplate. Many of the unfortunate girls who were constantly in the company of soldiers were not above seventeen or eighteen years of age, and some even younger than this. They were scantily dressed, and lay about in wretched hovels on the bare boards.'[54]

Widely regarded as a necessary sexual outlet for men, prostitution was not illegal in nineteenth-century Britain. However, by the 1860s, there was considerable public concern at the high incidence of venereal disease, especially among the armed forces, and governmental alarm was manifested in the Contagious Diseases Acts of 1864, 1866 and 1869. In certain garrison towns and ports in southern England, special policemen were empowered to challenge suspected prostitutes and require them to undergo medical examination. Should the woman refuse, and acceptance was tantamount to an admission of prostitution, she had to convince a magistrate of her respectability or meet the requirements of the law. If infected, the woman was treated in isolation at a 'lock' (that is, venereal disease) hospital. While some sections of society welcomed the legislation on public health grounds, others insisted on its injustice and the violation of women's civil liberties, and a national protest movement kept up an effective agitation for almost seventeen years until repeal in 1886. The campaign was spearheaded by two societies formed in late 1869, the male-dominated National Anti-Contagious Diseases Acts Association, subsequently the National Association for

---

[52] See, for example, K. Strange, 'In search of the celestial empire', *Llafur*, 3, No. 1 (1980), pp. 56–64; D. Jones and A. Bainbridge, 'The conquering of China: crime in an industrial community, 1842–64', ibid., 2, No. 4 (1979), pp. 23–5.
[53] F. W. Lowndes, *The Extension of the Contagious Diseases Acts to Liverpool and Other Seaports Practically Considered* (1876), p. 64.
[54] *South Wales Evening Telegram*, 9 Oct. 1872.

the Repeal of the Contagious Diseases Acts (N.A.), and the Ladies' National Association (L.N.A.) which admitted only females to membership and maintained a separate existence in order to 'express a woman's point of view', although the two bodies did work in close co-operation. The L.N.A. produced the movement's outstanding figure in the formidable and dynamic Josephine Butler. Other bodies such as the Midland Counties' and the Northern Counties' Electoral Leagues also came into being, so that by the end of 1873 there existed 'some dozen societies in the United Kingdom working in accord towards the one object and having committees and correspondents in more than six hundred towns'.[55] A South Wales Electoral Union had apparently been formed in the wake of Mrs Butler's visit early in that year, though it seems to have had only a short, nominal existence.[56]

Over the years the various repeal societies conducted a vigorous propaganda 'for the purpose of enlightening the community as to the immoral, unconstitutional, and inefficacious character of the Acts'. A total of more than 900 public meetings were organized, invariably addressed by one of the movement's itinerant agents, and 17,000 petitions with 2 ½ million signatures were generated.[57] Local committees and associations were also established; on disbandment in 1886 the N.A. had some 500 branches. A weekly journal, the *Shield*, performed an important co-ordinating role, offering powerful argument and news of all aspects of the campaign. In the House of Commons, the Liberal politician James Stansfeld led the cause,[58] while in the constituencies repealers sought to pressurize MPs, under threat of electoral action, as was effectively carried out in Colchester in 1870, into supporting parliamentary repeal initiatives. The agitation amounted to a potent political force and, moreover, a successful one, for the Acts were suspended in 1883 and repealed in 1886.

Indeed, there had been an initial triumph as early as 1872 when the government dropped the idea of extending the legislation to more towns. It was in this context that the movement first

[55] Josephine Butler, *Personal Reminiscences of a Great Crusade* (1896), p. 82.
[56] Ibid., p. 71; *Shield*, 1, 8 Feb. 1873.
[57] P. Hollis, *Women in Public*, p. 199.
[58] Henry Richard evidently declined the responsibility 'on grounds of health, want of time and having so many important matters on his hands'. N.A. Exec. Mins., Vol. III, Min. 86 (30 Mar. 1874). Richard was a vice-president of the Association throughout the campaign.

made a significant impression in Wales when, late in that year, Newport Town Council considered seeking the application of the Acts. This was in response to a communication from the commanding officer of the local barracks, drawing attention to the large number of soldiers 'suffering from a loathsome disease' ('ten out of every eleven cases in the military hospital') and urging 'steps by which the number of wretched girls on the streets be dealt with preventively'. Public alarm and protest were swiftly manifested and the aid of the national repeal bodies enlisted. Josephine Butler was incensed:

> The *men* suffer—so let us come down upon all those dirty girls, they (Newport town councillors) said, and cleanse them and make them *fit* for those dear men to consort with ... here is a warning of what we might expect from Town Councils, and the need there is for municipal agitation ... This evil thing will be *done*, if we don't look sharp ... If the present Town Council of Newport *could* be made to stink in the nostrils of the Municipal electors of Newport, before the 1st of November, a new and better Town Council might be elected.[59]

'Loads of papers' were immediately sent for distribution in the town and three agents dispatched. A crowded public meeting condemned both the Council's action and the Contagious Diseases Acts themselves; 'at the municipal election a few days after the chairman of our meeting was returned free of cost at the head of the poll' and the initiative was subsequently abandoned.[60] In Merthyr and Swansea, too, discussion by local officialdom on applying for extension of the Acts met with vociferous protest and went no further.[61] The military was not wholly to be defeated in Newport, however, for in November 1872 a War Office emissary working in co-operation with a local police inspector had thirteen girls consigned to a London hospital, apparently voluntarily. Newport activists were advised by the N.A. executive to be 'extremely alarmed and distrustful of the War Office interfering in this unprecedented manner to "get together" women of the most defenceless class, to convey them to a distant Lock Hospital under

---

[59] Josephine Butler Collection (JBC), Josephine Butler to Miss Priestman, late Oct. 1872.
[60] Ibid., Miss Mary Priestman to Mrs J. H. Wilson, 11 Feb. 1873; N.A., Exec. Mins., Vol. II, Mins. 503, 512 (21, 28 Oct. 1872); *Shield*, 26 Oct., 2, 9, 16 Nov. 1872; *South Wales Evening Telegram*, 8, 9 Oct. 1872;' *Monmouthshire Merlin*, 1 Nov. 1872; *Star of Gwent*, 2 Nov. 1872.
[61] *Merthyr Star*, 6 Aug. 1870; *Shield*, 21 June 1873.

charge of the police' and to be 'on the alert' for further attempts at 'putting the Contagious Diseases Acts into force by a sidewind'.[62]

The Newport meeting had called for the unconditional repeal of the Contagious Diseases Acts, which were 'subversive of the liberty of the subject, grossly unfair to women, and directly promotive of vice and immorality'. Elsewhere in Wales, the Acts were similarly denounced as 'immoral, one-sided and tyrannical' and such resolutions neatly compressed the main arguments of abolitionists. In the first place, the Acts, with their plain-clothes policemen ('a secret police') and compulsory inspection, seemed an infringement of basic liberty.[63] As the veteran Chartist George Morgan explained to fellow Merthyr radicals, he was

> virulently opposed to those Acts insomuch as it gave power to a policeman to take a female up if he suspected her of being a prostitute, and if the magistrate was satisfied with the policeman's evidence, which he generally is, he compels her to undergo an examination which to a modest female was shocking to her feelings ... We know there are good policemen, but we know there are some bad ones.[64]

Secondly, there was the issue of women's rights and the legal discrimination against women by a male-dominated State. 'While the male sex are to be allowed to indulge in vicious habits,' observed Revd Thornley Smith, a Swansea Wesleyan minister, 'the female sex is to be treated with the utmost indignity and subjected to the most vile and abominable discipline.'[65] A commonly held view was that if such legislation was to be on the statute book then it should apply to both sexes. Equal justice for rich and poor was another cry, for the victims were invariably working-class women, often driven to prostitution by desperate circumstances; 'class legislation in its worst form', declared a Caernarfon handbill.[66] The third objection centred on the relationship between the law and morality. Revd Henry Oliver, Independent minister of Newport, spoke for repealers everywhere when he emphasized that 'the object of the Acts was not to put down

[62] N.A., Exec. Mins., Vol. II, Min. 549 (25 Nov. 1872); *Shield*, 16 Nov. 1872; *South Wales Evening Telegram*, 5 Nov. 1872.

[63] The same objection was levelled against compulsory smallpox vaccination for infants and gave birth to the Anti-Compulsory Vaccination League. See *Merthyr Star*, 18 June 1870.

[64] *Merthyr Star*, 6 Aug. 1870.

[65] *Cambrian*, 10 Jan. 1873.

[66] *Shield*, 20 Dec. 1873.

prostitution but to cleanse the vessels'.[67] In this respect, 'they legalised vice', they encouraged men to sin and, accordingly, were contributing to the moral degeneration of society.

Supporters of the Acts countered with several lines of defence. Most obviously, there was the public health aspect. Thus the Denbighshire MP, Osborne Morgan, speaking in the 1883 parliamentary debate on the subject, argued that the measures 'have done much, very much, to alleviate the severity and check the growth of one of the most terrible diseases to which humanity is scourged'.[68] Stress was of course placed on the health of the nation's defenders and also on the drain on public expenditure as a result of the hospitalization of so many soldiers and sailors. At the same time, advocates could taunt opponents with the accusation that they disapproved of medical treatment for venereal disease. On a purely mercenary level, it was held that prostitutes were traders and therefore consumers had the right to expect them to be clean and safe. Finally, advocates contended that the legislation reduced prostitution through reclamation; hospital treatment for those infected was intended to be psychological as well as medical, with a heavy emphasis on social and moral re-education by such means as prayers and reading classes. If Cardiff were to be placed under the influence of the Acts, insisted the Chief Constable, it 'would tend more to the moral regeneration of the people than the present futile efforts of religious bodies. Here in Cardiff we have a patent fact of the inability of religion *per se* to cope with the evil of prostitution.'[69]

At the time, the effectiveness of the Acts was much disputed. The body of medical opinion believed that they were efficacious, and accordingly local doctors like Dr T. D. Griffiths of Swansea, Dr Burke of Cardiff, and Dr John Williams of Caernarfon came forward strongly to oppose repeal agitations in their areas; Griffiths, in fact, was involved in an organized public debate with the L.N.A. agent, Samuel Fothergill, at Swansea in 1873.[70] On the other hand, some members of the profession dissented from the majority view, adding weight to abolitionist refutations of

[67] Ibid., 9 Nov. 1872.
[68] *Hansard*, CCLXXVIII, col. 799 (20 Apr. 1883).
[69] F. W. Lowndes, op. cit., p. 64.
[70] *Swansea and Glamorgan Herald*, 12 Feb. 1873; *Cambrian*, 14, 21, 28 Feb. 1873; *Shield*, 22 Feb. 1873.

government statistics showing a reduction in prostitution and argu-ing that the evil was simply being driven underground. Thus, for example, two doctors from Liverpool hospitals lectured on behalf of the repeal movement at Mold, Holywell, Bagillt and Flint in 1872.[71] In any case, to many campaigners, this particular controversy was irrelevant for it was not the essential issue. Jose-phine Butler and like-minded men and women based their oppo-sition firmly on Christian principle; the law must be on the side of morality and virtue. 'I have', confessed Mrs Butler, 'no interest in the operation of the Acts. It is nothing to me whether they operate well or ill, but I will tell you what you wish to know as to my view of the principle of the Acts.'[72] Similarly, Lewis Williams, a leading Cardiff Wesleyan Methodist, submitted that 'no hygienic advantage, real or supposed, can justify the regulation of vice, or compensate for the destruction of social morality' which the Acts brought about.[73] To such moral reformers, reclamation of the prostitute was entirely dependent on voluntary effort.

The participation of Welsh localities in the contagious diseases campaign was most often initiated by public meetings held under the auspices of the various repeal organizations and addressed by one or more of their travelling agents. Wales was comprehensi-vely toured by L.N.A. lecturers Samuel Fothergill and William Burgess in 1873, while they and their co-workers appeared in other years too. At the end of the decade and in the early 1880s, deputations of ladies visited centres of population in north and south Wales seeking to enlist the active support of more Welsh women in the agitation. Josephine Butler herself spoke at large meetings in Cardiff, Newport and Swansea, 'all swarming places on the South Coast of Wales', in January 1873. Reports normally appeared in local newspapers, yet at the same time there were grounds for activists' complaints that 'a considerable portion of the public press' was to a large extent ignoring an important national agitation. Some editors clearly found the question too distasteful for lengthy discussion. 'Upon this subject of indecency we have very little to say,' confessed the *South Wales Daily News*. 'Prurrient [*sic*] details may have some attraction to those who

[71] *Shield*, 5 Oct. 1872.
[72] Quoted in B. Harrison, 'State intervention and moral reform', in P. Hollis (ed.), *Pressure from Without in Early Victorian England*, p. 314.
[73] *Protest* (formerly *Methodist Protest*), 21 Jan. 1882.

get up, and take part in, meetings ... but they have no interest for the general public.'[74] On several occasions the *Cambrian* felt obliged to apologize to readers before alluding to the campaign and early in 1873 called an abrupt halt to lively argument in its correspondence columns with the assertion that 'we cannot insert any more letters upon this nasty subject'.[75] Where Welsh newspapers did take a firm editorial stance they most commonly emphasized the paramountcy of public health considerations and supported the Acts. Only a few, like the *Star of Gwent* and the *Cardiff Times*, advocated repeal. One notable figure in this respect was the veteran radical, now a doughty champion of women's rights, Revd Samuel Roberts ('S. R.'), who attacked the Contagious Diseases Acts in *Y Cronicl*. Indeed, right at the end of his life, old and in poor health, he translated a leaflet explaining the nature and operation of the Acts into Welsh and took charge of printing and distributing 4,000 of them in Conwy, where he now lived, and in the slate-quarrying community in Bethesda.[76]

The unsavoury nature of the subject provided plenty of scope for often emotive local opposition. Thus, the Swansea ladies' committee of repealers met 'to patronise contagion' and repealers were condemned for placarding 'our walls with sentences of a decidedly immoral and indecent character'.[77] Similarly, a north Wales magistrate assailed those 'who have poisoned the minds of the young of Caernarvon by the introduction of the subject of those filthy and loathsome diseases'.[78] Elsewhere, campaigners were denigrated as 'free traders in vice and disease', 'unscrupulous and ignorant agitators', 'the shrieking sisterhood' and, indeed, by means of a whole vocabulary of abusive terminology. In Parliament, Osborne Morgan spoke of 'the miserable agitation which ... was a disgrace to the country, as it flooded gentlemen's breakfast tables with abominable literature, not addressed to themselves only but also their wives and daughters'.[79] Accordingly, throughout Wales, agents faced rival spokesmen, counter-resolutions and often persistent disruption, some meetings degenerating into chaos. After a stormy meeting in Cardiff, Josephine Butler was 'followed

[74] *South Wales Daily News*, 30 Jan. 1873.
[75] *Cambrian*, 31 Jan., 7, 24 Feb. 1873.
[76] N.A., Exec. Mins., Vol. VI, Mins. 4478, 4498 (15 June, 6 July 1885).
[77] *Cambrian*, 17 Jan., 7 Feb. 1873.
[78] *Shield*, 20 Dec. 1873; *Carnarvon and Denbigh Herald*, 6 Dec. 1873.
[79] *Hansard*, Vol. CCXI, col. 56, 1 May 1872.

to her hotel by a small but vociferous band of ruffians, uttering unmanly threats and indecent shouts', while a court case for assault followed one of Samuel Fothergill's Swansea lectures.[80] Indeed, Mrs Butler's own experience and her agent's subsequent defeat in a public debate with a Swansea doctor (though he consoled himself that the 'truly packed audience' comprised 'a remarkable number of *fast young men*, very few heads of families or earnest Christian workers'[81]) made her greatly concerned about south Wales:

> Fothergill has been tremendously beaten there again at a meeting and it is bad to leave the place having been apparently driven out of it. Our friends there are also much distressed. We *never* were so beaten in any of the subjected towns.[82]

The methods adopted by repealers were typical of most Victorian reform movements—the centrally administered and subscription-based popular organization, itinerant agents, public meetings, distribution of publications, petitioning, election and parliamentary activity. Local supporters expended considerable energy on getting up repeal petitions, taking them from house to house, depositing them on shop counters and urging public meetings and chapel congregations to sign them. During the campaign scores were sent forth from Wales.[83] This suggests a substantial number of local committees, though the degree of permanence is unclear. The most active centres were certainly Newport, Cardiff and Swansea, where at various times both male and female committees flourished; those at Newport totalled seventy ladies and gentlemen at the end of 1872.[84] These three towns also supplied most of the Welsh members on the General Committee of the N.A.—as many as twenty in 1879.[85] Local sympathizers were also urged to press municipal and parliamentary candidates on repeal, as was done at the Flintshire by-election in September 1872,[86] and exercise their vote accordingly. Within Parliament, a scrutiny was made of the voting on repeal bills, eleven of which were unsuccessfully introduced between 1873 and 1886. On the first occasion

[80] *Shield*, 8 Feb. 1873; *Swansea and Glamorgan Herald*, 26 Feb. 1873.
[81] JBC, S. Fothergill to H. J. Wilson, 12 Feb. 1873.
[82] Ibid., Josephine Butler to H. J. Wilson, 17 Feb. 1873.
[83] See, for example, N.A., *Annual Report*, 1875.
[84] *Shield*, 21 Dec. 1872.
[85] N.A., *Annual Report*, 1879.
[86] *Shield*, 14 Sept. 1872.

only 4 Welsh members (all Liberals) voted in favour of repeal while 16 (11 Liberals and 5 Conservatives) opposed. A decade later, in 1883, the pattern was reversed with 14 for (again all Liberals) and 6 (5 Liberals and 1 Conservative) against.[87]

A central figure in the controversy was the Denbighshire MP, Osborne Morgan, who registered five votes against repeal in the 1870s and, as Judge Advocate General in Gladstone's second administration of 1880 to 1885, emerged as 'the ardent champion of the Acts'.[88] A vigorous reformer in many areas, especially on Nonconformist issues, and indeed a promoter of women's education and married women's property rights, Morgan was nevertheless resolutely opposed to repeal of the Contagious Diseases Acts and to women's suffrage, thereby incurring 'the undying hostility of all the good women of England'.[89] As he became the chief defender of the Acts in the early 1880s, proclaiming their worth in terms of public health and reclamation in particular, the repeal movement quite naturally sought to place him under constituency pressure to reconsider his position. However, as the N.A. executive acknowledged, 'effective work in Denbighshire could only be done with the help of local Liberals' and this was never unreservedly given. They were prepared to use 'quiet influences' and at one stage Osborne Morgan was 'severely so written to respecting the action he took in regard to the Acts' but to no avail. Indeed, so strongly did the member defend his stance that several of his most prominent supporters were induced 'to turn around upon repealers and to declare that they would make it hot for them if they attempted to weaken the Liberal cause which had taken so many years to establish'.[90] And this was the crux of the matter. Despite the repeated efforts of various repeal bodies, dispatching agents and written communications, local Liberals, however sympathetic to the contagious diseases campaign, were averse to any public action against an otherwise wholly satisfactory representative.

In common with other Victorian reform movements, repealers sought to demonstrate working-class support. Indeed, a separate

---

[87] P. McHugh, *Prostitution and Victorian Social Reform* (1980), p. 237.
[88] N.A., Letter Book 1883–6, p. 7 (Triennial Report).
[89] *Hansard*, CCLXXVII, col. 780, 20 Apr. 1883; see also P. McHugh, op. cit., pp. 205, 222, 239–40.
[90] N.A., Exec. Mins., Vols. IV, V, VI (Oct. 1881–Mar. 1885).

organization for workers, the Working Men's National League, involving prominent labour figures like George Howell, Joseph Arch and Henry Broadhurst, came into being in 1875 and a monthly paper, the *National League Journal*, was launched. Representatives occasionally spoke in Wales, a few Welshmen were members of its National Council, and several hundred working men (and a few dozen women) from the industrial south enrolled as members.[91] The League certainly helped to rally working-class opposition to the Acts though, hamstrung by financial weakness, it never became the force it aspired to be.[92] At a national and local level the campaign was dominated throughout by middle-class men and women. At Newport, the president of the N.A. branch was a timber merchant and the secretary an iron merchant and wharf-owner; their wives were active on the ladies' committee. Other prominent repealers in the town included a dentist, a surgeon, a coal merchant, a printer and several shopkeepers, 'gentlemen well known for taking a lead in philanthropic measures'.[93] Similarly, at Cardiff, leading figures were the industrialists Richard and John Cory, and the shipowning businessman John Batchelor. Above all though, it was Nonconformist ministers, and occasionally Anglican vicars, who were foremost in the campaign. After an extensive tour of north Wales in 1873, L.N.A. lecturer William Burgess reported that he had been 'received well... especially among the Nonconformists'.[94] At Swansea, the local movement was almost entirely in the hands of ministers, while in Cardiff in 1873 twenty ministers of various denominations formed a local ministers' union, to co-operate with the N.A. and the L.N.A.[95] At Newport and elsewhere too, a considerable number were actively involved, while Dissenting bodies like the Welsh Congregational Union, meeting at Denbigh in 1881, the Welsh Baptist Union, at Llandudno in 1882, and Carmarthenshire Independents, at Llanelli the same year, passed formal resolutions condemning the Contagious Diseases Acts.[96] Nationally, the Wesleyan Society for Securing Repeal was founded and a number

[91] Scattered references in *National League Journal*, 1875–83.
[92] See P. McHugh, op.cit., pp. 112–19.
[93] *Star of Gwent*, 1 Feb. 1873.
[94] L.N.A., *Annual Report*, 1873, p. 6.
[95] N.A., Exec. Mins., Vol. II, Min. 695 (24 Feb. 1873); see also NLW, MS 15441B, Minutes of the Cardiff Nonconformist Ministerial Union, Dec. 1881.
[96] N.A., Exec. Mins., Vol. IV, Mins. 2999 (9 Jan. 1882), 3091 (13 Mar. 1882); *Shield*, 8 Apr., 9 Dec. 1882.

of Welsh ministers and laymen served on its General Committee.[97] The agitation was also conducted with a religious fervour, prayers and rousing hymns like 'Onward, Christian soldiers' being features of meetings. 'May God help and defend the right of the often innocent and oppressed victims of the cause we plead,' entreated the Cardiff ladies' committee led by Christine Hollyer.[98] Similarly, the president of the Newport Auxiliary Association, Councillor Nelson Hewertson, opened Josephine Butler's lecture in the town by kneeling for prayer and calling for God's blessing and aid for the cause.[99] There were exceptions to the pattern. At Cardiff in 1873 the Baptist minister, Revd Thomas Rees, led the opposition at Mrs Butler's meeting, registering his 'indignant protest against the convening of promiscuous assemblies',[100] while, after several visits to Denbighshire and Flintshire in the early eighties, the repeal agent, Revd J. P. Gledstone of Sheffield, concluded that 'the strongest denomination in Wales [the Welsh Calvinistic Methodists] has yet to be won'.[101] Nevertheless, Nonconformist ministers were at the heart of the campaign everywhere in Wales.

In the local press, the involvement of Welsh women in the repeal movement was invariably reported with a mixture of surprise, condescension and frivolity. Yet clearly in several places women did come forward and play an important, and above all independent, role in the protest. Spurred by female deputations from English repeal bodies, ladies' organizations were certainly formed at Newport, Swansea and Cardiff; committees may well have been set up in Conwy, Caernarfon, Aberdare and other places too. This was a significant political development. In March 1879, under the headline 'A Women's Conference about Women in Cardiff', the *Cardiff Times* reported 'a novelty' and 'a large and fashionable audience' attending 'the first public meeting here to which ladies alone were invited'.[102] Elsewhere in Wales there were similar meetings. Ladies also collected funds, circulated pamphlets and raised petitions. The national repeal petition from women presented to Parliament in May 1878, for example, contained

[97] Scattered references in *Methodist Protest*, 1876–83.
[98] L.N.A., *Annual Report*, 1882, p. 22.
[99] *Star of Gwent*, 1 Feb. 1873; *Shield*, 8 Feb. 1873.
[100] *Shield*, 8 Feb. 1873.
[101] N.A., Exec.Mins., Vol. IV, Min. 3149 (8 Mar. 1882).
[102] *Cardiff Times*, 29 Mar. 1879.

2,447 signatures from Wales, the largest number of contributions coming from Swansea and Caernarfon.[103] Cardiff ladies went a stage further; a deputation waited on the local MP to argue their case in 1882.[104] Nevertheless, the number of paid-up members of the L.N.A. in Wales was always small, never exceeding more than a few dozen a year. Most came from Newport, more than a hundred subscriptions being forwarded from the town between the years 1879 and 1885. Elsewhere, there were rarely block payments, though scattered around Wales there were long-standing individual subscribers, women like Mrs C. H. James, wife of the Merthyr lawyer and MP, and Mrs Owens of Conwy who, along with Revd Samuel Roberts, undertook the distribution of thousands of Welsh-language leaflets in the area.[105]

Who precisely were these female activists? Most certainly they were middle-class, able to afford a sizeable membership contribution, and wives of professional men and businessmen; husbands at Newport, for example, included an auctioneer, a botanist, a timber merchant and an iron merchant and wharf-owner. Often, they were the wives of activists; at Newport, the wives of the president, secretary and treasurer of the male association served on the ladies' committee. Religion was also an influence; the leading figures at Swansea were Mrs Catherine Smith and Mrs Emily Higginson, wives of Nonconformist ministers (who themselves were active campaigners), and this was so elsewhere too. In addition, as already noted, the conduct of meetings was often strongly religious.

As in other parts of Britain, there were links in personnel between the repeal and suffragist movements. In south Wales, striking examples of dual activists were Gertrude Jenner, Emily Higginson, Mrs C. H. James, Richard Cory and Revds Alfred Tilly and James Waite. There were others too.[106] Such an interconnection was common but by no means uniform, and some Welsh repealers do not seem to have participated in the suffragist campaign and vice versa; indeed, at a national level, association with the contagious diseases movement caused a split within the ranks

---

[103] L.N.A., *Annual Report*, 1878, pp. 21–3.
[104] Ibid., 1882, p. 22.
[105] N.A., Exec. Mins., Vol. VI, Min. 4478 (15 June 1885).
[106] Osborne Morgan and J. H. Scourfield, on the other hand, were prominent anti-suffragists and leading supporters of the Contagious Diseases Acts.

of campaigners for women's rights in the 1870s. Women's rights activists in Wales often had links with other agitations too, especially those directed by the Liberation Society, the United Kingdom Alliance and the National Education League, those pressure groups associated with political Nonconformity.

Women's rights therefore made some impression in Wales in the seventies and eighties via the campaigns for suffrage and against the Contagious Diseases Acts. Men were prominent in local movements but, most significantly, the agitations brought female involvement, often in the face of considerable prejudice. Established Victorian attitudes to women's role in society were thereby challenged and the idea that women could be significant participants in political activity was implanted. The development of course continued; by the early 1890s Women's Liberal Associations were springing up throughout Wales and serving as agencies for the promotion of women's suffrage.[107]

[107] N.S.W.S., *Annual Reports*, 1892.

XII

RADICAL DISSENT

Welsh radical Dissent achieved a significant electoral breakthrough in 1868 and this advance continued in successive elections. In the seventies and eighties Welsh Nonconformity spearheaded political activity on a number of fronts—temperance, land reform, tithes, education and, above all, disestablishment.[1] These were essentially the demands of the later nineteenth-century 'crocheteers' or 'faddists', to use the disparaging language of their opponents.

Tenant farmer exploitation and tithes had long been emotive issues in Welsh Nonconformist politics. These agitations gained momentum with the agricultural depression from 1879 but did not achieve full force until after 1886. Disestablishment campaigners naturally sought to exploit the increasing tension over tithes, 'to loosen the foundations of the existing system'.[2] Thus, tithe became a salient topic in Liberationist councils, conferences, branches and public meetings in Wales in the eighties, and local farmers invited Society agents to speak on the subject.[3] Land reform centred on the demands of tenant farmers for fair rent, security of tenure, and compensation for improvements, a programme which was given organizational expression in Thomas Gee's Welsh Land League, founded at Rhyl in 1886. This quickly incorporated the Anti-Tithe Leagues which had recently mushroomed in most of the counties of Wales.

It was in the field of temperance reform that Welsh Nonconformity achieved its major legislative triumph in the period 1868–86. The Welsh Sunday Closing Act of 1881 was the culmination of a vigorous agitation by temperance organizations, backed by Church and chapel, over the previous decade. Public opinion in the Principality appeared almost unanimously in favour of the Sunday closure of public houses, while Welsh MPs, particularly

---

[1] See K. O. Morgan, *Wales in British Politics*, Chs. II, III; idem, *Rebirth of a Nation*, pp. 36–45.

[2] *Liberator*, Oct. 1866.

[3] Ibid., Apr. 1881; Lib. Soc. Mins., Vol. VIII, A/LIB/7, Min. 1880 (11 Oct. 1886).

Liberals, overwhelmingly supported temperance legislation. The United Kingdom Alliance, demanding legislative restriction on the sale of liquor throughout the week, was not responsible for the agitation though inevitably Welsh supporters were active. During the 1870s and the 1880s the Alliance continued to make significant progress in Wales, more auxiliaries being formed and numbers of subscribers and total subscriptions increasing. Nevertheless, marked disagreements on policy surfaced from time to time, largely centring on the Alliance's uncompromising all-or-nothing stance on local option (its insistence on the total prohibition of liquor traffic as opposed to the willingness of Welsh temperance reformers to accept the reduction or limitation of licences, if prohibition proved impracticable). At the same time, temperance, like a number of other issues, was gravitating towards the Liberal Party, the cause being embraced by the North Wales and South Wales Liberal Federations in the mid eighties and appearing in the 1891 Newcastle Programme.[4]

The Welsh Sunday Closing Act represented a political landmark in Wales, for the first time bestowing separate legislative treatment on Wales as an entity. Inevitably it acted as a precedent for similar demands, not only for a Welsh local option bill but for legislation on themes like education and disestablishment. Educational demands in part revolved around the provision of secondary and higher education in Wales, areas where Liberals and Conservatives were in broad sympathy. Elementary schooling, on the other hand, was fiercely contentious. Disestablishment of the Church eventually emerged as the overrriding issue in Welsh politics. But in the years immediately after 1868 it was public education which most stirred passions and in the early seventies the Liberation Society was to a large degree overshadowed by the National Education League and the Welsh Educational Alliance.

I THE NATIONAL EDUCATION LEAGUE

By the late 1860s there was mounting pressure on central government to take a more direct role in elementary education. The efforts of the voluntary religious societies, despite increasing state subsidies (where they would be accepted), were clearly inadequate, children in some areas receiving little or no schooling and illiteracy

[4] On these points, see W. R. Lambert, *Drink and Sobriety in Victorian Wales*, Chs. V, VI.

remaining widespread. In educational provision, Britain lagged behind other countries, notably the triumphant Prussians, to the detriment of industrial prosperity and national power, while the enfranchisement of large numbers of working-class voters by the Second Reform Act of 1867 made an improved system imperative. Some advocates also argued that educational opportunity was a basic human right, while others looked to the reduction of drunkenness and crime among the lower orders. The likelihood of Gladstone's Liberal administration introducing a major educational measure led to the formation of two pressure groups in 1869, the National Education League (N.E.L.) and later, its rival, the National Education Union (N.E.U.). Religion lay at the heart of the debate. The N.E.U. was Manchester-based and wished to maintain denominational teaching. Much the more powerful was the N.E.L., formed by Joseph Chamberlain and other Nonconformist radicals in Birmingham, where an Education Society had existed since 1867. It wanted the creation of a nation-wide system of state elementary schools, providing free, compulsory and, initially, undenominational education, which would permit use of the Bible without commentary. Welsh people went eagerly into the fray, positively responding to the League's initiative and, in a significant parallel development, forming an independent pressure organization, the Welsh Educational Alliance (W.E.A.).[5]

In organizational structure and conduct of campaign, the N.E.L. mirrored other nineteenth-century reform societies, most obviously the A.C.L.L. and the Liberation Society. An executive committee, under the chairmanship of Joseph Chamberlain, operated from central offices in Birmingham, the city which remained the backbone of the agitation throughout the eight years of its existence. An unwieldy council, consisting of all MPs who joined the League, donors of £500 or more, delegates appointed by branches, and many more ladies and gentlemen chosen from the membership, met once a year and acted as a consultative body. William Simons, the Merthyr solicitor and former High Constable, sat on the first executive; S. C. Evans-Williams of Rhayader, magistrate and Liberal MP for Radnor District in 1880-4, and John Batchelor of Cardiff were later members. At the League's first

<hr>

[5] For this organization, see Leighton Hargest, 'The Welsh Educational Alliance and the 1870 Elementary Education Act', *Welsh History Review*, 10, No. 2 (Dec. 1980), pp. 172-206.

annual general meeting in October 1869 twenty-two Welsh representatives, including three MPs, George Osborne Morgan (Denbighshire), Thomas Love Jones-Parry (Caernarfonshire), and Watkin Williams (Denbigh District), were named as members of the council. Among the earliest League branches, established in 1869, were those at Merthyr and Newport, while the Welsh quickly began contributing to funds on an individual and group basis. An agent for the Principality, Revd David Dudley Evans of Newport, was speedily appointed, and early in 1870 Lloyd Jones of London was specially deputed to conduct a lecture tour there. Increasingly, Wales became a stronghold of N.E.L. support, by October 1871 harbouring fifty-seven branches and eventually almost a third of the total of more than four hundred.[6] In contrast, the Anglican-led N.E.U. apparently inspired only a handful.

From the very first, however, there was a division between the N.E.L. and many Welsh Nonconformists who took a more extreme stance on religious instruction in schools. Support for a completely secular education system evolved from a strong attachment to voluntaryism in various parts of the Principality. In 1868 it emerged publicly in Merthyr where the chief advocates were William Simons and the Congregational minister, Revd F. Sonley Johnstone.[7] Similar concern in Cardiff led Nonconformist radicals to initiate an education conference at Aberystwyth in January 1870, where the W.E.A. was created. Thereafter, this organization attracted determined support, particularly in south Wales urban centres like Merthyr, Cardiff and Carmarthen, and represented a rift with the N.E.L. chiefly over the secular principle. The League, at this time adopting the ambiguous words 'undenominational' or 'unsectarian', was prepared to allow the use of the Bible as a class book 'without note or comment' and denominational teaching outside school hours. Secularists insisted on the exclusion of the Bible altogether, leaving religious teaching to the various Sunday schools. Accordingly, the 'strictly secular' Merthyr

---

[6] *N.E.L. Monthly Paper*, Dec. 1869, Jan. 1870; Francis Adams, *History of the Elementary School Conflict* (1882), p. 200; N.E.L., *First and Third Annual Meeting Reports*, 1869 and 1871. A precursor of the N.E.L. was the National Public School Association (1850–62), itself a descendant of the A.C.L.L. In Wales, John Jenkins, former A.C.L.L. lecturer and editor of the *Swansea and Glamorgan Herald* (1847–57), was involved. A secular committee was founded in Swansea but apparently attracted little public support. There was also interest in the movement from Chirk and Carmarthen. Wilson Papers, M. 136/2/3, Nos. 1799–1805, 1854–7, 2492; WSRO, Cobden Papers 42, Cobden to John Jenkins, 1 May 1850.

[7] L. Hargest, op. cit., pp. 178–9, 181.

Education Committee withdrew as a branch of the League and Simons resigned as a member of its executive in January 1870, while meetings in Carmarthen expressed adhesion to the general principles of the Birmingham organization but voiced a 'decided preference for a perfectly secular system'.[8]

Yet there was by no means universal support for secularism in Wales. Lengthy debate and heated exchanges on the issue at the Aberystwyth conference ultimately brought no clear majority in favour of the secular principle. Speeches revealed the split within communities. Thus, William Simons and the Revd F. S. Johnstone argued passionately against their fellow townsmen, Revd John Griffith, rector of Merthyr, and C. H. James. It was at the same gathering that secularists founded the W.E.A. to promote their cause even though the principle had failed to win general approval. This failure, based on the deep reluctance of many Welshmen to exclude the Bible entirely from schools, inevitably severely damaged the Alliance's effectiveness.[9]

An uneasy relationship with the League was another problem. Addressing a public meeting in Cardiff, a major centre of Alliance support, in May 1871, Revd D. D. Evans, N.E.L. agent for the Principality, argued 'though his Welsh friends went a step beyond the League, that there was no reason why they should not support the League as far as it went'.[10] For the most part, Alliance leaders seem to have accepted this as being in their best interests; moreover, there was, of course, much common ground. Thus, while rigidly adhering to the exclusion of religion from any part of the state-supported system of education and independently discussing developments in the controversy, the secularists also sought to work out strategy and effective pressure in conjunction with the League as far as possible. The Aberystwyth conference had appointed a deputation to wait upon the Birmingham executive so that 'some means may be found to secure concurrent, if not united, action between the League and the Welsh educational reformers'.[11] When the government's detailed proposals were

[8] N.E.L. Monthly Paper, Feb. 1870.
[9] Cardiff and Merthyr Guardian, 29 Jan., 5 Feb. 1870; L. Hargest, op. cit., pp. 182–5. For a detailed discussion of the divide between secularists and non-denominationalists and, indeed, the whole controversy surrounding the 1870 Education Act and Welsh politics, see H. G. Williams, 'The Forster Education Act and Welsh politics, 1870–1874', Welsh History Review, 14, No. 2 (Dec. 1988), pp. 242–68.
[10] N.E.L. Monthly Paper, June 1871.
[11] Ibid., Feb. 1870.

announced by W. E. Forster in February 1870, an Alliance executive meeting in Llanidloes swiftly dispatched representatives to Birmingham to co-operate in a campaign of protest though, subsequently, separate delegations met ministers on 9 March.[12] Later in the year, the executive, meeting in Brecon to discuss various amendments being debated in Parliament, deputed Revd Daniel Rowlands, Principal of Bangor Normal College, and Revd F. Sonley Johnstone to go to London to watch the progress of the Bill through Committee and to act in concert with officers of the N.E.L. 'as far as they can consistently do so'.[13] Thus, Alliance policy throughout was to uphold its independent stance, indeed to press the League towards a secularist position, while at the same time seeking political headway through co-operation with their powerful counterpart.

Secularist or unsectarian, Alliance or League, Welsh Nonconformists were at one in condemnation of the Liberal Government's education scheme, which rejected their basic principles. Introducing the Education Bill in February 1870, W. E. Forster's declared aim was 'not to injure existing and efficient schools [but] to complete the present voluntary system, to fill up gaps ...' The final version, approved by the Commons in June, created a dual system of voluntary and board schools, the former administered by the religious societies, the latter by locally elected School Boards. Both received government grants and could charge fees, but only the board schools had rate-aid. The religious question roused intense parliamentary debate. Eventually, the Cowper-Temple clause stipulated that religious teaching in board schools was to be 'undenominational' (though the teacher was free 'to explain the Bible according to his own views').[14] In voluntary schools, parents were allowed to withdraw their children from religious instruction on grounds of conscience.

The introduction of the Bill in the Commons had brought immediate Nonconformist protest. Chamberlain condemned the original draft as 'detestably bad ... not National Education at all [but] a trick to strengthen the Church of England against the Liberation

---

[12] *Cardiff Times*, 12 Mar. 1870; L. Hargest, op. cit., pp. 187–9.

[13] *Aberdare Times*, 18 June 1870.

[14] W. F. Cowper-Temple was chairman of the N.E.U.

Society'.[15] Both the N.E.L. and the W.E.A. formulated criticisms but their representations to government ministers found little favour. Despite substantial amendment, the final measure remained a great disappointment to these two pressure organizations and, indeed, to Nonconformists generally. Elementary education was neither free nor universally compulsory, School Boards having the option of compelling attendance in their districts. Above all, the religious aspects caused resentment, nowhere more deeply than in Wales where in many rural, overwhelmingly Nonconformist areas Anglican 'National' Schools held, and by Forster's Act retained, a monopoly. Most invidious was the teaching of the Catechism to Nonconformist children and other efforts by some Anglican schoolmasters to influence minds. As Henry Richard pointed out to the Commons, a conscience clause applying to the vast majority of the population was absurd;[16] in the words of William Simons to the N.E.L., it was 'a delusion and a snare'.[17]

Radical Nonconformists in Wales, as elsewhere, therefore found much to object to in the measure. Indeed, some zealots argued that it was too reprehensible to be altered; 'the tree', insisted one Cardiff militant, 'instead of being pruned, must be burnt'.[18] Disillusionment was made complete as the effects of clause twenty-five, which permitted payment of the school fees of poor children out of the rates, became apparent. This could mean rate aid to denominational schools, anathema to many Nonconformists. As Revd Alfred Tilly, Cardiff Baptist minister and a W.E.A. stalwart, told the N.E.L annual meeting in 1871, whereas activists in his town had initially agitated for a School Board, 'since the discovery of the twenty-fifth clause' they were not sure whether one was desirable; his proposed strategy was refusal to pay rates until the clause was repealed.[19]

Following the passage of the Education Act in July 1870 the focus of attention on the issue shifted from Westminster to the country, to a nation-wide campaign spearheaded by the N.E.L.

[15] Chamberlain Papers, Chamberlain to Dixon, 3 Mar. 1870, quoted in Peter Griffiths, 'Pressure groups and parties in late Victorian England', *Midland History*, III, No. 3 (1976), p. 194.
[16] Hansard, CC, cols. 263–74, 18 Mar. 1870; K. O. Morgan, *Wales in British Politics*, p. 45; L. Hargest, op. cit., p. 190.
[17] N.E.L., *First Annual Meeting Report*, 1869, pp. 85–6.
[18] *N.E.L. Monthly Paper*, June 1871.
[19] N.E.L., *Third Annual Meeting Report*, 1871, pp. 56–8.

aimed at forcing revision. This agitation, and in particular the demand for repeal of clause twenty-five, brought the Alliance and the League into closer association. Thus Revd Alfred Tilly, representative of the W.E.A. or, as he put it, 'the Nonconformists of Wales', at the N.E.L annual meeting in October 1871, 'publicly identified himself with the League ... though somewhat reluctant to do so before'.[20] Indeed, during that summer, following an extensive lecturing tour by N.E.L. agent Revd D. D. Evans, over fifty branches were formed in Wales. Men like Tilly 'still differed with them [League leaders] by advocating a purely secular system of education', but early in 1872 this disparity was removed when the League finally committed itself to a secularist position, demanding universal school boards to govern all schools with religious teaching being supplied only in out-of-school hours. This completed a development noted earlier by the *Cardiff Times*: 'we find that the latter (the Birmingham League) has made a great advance towards the position of the Welsh association'.[21] There was now no impediment to full integration of Welsh educational radicals into the N.E.L., though the Alliance continued to function.

The League's efforts in the country at large were based on a network of local agents, who were expected to perform a wide range of duties. Agents travelled the districts assigned to them, addressed public meetings, distributed publications, enrolled members and collected subscriptions, formed and revitalized branches, promoted the formation of School Boards and participated in local contests, and collected constituency information with a view to electoral action. One of the first appointments was Revd D. D. Evans of Newport, who served as Welsh agent for almost four years until his death in 1873. During these years he visited every part of Wales, the remarkable number of branches instigated testifying to the enthusiastic response. Largely due to Evans's exertions, branches were in operation in all thirteen counties by the summer of 1872. At this same time, Revd John Rhys Morgan of Llanelli became agent in south Wales, and later Revd J. Spinther James of Llandudno and Revd J. 'Kilsby' Jones of Llanwrtyd Wells took up similar positions, enabling a systematic coverage of the whole

[20] Ibid.
[21] *Cardiff Times*, 20 May 1871. See also ibid., 25 Jan. 1873.

of the Principality. Thus, in 1875, three of the League's ten local agents were based in Wales.[22]

But agents were essentially stimulants to protest. 'The strength of the League', insisted the executive, 'consists in the multiplication of efforts throughout the country and in the effect produced by the simultaneous action of 400 local centres.'[23] Branches indeed totalled 430 by the end of 1872, the peak year of the agitation. A heavy concentration of these was in Wales—121 by this date, with more formed later. They were founded not only in many of the bustling industrial communities of the Principality but also in sleepy rural villages like St Harmon and Newbridge-on-Wye in Radnorshire. It is difficult to determine the degree of activity and durability of most of these organizations. The majority were inspired by one of the League's itinerant agents, lecturing to a public meeting in the community, often in a Nonconformist school-room or chapel; a committee and officers would be appointed, members enrolled and a subscription list opened (the membership fee was one shilling per annum). Branch activities included house-to-house canvassing, circulating League papers and pamphlets, holding local meetings, collecting petition signatures and keeping a watchful eye on parliamentary representatives. Subscription lists indicate that branch memberships usually totalled no more than a few dozen, though public meetings often attracted attendances of several hundred and in places like Merthyr and Cardiff could be very large gatherings indeed. A considerable number of Welsh branches were no doubt short-lived affairs, the impetus given by an outside speaker perhaps proving hard to sustain. In some centres, however, local organizations showed a marked resilience, treasurers continuing to forward their handfuls of subscriptions for a number of years. League representatives in Wales continued to enliven activity, Spinther James and J. Rhys Morgan remaining busy throughout 1876, the last full year of the N.E.L.'s life.

Like other pressure groups, the League also sought to solidify Nonconformist discontent over the Elementary Education Act of 1870 by penetrating official denominational bodies. Agents addressed county association meetings and elicited pledges of

---

[22] N.E.L., *Seventh Annual Report*, 1875, pp. 14–16. During 1873 Revd D. Jones of Liverpool also acted as agent for Liverpool and north Wales. Ibid., *Fifth Annual Report*, 1873, p. 14.

[23] N.E.L., Miscellaneous Papers, Circular No. 253.

co-operation with the N.E.L.[24] Ministers were invariably a solid source of support. Thus, when Forster's Bill was first placed before Parliament, a petition organized by the Central Nonconformist Committee, which was Birmingham-based and an inspiration of the N.E.L., protesting against rate-aid for denominational schools was signed by 'over two-thirds of all the Nonconformist ministers in England and Wales, of all denominations'.[25] Beyond this section of the community, League membership and contribution lists indicate the support and participation of prominent local businessmen and professional men in various parts of Wales, though in some places there was undoubtedly a considerable social mix.

The League's *Monthly Paper*, selling 20,000 copies a week, played an important unifying role in the movement. Thousands of pamphlets were also distributed—250,000 within a few months of the N.E.L.'s formation. A substantial income enabled this: over £6,000 a year by 1870, a peak of £7,483 in 1872, declining to £3,741 by 1876. Funds came partly from membership subscriptions but essentially from donations, Birmingham businessmen and manufacturers being most conspicuous.[26] Relatively few sizeable donations came from Wales but there were, from 1870 onwards, a very large number of subscribers throughout the country contributing their few shillings, and this kind of support continued over the years. Thus, the very last issues of the *Monthly Paper* in 1876 recorded sums forwarded by branch secretaries at Rhayader (8 subscribers), Pontypridd (15) and Tenby (35), as well as various monies collected by the Welsh travelling agents.[27] In this respect the Welsh showed a commitment to the cause of education comparable to that for almost all other reform campaigns of the period.

Following enactment of the Education Bill and despite acute disappointment with its terms, the League and the Alliance instructed branch committees and supporters to agitate for the creation of School Boards. In this, campaigners often faced the powerful resistance of local landowners operating as staunch defenders of the Church's favoured educational position in many parts of Wales. There was certainly no mistaking the directive of one Merioneth landlord to his tenants: 'I shall be extremely

[24] *N.E.L. Monthly Paper*, May, July 1871.
[25] F. Adams, op. cit., pp. 221.
[26] Ibid., p. 200; D. A. Hamer, *The Politics of Electoral Pressure*, p. 335; D. Read, *England 1868–1914* (1979), p. 97–8.
[27] *N.E.L. Monthly Paper*, Oct., Nov. 1876.

displeased if you do not vote against a School Board in Arthog parish, and do all in your power to oppose it ... The land is mine and from me you derive your vote.[28] Similar reports came from other areas. In one Cardiganshire parish it was recounted that:

> ... every possible power and every agency of tyranny were set to work—letters from all the Tory landlords, all the scheming pressure of their agents, all the influence, high and low, of Church patronage, all benevolence to the poor—in the shape of soap, sugar and candles—were brought up, and the cottagers agreed to vote against the School Board. Farmers were reminded who their landlords were. It was ten times hotter than during the election of 1868. There are now eight evictions here ... and it is believed the School Board contest had quite as much to do with them as the election of '68.[29]

School Boards, according to some opponents, 'would propagate infidelity and atheism', while scaremongering on the size of the rates was a frequent tactic. In Builth Wells opponents estimated the rate as high as 16s. in the £; N.E.L. activists insisted a rate of 2d. or 3d. would be sufficient. The efforts to get a Board in the town were ultimately unsuccessful, owing, it was said, 'to the treating and the intimidation of the Church party'.[30] Cardiff radicals were similarly thwarted by the Anglican and Catholic clergy, backed by Bute influence.

Elsewhere, in such places as Aberystwyth, Carmarthen, Brecon and Wrexham, School Boards were swiftly established and elections duly held in late 1870 or early 1871; many more followed over the next few years, though at the cost of 'desperate party conflict and angry feeling and passion between sect and sect, priest and people, landlord and tenant'.[31] In many localities, contests exhibited 'bad feeling and unwholesome excitement' between the rival factions. The Carmarthen election of late 1870 took the form of a struggle 'between a committee, composed of the members of the local branch of the League and other friends of unsectarian education, and the local committee of the Manchester Union', the result, according to an N.E.L. activist, being 'the formation

---

[28] Ibid., Apr. 1871.
[29] N.E.L., *Third Annual Report*, 1871, pp. 93–4, Revd F. Sonley Johnstone delivering a paper entitled, 'The Education Act and its Working in Wales'.
[30] *N.E.L. Monthly Paper*, May 1871.
[31] N.E.L., *Third Annual Report*, 1871, p. 93. For the formation of School Boards in Wales, 1870–6, see L. Hargest, op. cit., pp. 197–9, 203–6.

of an excellent Board'.[32] Similarly, Leaguers trumpeted the election of the Rhayader branch president as first chairman of the School Board and in Colwyn Bay the 'triumph of the north Wales agent at the expense of the local vicar'.[33] But the results were not always so agreeable to Nonconformists. In some places elections took the form of a 'distressing war of sects', with Nonconformists failing to act concordantly, promoting too many candidates and thereby allowing Anglican and Catholic majorities on boards. Accordingly, supporters of denominational education in the parishes of Merthyr and Vaynor were able to make the highly contentious decision to put clause twenty-five of Forster's Act into operation. The overall experience of the early implementation of the Act, 'the partiality and injustice which deforms it', turned the W.E.A. against applying for boards.[34] Nevertheless, School Board elections in Wales over the years did generally reflect Nonconformist preponderance, sentiment and ardour, and the majority of board schools either provided no religious instruction or permitted only the reading of the Bible without interpretation.

N.E.L. partisans were also inevitably drawn towards parliamentary electoral activity, aimed at the return of members pledged to support their principles. In 1872, the League, like the Liberation Society before it, opened a parliamentary register 'containing the fullest particulars which could be collected respecting the various constituencies', information being obtained through correspondence with members and friends and through visits by agents. The latter now took on much more electoral work. In the summer of 1872, Revd D. D. Evans was 'exclusively occupied in visiting the Welsh constituencies', concluding that 'several boroughs with the Ballot could be carried for Radicals against the present representatives'.[35] During the first half of 1873 Francis Adams, the League's travelling agent in the southern counties, conducted a lecture tour of Wales but gave his time 'chiefly to Parliamentary work, relating to various constituencies'.[36]

League members were also encouraged to pressurize parliamentary representatives. Welsh branches organized public meetings

[32] *N.E.L. Monthly Paper,* Jan. 1871.
[33] Ibid., July, Sept. 1875.
[34] N.E.L., *Third Annual Report,* 1871, p. 96 (Revd F. Sonley Johnstone).
[35] N.E.L., *Fourth Annual Report,* 1872, pp. 12–13; J. L. Garvin, *The Life of Chamberlain* (1932), Vol. I, pp. 129–30. See also D. A. Hamer, op.cit., pp. 128–9.
[36] *N.E.L. Monthly Paper,* Feb., Mar., Apr., May 1873.

prior to George Dixon's parliamentary motion of March 1872 criticizing the existing educational system and then took note of members' voting; the Cardigan branch subsequently passed a resolution acknowledging the services of those MPs who backed Dixon but condemning the conduct of their own borough member, Sir Thomas Lloyd, who 'absented himself'.[37] The failure of Dixon's motion and of another presented by John Candlish the following month for the repeal of clause twenty-five induced the League to adopt a militant policy of intervention in by-elections in an effort to ensure that all Liberals returned were in support of its principles. The strategy was implemented in Bath and other places; Wales was unaffected, there being no contests at this time. Finding little profit, the League dropped electoral opposition to the Liberal Party in August 1873, some six months before the Conservative general election victory.[38]

At the general election, the N.E.L. executive determined upon a hardline stance towards the Liberal Party, threatening to withdraw support from candidates who did not pledge repeal of clause twenty-five, a tactic taken up by radicals in parts of Wales. This produced 300 firm promises from the 425 Liberal candidates in England and Wales, though the League did not actively oppose recalcitrants. Of these 300, 167 were elected but only about one-third accepted the full League programme of secularism, universal School Boards, free education, and compulsion.[39] In Wales, government education policy seems to have been one factor in the poor performance of a number of Liberal candidates.[40] For the League, the 1874 election represented a disappointing return on over four years' labour, though publicly it remained undaunted, taking solace in the memory of the venerated A.C.L.L.:

> The existence of a decisive majority in the House of Commons against any alteration in the Act of 1870 … is only really discouraging to the people who despair of a cause if it fails to triumph the day after their own awakening to a sense of its justice and expediency. Let such persons remember that in 1841 the Anti-Corn Law League, after years of strenuous effort, had the mortification of seeing the country send to Parliament a majority of ninety against the cause of science and common sense, and

[37] Ibid., Mar., Apr. 1872. For the voting of Welsh members see L. Hargest, op.cit., p. 200.
[38] D. Hamer, op. cit., p. 137; P. Griffiths, op. cit., pp. 195–6.
[39] F. Adams, op. cit., p. 301; P. Griffiths, op. cit., pp. 197–8.
[40] L. Hargest, op.cit., pp. 202–3.

the commonweal. Yet in 1846 the League was triumphant and the Corn Laws vanished into the limbo of legislative blunders.[41]

Nevertheless, the mid 1870s witnessed increasing disillusionment, among both leadership and rank and file, with the N.E.L.'s effectiveness as a pressure group and early in 1877 it merged into the newly created National Liberal Federation, with its comprehensive programme of radical, and indeed Nonconformist, demands. While the League failed to achieve its ultimate objectives, its propaganda campaign over the years had an effect on public opinion. The strengthening case for compulsory and free education was reflected in a substantial growth in parliamentary support in the decade. Adherence to denominational education, however, proved much more resolute, though in Wales, as elsewhere, it remained a central, frequently acrimonious, issue in local politics for many years.

II THE LIBERATION SOCIETY

The central issue of the 1868 general election (as defined by Gladstone) was disestablishment of the Irish Church and, accordingly, this was the first major measure tackled by the newly elected Liberal Government. Welsh people were very much behind Gladstone in his proposals, and meetings expressing support, often under the auspices of the Liberation Society, were held throughout the Principality during 1868–9. In such debate the analogy between the Church in Ireland and the Church in Wales was inevitably and frequently drawn, and indeed, within a few weeks of the enactment of Irish disestablishment in July 1869, the new member for Denbigh District, Watkin Williams, gave notice of a motion for Welsh disestablishment.

From the first, the move proved a contentious one, for Williams was acting independently, offending both his parliamentary colleagues and the Liberation Society.[42] A rift emerged among Welsh Liberationists themselves and between the Society and a proportion of its leading supporters in Wales. Williams's defenders envisaged substantial benefits from a stirring debate on the motion; in the Principality enthusiasm for the subject would be greatly intensified and considerable advance could be made generally by

---

[41] *N.E.L. Monthly Paper*, Mar. 1874.
[42] For this episode, see K. O. Morgan, *Wales in British Politics*, pp. 28–36.

using Wales 'as the best platform for attacking the whole system'.[43] The Liberation Society executive, on the other hand, promptly denounced the step as 'premature and inexpedient'. It feared a heavy defeat in the Commons and a subsequent assertion by opponents that the Welsh people, speaking through their parliamentary representatives, manifestly did not want disestablishment. To Carvell Williams, the parliamentary initiative assumed 'a much more advanced state of preparedness than at present exists'. Essentially the Society counselled patience; haste would drive Gladstone into an intransigent position. Williams's Welsh disestablishment motion was inopportune and, in any case, should constitute part of an assault on the establishment as a whole; settlement independently of England was unrealistic.[44]

Vocal in Williams's camp was the north Wales Liberationist Thomas Gee, and the Society sought to enlist his influence in inducing a withdrawal of the motion. This was difficult, not least because he and his compatriots were, in part, asserting nationalist sentiments and aspirations, thus giving the dispute a more complex character. Antagonists denied the claim of separate legislation for Wales, since it had no greater prerogative than any other region of the country. Nevertheless, an interview between Carvell Williams and Gee seems to have had some effect and, apparently, Watkin Williams intended to withdraw the motion.[45] But in the event, the opposition forced a division, in which the resolution was rejected by 209 votes to 45. The debate lasted a mere two hours and was restricted to four speakers (Watkin Williams, Gladstone, Osborne Morgan and J. H. Scourfield). Reflecting on 'the late Parliamentary fiasco', the *Nonconformist* was severely critical of Williams's initiative: 'A whole army may be dragged into action by the premature foolhardiness of a corporal's conduct.'[46]

In the mean time, in Wales itself, the Liberation Society was seeking to extend and develop its provincial organization. District agents were the hub of the machinery. In 1868 two of the eight

[43] NLW, MS 8311D, J. Carvell Williams to Gee, 30 Sept. 1869.

[44] NLW, MS 8310E, 'Gohebydd' (John Griffiths) to Gee, 11 Aug. 1869; NLW, MS 8311D, J. C. Williams to Gee, 25, 30 Sept. 1869; NLW, MS 8308D, Henry Richard to Gee, 17 Aug. 1869; Lib. Soc. Mins., Vol. V, A/LIB/4, Min. 360 (1 Oct. 1869); *Liberator*, June 1870.

[45] Lib. Soc. Mins., Vol. V A/LIB/4, Mins. 361, 362 (1 Oct. 1869), 372 (22 Oct. 1869), 850 (27 May 1870).

[46] *Nonconformist*, 1 June 1870.

were in Wales, Revd Watkin Williams in the south and Revd D. Milton Davies in the north. Appointments were made by the Society's Finance Subcommittee in consultation with local supporters. Changes of personnel inevitably occurred over the years; the number of agents also increased though difficulties sometimes arose in finding a qualified person to take on the demanding position and agencies could be vacant for many months. Agents were salaried according to qualifications and the work required in each district. All were part-time. In 1868 Milton Davies was paid £50 for a minimum of three months' work while Watkin Williams received £80 plus ten per cent commission on subscriptions. Travelling expenses were also allowed. Terms of contract were negotiated individually between agent and the Finance Subcommittee—Milton Davies refused employment on the original £30 salary. Appointments were initially for a probationary year, whereupon the position was reviewed. In Wales the Society sought bilingual men with strong local connections.[47] Agents were required to keep expense accounts and submit regular reports of activities. These entailed much public speaking throughout the district, although they could use deputies, hire and payment of whom rested in their own hands; at the same time, Society lecturers from England made periodic tours. The agents' primary function remained the levying of subscriptions. During the seventies and eighties Welsh agents were industrious, penetrating even the remotest villages. Subscription lists reveal enclaves of support in every corner of the Principality. The agents seem to have been far less successful in vitalizing sustained local action through the operation of committees. Indeed, this lack of organization may have contributed to some of the disappointments of the 1874 election; certainly the discontinuation of the South Wales Committee meetings in the late 1860s appears damaging.

Although three more Nonconformists were returned in the 1874 general election, including a Liberationist, Peter Eyton, in Flint District, the Liberal Party suffered a net loss of four seats in Wales.[48] For the Liberation Society, the defeat of E. M. Richards in Cardiganshire, 'the second best Nonconformist representative

[47] Lib. Soc. Mins., Vol. IV, A/LIB/3, Min. 535a (30 Aug. 1867); Vol. V, A/LIB/4, Mins. 145 (24 July 1868), 386 (19 Nov. 1869), 1024 (22 May 1870); Vol. VI, A/LIB/5, Min. 527 (13 Aug. 1874).
[48] K. O. Morgan, *Wales in British Politics*, pp. 37–9.

to Henry Richard', was the most severe blow. Liberal unpopularity over issues such as education played a part in the Welsh contests while in some county constituencies landlord power was influential. A Cardiganshire man claimed that 'the Tivyside squirearchy were allowed to mislead and terrify illiterate voters' and called for an amended Ballot Act.[49] Certainly, the secret ballot was not yet sufficiently understood and effective. Some of the blame for the setbacks can also be attributed to the negligence of local Liberals and Liberationists. In the wake of the Caernarfonshire defeat, W. J. Parry, head of Thomas Love Jones-Parry's campaign, spoke of complacency, non-attendance to the register, and over-optimism concerning the ballot at a time when local Tories had been overhauling their organization.[50] Thorough canvassing was vital, especially in deep rural areas where ignorance of political issues was most prevalent. Indeed, local activists in many parts of Wales may well have been caught unprepared by the snap election, while the two Liberationist bodies, the Welsh Reform Association and the South Wales Liberal Registration Society, suffering financial problems, were apparently ineffectual.[51]

In response to the election results, the Liberation Society intensified its propaganda campaign throughout the United Kingdom. A series of county conferences and public meetings during 1875 represented one aspect of its invigorated operations in Wales. At the same time, an increase in the number of Welsh agencies, from 4 to 7, afforded a more systematic coverage of the 13 counties. By assigning eastern Monmouthshire to the Bristol agency in October 1876, this was further extended.[52] Only briefly in late 1877 was the full complement in operation because of problems in filling posts. Thus, vacant districts were temporarily added to neighbouring ones. Nevertheless, in the decade or so before 1886, the number of agents at work in Wales rarely fell below 5 or 6, certainly sufficient to allow the system to work effectively. Denbighshire and Flintshire proved particularly troublesome, being

---

[49] *Nonconformist*, 18, 25 Feb. 1874.
[50] J. R. Williams, *Quarryman's Champion: The Life and Activities of William John Parry of Coetmor* (Denbigh, 1978), pp. 100–4; see also R. Merfyn Jones, *The North Wales Quarrymen* (Cardiff, 1981), p. 52.
[51] Lib. Soc. Mins., Vol. V, A/LIB/4, Min. 106 (15 July 1870).
[52] Ibid., Vol. VI, A/LIB/5, Min. 808 (5 Oct. 1876). An agent was also appointed for the Welsh populations of Liverpool, Manchester, Chester and Shrewsbury. Ibid., Min. 327 (13 Aug. 1874).

unoccupied from 1869 to 1875 and again from 1879 to 1883, and changing hands three times in as many years in the interim. Other agencies were very stable. Men like C. R. Jones of Llanfyllin (agent in Montgomeryshire and Merioneth, 1875–86), Revd J. Eiddon Jones of Llanrug (Caernarfonshire and Anglesey, 1875–86), Thomas Davies of Cardiff and Revd John Matthews of Swansea (east Glamorgan, 1875–81 and 1881–6, respectively), were stalwart servants. Outstanding in this respect was Revd J. E. Jones of Llanelli, who served south-west Wales for over fifteen years from 1871, having previously acted as agent in Denbighshire and Flintshire for the previous two years. Throughout, a high proportion of Welsh agents were Nonconformist ministers: 13 out of 17 in the period 1868–86.

Wales also benefited from reform of the whole agency system in the mid seventies. At the Society's first Agency Conference in June 1875, by which time there were 30 agents (and 38 by the end of the year, compared with 8 in 1868), the whole span of duties was detailed—the arrangement of meetings, the circulation of the *Liberator* and other literature, use of the local press, the formation of local committees, the collection of monies (a special £100,000 fund had recently been launched), electoral work, the organization of district delegates for triennial conferences—and subsequently a book of instructions was issued.[53] The Executive also set up a permanent Agency Subcommittee to nominate and correspond with local officials and appointed a full-time 'Travelling and Organising Secretary', Revd John Fisher of Sheffield, who was to assist, supervise and co-ordinate agents' work. In the late seventies and early eighties Fisher made a number of visits to the Principality, examining the state of the agencies, organizing and attending conferences, and addressing public meetings. In addition, Welsh agents were aided by regular communications on current policy from the Subcommittee, to whom they had to forward monthly accounts and reports.

As a supplement to the agents' work, increasing efforts were made during the 1870s to provide propaganda in the Welsh language, a requirement to which the Society had long paid lip-service but had turned to little practical effect. Liberationist literature

---

[53] Ibid., Min. 546 (8 July 1875).

was translated, while more and more treatises and articles by prominent Welsh supporters were printed—10,000 copies of eight Welsh tracts in 1877, for example.[54] For distribution, the Society sometimes paid men on a casual basis, as the A.C.L.L. had done years before. In most cases, however, reliance was placed upon the district agents and the voluntary efforts of local friends who delivered the publications from house to house. Others were sent directly to influential members of the community who were not yet committed to the movement, to 'Methodist ministers, local preachers, leaders of working men and intelligent persons'; selections were carefully adapted to each class.[55] Tracts were also advertised by provincial newspapers and, in the summer months, by posting placards at holiday resorts.

The Agency Subcommittee's annual reports, listing the number of meetings and lectures arranged by the Society, testified to the increased activity in the late seventies. In the five years between 1875 and 1880, Wales's total was 139, comparing very favourably with Scotland (81) and some of the regions of England.[56] Liberationists now looked to the next general election for a return on these efforts. And indeed, following the 1880 results, the executive claimed that 47 MPs, including 8 from Wales, had either supported the Society as subscribers or speakers, while a further 139 members, including 10 from Wales, were believed to be in sympathy with disestablishment.[57] In all, Wales returned 29 Liberals, including 8 Nonconformists, and only 4 Conservatives, a net Liberal gain of 9 seats.[58] To the Society's Parliamentary Subcommittee the electoral changes demonstrated not only the great advance made in the 'spirit and organisation' of Welsh Liberalism but also a more profound phenomenon, 'the manifestation of a spirit of self-assertion in regard to the wants of the Principality as distinguished from the rest of the Kingdom'. The passage of the Welsh Sunday Closing Act in 1881 was a major landmark

[54] Ibid., Vol. V, A/LIB/4, Mins. 326 (9 July 1869), 398 (3 Dec. 1869), 436 (25 Feb. 1870), 536 (18 Mar. 1870), 957 (17 Feb. 1871), 969 (17 Mar. 1871); Vol. VI, A/LIB/5, Min. 18 (12 Oct. 1877); Vol. VII, A/LIB/6, Min. 1050 (19 Jan. 1880).

[55] Ibid., Vol. VI, A/LIB/5, Min. 306 (9 July 1874).

[56] Lib. Soc. Mins., Vol. VI, A/LIB//5, Mins. 510 (4 May 1875), 730 (18 May 1875); Vol. VII, A/LIB/6, Mins. 775 (20 May 1878), 1416 (30 May 1881).

[57] Ibid., Vol. VII, A/LIB/6, Min. 1102 (12 Apr. 1880).

[58] For more detail on the election in Wales, see K. O. Morgan, *Wales in British Politics*, pp. 39–40.

in this development, creating, as the Subcommittee's report recognized, 'a precedent for legislation especially affecting Wales, and will stimulate the Welsh to make further demands on the same principle'. Thus it was maintained that 'an agitation for the *Disest. of the Church of England in Wales* would be entered upon with enthusiasm by Welsh Nonconformists and the Society would thereby be furnished with a leverage in Wales such as it had not hitherto possessed'. The report did not believe that the enactment of a Welsh Disestablishment Bill would result 'but it would be a new and forceful demonstration against the English Establishment as a whole, and the events in the Church of England would deepen the impression that the adoption of a Disestablishment policy was inevitable'.[59] This was not recognition of the separate status of Wales but from now on, under pressure from supporters inside and outside Parliament, the Liberation Society was to be carried along by the Welsh disestablishment campaign rather than being in control of it.

The launch of such an agitation in the early 1880s was apparently delayed by the issue of higher education which was consuming attention in Wales, but following the Triennial Conference of 1883, which allotted time for debate on Welsh disestablishment in its own right, a new Liberationist campaign got under way.[60] The most significant innovation was the formation of regional councils in north and south Wales, made up of local delegates. The councils had their own elected officials, met annually or more often and were to direct the agitation for disestablishment. Nevertheless, the London executive sought to exercise a controlling influence, claiming a nominee at meetings and authorization of plans and expenditure. There were other aspects to the new Welsh enterprise. Delegate conferences and public meetings were held in many of the larger towns.[61] Again, emphasis was placed on publishing material relating specifically to the Principality.[62] At the same time, arrangements were made for frequent visits by deputations from England, while agency work was also stepped

[59] Ibid., Min. 1466 (12 Sept. 1881).
[60] Ibid., Mins. 1473 (26 Sept. 1881), 1486 (10 Oct. 1881), 1878 (19 Mar. 1883), 1892 (16 Apr. 1883); Vol. VIII, A/LIB/7, Min. 34 (7 May 1883).
[61] Ibid., Mins. 168 (19 Nov. 1883), 178 (3 Dec. 1883); *Liberator*, Dec. 1883; NLW, MS 8319E, circular on the Caernarfon conference, dated 30 Oct. 1883.
[62] Lib. Soc. Mins., Vol. VIII, A/LIB/7, Mins. 179, 180 (3 Dec. 1883), 184, 186, 187 (17 Dec. 1883).

up. Accordingly, the number of meetings and lectures arranged by the Society in Wales strikingly increased and in 1883–5 comprised as much as one-third of the total for the whole country.[63]

To finance these operations the Society launched a special fund in Wales, aimed at collecting £3,000 during the three years 1884–6. The appeal was extended to Welsh people residing in English towns. For this purpose C. R. Jones of Llanfyllin, a district agent and recently appointed secretary of the North Wales Council, was employed in canvassing and speaking in England. During 1884, meetings of Welsh exiles were held in London, Manchester and Liverpool and, indeed, in that year more *émigré* than native Welsh people, particularly from Liverpool, donated to the fund.[64] The new agitation resulted in a dramatic increase in Welsh contributions to the central authority. In the years 1871–82 subscriptions from Wales fluctuated between £150 and £300 per annum, climbing steeply prior to the 1874 general election and with the Society's renewed vigour in the Principality in 1876 and 1877. During this period Wales broadly corresponded to the British trend. After 1882, however, major discrepancies appeared. Over the next two years Welsh donations almost trebled and reached an all-time high of £624 in 1886, after a slight fall in 1885. In Britain, meanwhile, between 1882 and 1886 the Society's income wavered between £9,000 and £10,000, but the general motion was a downward one and in 1886 it reached its lowest ebb for twelve years. In the year 1883–4 Wales achieved its highest ever annual increase of £273, while the Society's total income fell by £1,642. Some towns like Aberdare and Cardiff showed substantial increases in the size of donations but generally the growth in Welsh subscriptions after 1882 was due to the greater number of people contributing. In communities throughout the Principality more people gave their shillings and pence. While the Principality's largest towns

---

[63] In 1883–4 89 out of 284 and 94 out of 327 in 1884–5. Ibid., Mins. 28 (7 May 1883), 584 (1 June 1885).

[64] Ibid., Mins. 134, 135 (17 Dec. 1883), 224 (10 Mar. 1884), 257 (24 Mar. 1884), 265 (7 Apr. 1884), 307 (9 June 1884); Lib. Soc., *Annual Report*, 1884, pp. 22–3. One organized society was the Manchester, Salford and District Welsh Liberal Association (which had evolved from the Welsh branch of the Manchester and Salford Auxiliary of the Liberation Society of the 1870s). It aimed to 'further Welsh political movements (especially disestablishment and disendowment, educational reform and Nonconformist parliamentary representation) and assist in a more complete organisation of Welsh voters in the district'. *Nonconformist*, 4 Apr. 1877; *Cambrian News*, 15 Aug. 1884.

provided the bulwarks of Liberationism in the seventies and eighties, the rural towns also furnished solid bedrock.[65]

Though there were some very substantial contributions, the size of subscriptions confirms the essentially middle-class support which had long spearheaded the cause. In Wales more than elsewhere the movement relied heavily on the vigour of the Dissenting clergy. Appreciating this, the Society was always anxious to court the Nonconformist colleges, thereby enlisting the allegiance of prospective ministers. Copies of the principal Liberationist publications were deposited in college libraries, while official representatives were frequent visitors to these institutions.[66] Students and tutors at Bala, Pontypool, Haverfordwest and Carmarthen were particularly staunch supporters. Liberationism never became a working-class movement, though the leadership did make efforts to generate such support, especially in the seventies and eighties. The Working Men's Committee for Promoting the Separation of Church and State, comprising London labour leaders, functioned between 1871 and 1873, and over the following years men like George Howell and Joseph Arch were occasionally engaged as lecturers of the Liberation Society. In Wales, too, prominent trade unionists like Robert Parry and W. J. Parry of the North Wales Quarrymen's Union, and William Abraham ('Mabon') of the south Wales miners were active Liberationists.

As ever, the Liberation Society called for 'organised and sustained action' on the part of supporters. Local committees are not easily detectable; certainly, those which existed made little attempt to develop their organizations on a popular level. It was precisely for this purpose that the executive sought to stimulate the formation of branch associations in 1886—bodies of a broader nature, embracing not only subscribers but sympathizers too. Their role was generally to further the disestablishment campaign and also to attend to local matters of religious inequality like burial disputes. Such a branch was established in Cardiff in February

---

[65] The largest membership increases were at Dowlais, Neath, Swansea, Bridgend, Brynmawr, Merthyr, Rhyl and Pontypridd. Elsewhere, money came from localities, like Mountain Ash, which had not previously contributed or, like Abergele, which had not done so for some time. Subscriptions lists still showed irregular centres of support and sometimes glaring fluctuations, as at Tanygrisiau, near Blaenau Ffestiniog: no subscribers 1871–5, 1878, 1880–2 and 1894–6; 21 subscribers in 1876, 103 in 1877, 66 in 1879 and 5 in 1883.

[66] Lib. Soc. Mins., Vol. VI, A/LIB/5, Min. 806 (5 Oct. 1876).

1886.[67] The Society also continued to operate through the various denominations, regularly circulating associations on policy and using them as focuses for agitation. Local committees and religious bodies were long-established organs of Liberationist pressure. In the seventies and eighties Liberal associations, which had mushroomed in Wales, began to fulfil a similar role. The Llanelli Liberal Registration Association had functioned as such since 1876, while in June 1878 a Liberationist lecture at Bethesda 'led to the formation of a Liberal Society amongst the quarrymen of Lord Penrhyn'.[68] Nationally, the Liberation Society worked to get disestablishment and disendowment on the official programme of the N.L.F. and at a local level to get political bodies to take up the cause.[69] Agents and lecturers took every opportunity to address Liberal committees and clubs, while the local activists worked for the fusion of Liberationism with Liberalism.[70] Increasingly, too, the emphasis was on the specific claims of Wales and, here, Joseph Chamberlain's declarations for Welsh disestablishment at Newtown and Denbigh in 1884 marked an important advance, the first commitment of a cabinet minister to the cause. On the inception of the North Wales Liberal Federation in December 1886, pride of place in its platform was given to disestablishment and disendowment in Wales.[71] Thus, the fulcrum of pressure was shifting to 'new and important circles', to Liberal Party organizations and within the walls of Parliament.

This development was so because of the changed nature of Welsh parliamentary representation, itself much facilitated by the further advance of democracy in 1884-5. As in earlier decades, Liberationists around Wales took part in the parliamentary reform agitation and welcomed the newly enfranchised as 'a powerful contingent in the attack on the ancient strongholds of ecclesiastical injustice'.[72] At the Welsh polls in November 1885 the Liberals were triumphant, the Conservatives again winning only 4 of the

---

[67] *Liberator*, Feb., Dec. 1886.
[68] Ibid., Oct. 1876, June 1878; *Nonconformist*, 27 Sept. 1876.
[69] Five Welsh Liberal associations—those of Brymbo, Cardiganshire, Llechryd, St Dogmaels and Swansea—were represented at the 1883 Triennial Conference. *Liberator*, June 1883.
[70] See, for example, the address of W. J. Parry to the North Wales Council of the Liberation Society at Blaenau Ffestiniog in December 1884. W.J. Parry, *Cymru a Datgysylltiad: Cymdeithas Rhyddhad Crefydd* (Caernarfon, 1885). See also, J. R. Williams, op. cit., pp. 132–4.
[71] Lib. Soc. Mins., Vol. VIII, A/LIB/7, Min. 926 (20 Dec. 1886).
[72] *Nonconformist*, 11 Oct. 1886.

now 34 seats. Equally striking was the continued increase in Non-conformist representation, from 8 in 1880 to 14, among whom were several important figures in Welsh Dissent.[73] The Liberation Society now claimed that 29 of the 30 Welsh Liberal members were in favour of disestablishment.[74] Welsh questions, especially disestablishment, were also prominent in the 'Irish home rule' election of the following year, when Liberal ascendancy in the Principality was re-affirmed.

Though its agents and supporters involved themselves in electoral activity in parts of Wales in 1885–6, the Liberation Society's influence was evidently diminishing. Organizationally, severe financial problems necessitated economies while home rule for Ireland generated internal dissension.[75] At the same time, the Society's role in providing a structural framework for Welsh Liberalism was now being very much appropriated by local Liberal associations. Indeed, the Society's policy of penetrating such bodies naturally contributed to this transition. The formation of Liberal Federations in north and south Wales, in 1886 and 1887 respectively, co-ordinating most local associations and pledged to disestablishment, both endorsed and speeded up the supersession of the Liberation Society.

The initiative shifted to Westminster, too. In March 1886 L.Ll. Dillwyn presented his long-promised resolution for Welsh disestablishment. It failed by just twelve votes (229 to 241), a great advance on Watkin Williams's motion of sixteen years earlier. Welsh Liberals voted by 27 votes to 3 in favour as compared with 7 to 16 against in 1870. The progress made by the disestablishment movement in the Principality was now reflected in its parliamentary representation. And certainly, the emphasis was now increasingly on the separate claims of Wales: disestablishment on the grounds of nationality. The transformation owed much to the vigorous efforts of the dynamic Montgomeryshire MP Stuart Rendel to focus the campaign on a Welsh national party within the Liberal Party in the House of Commons. This design involved the severance of the inveterate bond between the disestablishment agitation in Wales and the Liberation Society, whose policy of attacking

[73] See K. O. Morgan, *Wales in British Politics*, pp. 65–6.
[74] Lib. Soc. Mins., Vol. VIII, A/LIB/7, Min. 666 (14 Dec. 1885).
[75] Ibid., Min. 823 (16 June 1886); see also, D. A. Hamer, op. cit., p. 141; W. H. Mackintosh, *Disestablishment and Liberation. The Movement for the Separation of the Anglican Church from State Control* (1972), pp. 295–6.

the Church establishment as a whole was now seen as detrimental to the Welsh cause. After 1886 disestablishment of the Welsh Church was essentially in the realm of party politics, winning the support of the National Liberal Federation in 1887 and appearing high on the Liberals' Newcastle Programme in 1891.[76]

In the 1880s disestablishment thus emerged as the principal question in Welsh politics. This was ensured not only by the stepping up of Liberationist efforts and developments within the Welsh disestablishment movement but also by a parallel reaction from the Church. In the middle decades of the century such counter-action by Churchmen in Wales had been confined to isolated and largely insignificant opposition at public meetings. Nevertheless, though as yet disorganized, anti-Liberationists, enjoying the bulk of landlord influence and having powerful press support, clearly constituted a potentially vehement force. In Wales they began to emerge as such in the seventies; the reality of disestablishment motions in Parliament, both Welsh and general, with the attendant demonstrations of support in the country, seems to have brought home the seriousness of the position to Churchmen. But it was not until the eighties that the national pressure group, the Church Defence Institution (C.D.I.), made any attempt to organize itself on a large scale in the Principality.[77]

This society had been founded as the Church Institution in London in 1859 'to oppose and imitate the Liberation Society'. Beset with organizational and financial weaknesses, its efforts met with little success during its first decade; accordingly, in 1871 it was completely restructured with a new constitution, executive committee and name—the C.D.I. The aim was to incorporate clergy and laity into an efficient national organization, capable of influencing and mobilizing public opinion and exerting various modes of pressure in defence of the political status of the Church. For various reasons—most significantly, continuing financial problems and structural deficiencies and also the reluctance of the bishops and other Churchmen to support political action—an elaborate system comprising a network of local associations looking

[76] See K. O. Morgan, *Wales in British Politics*, pp. 66–8, 77–8; idem, *Freedom or Sacrilege: A History of the Campaign for Welsh Disestablishment*, pp. 12–13; D. A. Hamer, *Liberal Politics in the Age of Gladstone and Rosebery* (Oxford, 1972), pp. 32–3.

[77] For the C.D.I., see Adrian Parry, 'The Church Defence Institution 1859–96, with special reference to Wales' (University of Wales MA thesis, 1982).

to the London parent body for lecturers, literature, information and direction was never successfully achieved. Nevertheless, the revitalized C.D.I. was an important influence in the manifestation of more consistent and coherent anti-Liberationist activity in the country.

At the same time, counter-activities by Churchmen were not necessarily disadvantageous to the Liberationist cause; on the contrary, they could be useful 'both in stimulating its friends and in rousing the attention of the public'.[78] Revd D. Milton Davies reported thus from Caernarfonshire in 1868:

> Our meetings, especially the one at Bethesda, have produced good effects. The clergy are alarmed, and are having lectures and meetings in defence of the Church, and lectures by way of rejoinder are being delivered by the Rev Mr Jones of Bethesda. At a clerical meeting held at Bangor last week, under the presidency of the Bishop, the clergy urged one another to come forward as a man, to counteract the influence of the Liberation Society.[79]

Such rivalry received extensive coverage in the local newspapers and invariably gave rise to a lively correspondence. In this way the Society gained invaluable publicity from a provincial press whose readership was always more interested in local controversies than in perennial national questions.

During the general election of 1874, lecturers of the Liberation Society and the C.D.I., J. H. Gordon and J. E. Lyon respectively, did battle in the Rhyl area: 'Lectures, and reply lectures, were thick in the neighbourhood all the week.' A formal debate between the two officials, supported by Welsh-language speakers, John Evans, Society agent, and Revd M. Edwards, vicar of Caernarfon, was subsequently held in May, attended by 1,200 people. The Liberation Society later subsidized the publication and circulation of a pamphlet on the discussion. In this manner, tremendous interest extending over several months was evoked. The local clergy

---

[78] *Nonconformist*, 8 May 1862; cf. the observation of the Chartist leader, Ernest Jones: 'In political agitations, and indeed, in the contest of all questions, open enmity is preferable to sluggish and apathetic neutrality. The one is vague, insidious, and apt to engender a corresponding dullness of advocacy. The other is fair and open, and eminently stimulative of eager exertion.' *London News*, 28 Aug. 1858.

[79] *Liberator*, Sept. 1868.

proved uncommonly active and several Church Defence associations were formed.[80] Other towns, too, like Newtown and Llandudno, held public debates of a similar character.[81] Elsewhere,
as at Machynlleth and Bethesda, oppositionists were allowed to
voice their opinions at Liberationist meetings.[82] More commonly,
Churchmen convened separate meetings, where speakers could
address sympathetic audiences. Dean H. T. Edwards of Bangor
was a zealous campaigner against disestablishment and sufficiently
effective to cause the Society executive itself, in 1884, to arrange
special replies to his speeches.[83]

Clashes became more belligerent with the generation of a fervour and the adoption of tactics which echoed the most intense
days of A.C.L.L.–Chartist confrontation. Rival factions attended
the others' gatherings, either to pass their own resolutions or simply
to heckle; W. E. Helm, the C.D.I. lecturer, completely failed to
gain a hearing at Newtown in April 1884.[84] Increasingly, revenge
became a motive for disrupting opponents' functions.[85] Physical
encounters sometimes developed; Liberationists scuffled with their
antagonists at Newtown in April 1884 and at Bethesda early the
following year before taking over the meetings.[86] Local elections
were more temperate trials of strength between the two parties,
though some became extremely hard-fought contests.

Having for many years paid little attention to the Principality,
the Institution's efforts eventually became focused there, in
response to the shift in the disestablishment agitation. In May
1883 the executive set up a Welsh subcommittee to direct a Church
Defence campaign. With the Liberationist movement reaching
its peak and the threat of disestablishment very real, the four
Welsh bishops, all members of the committee, now exerted their
influence in creating the C.D.I. branches in the rural deaneries.
The number of English- and Welsh-language publications disseminated also greatly increased, while in 1886 W. E. Helm was

---

[80] Ibid., Apr., Aug., Sept. 1874; *Nonconformist*, 25 Mar. 1874; Lib. Soc. Mins., Vol. VI, A/LIB/5, Min. 329 (13 Aug. 1874).

[81] *Nonconformist*, 21 Mar. 1877; Lib. Soc. Mins., Vol. VIII, A/LIB/7, Min. 432 (15 Dec. 1884).

[82] *Liberator*, May 1875, Mar. 1885.

[83] Lib. Soc. Mins., Vol. VIII, A/LIB/7, Min. 201 (7 Jan. 1884).

[84] NLW, MS 19460C (Rendel Papers), 14, no. 221, A. C. Humphreys Owen to Rendel, 6 Apr. 1884.

[85] See for example, *Montgomeryshire Express*, 25 Mar., 1, 8 Apr. 1884 for events in Llanidloes.

[86] *Liberator*, Mar. 1885; J. R. Williams, op. cit., p. 121.

appointed Organizing Secretary for Wales and a Welsh-speaking lecturer, W. Richards of Port Talbot, was engaged.[87] These initiatives were reflected in Welsh financial contributions to the Institution, which before the 1880s had been insignificant—five per cent or less of the total income. During the decade, receipts from Wales rose substantially (essentially through an increase in the number of small subscriptions rather than large donations) and, following two special appeals for Welsh Church Defence, reached a peak of £1,618 in 1893, one-sixth of the total income for the year.[88] By this time, Welsh Churchmen were influential on the executive committee and a large number of its 600 branches were located in the Principality. Over the years the C.D.I. had not achieved the financial resources, organizational sophistication or political effectiveness of its arch-rival, the Liberation Society; by the 1890s, with the latter in decline and Churchmen actively involved, the Institution was as powerful a pressure group. In many communities the relationship between Church assailants and defenders was frequently the most crucial, certainly the most enduring, aspect of political life in late nineteenth-century Wales.

[87] A. Parry, op. cit., pp. 34–5.
[88] Ibid., pp. 39–46.

XIII
LABOUR POLITICS

While Churchmen and Nonconformists were locked in battle, a new industrial and political force, the labour movement, was emerging in Welsh society. Trade unionism, albeit in a slow and fragmentary manner, gathered strength and ventured uncertainly into the political arena, while the idea of independent working-class representation in Parliament and on local bodies took root.

I TRADE UNIONS AND POLITICS

Trade unions in Wales were rooted in working-class friendly or benefit societies, which provided relief through savings at times of death, old age and sickness but became inevitably drawn into a response to such conditions of employment as wage levels and hours of work.[1] Following repeal of the Combination Acts in 1824, trade unions were able to exist overtly and amid the depression and unrest of the early 1830s the industrial regions of the Principality were significantly affected for the first time. Lodges of John Doherty's National Association for the Protection of Labour were formed, initially among the textile workers of Newtown and then in the coalfields of north-east and south Wales. By 1832 the movement had virtually disappeared, but its attempt at a general union of workers was soon taken up by Robert Owen's Grand National Consolidated Trades Union.[2] Owenite unions sprang into existence in industrial south Wales in 1833–4. Again, the initiative quickly collapsed in the face of endemic difficulties. Such factors as irregular employment and the subsequent debt run up at the company shop, by denying workers their independence, reinforced the overwhelming power of the employers and

[1] For friendly societies, see Gwyn A. Williams, 'Friendly Societies in Glamorgan, 1793–1832', *Bulletin of the Board of Celtic Studies*, XVIII (1959), pp. 275–83; Dot Jones, 'Self-help in nineteenth-century Wales: the rise and fall of the female friendly society', *Llafur*, 4, No. 1 (1984), pp. 14–26; idem, 'Did friendly societies matter? A study of friendly societies in Glamorgan, 1794–1910', *Welsh History Review*, 12, No. 3 (June 1985), pp. 324–49; P. H. J. H. Gosden, *The Friendly Societies in England, 1815–75* (Manchester, 1961).
[2] See G. A. Williams, 'Lord Melbourne and the trade unions', *Llafur*, 1, No. 1 (1972), pp. 3–15; D. J. V. Jones, *Before Rebecca*, pp. 118–20; idem, *The Last Rising*, pp. 41–2.

precluded the establishment of strong and permanent trade unions for several decades. Until the 1870s, unionism in the south Wales coalfield was essentially short-lived, local and tenuous, usually confined to times of crisis and often enforced by violence and intimidation.[3]

In the mean time, craft societies were successfully spreading among the skilled artisans of the towns of Wales. *The United Kingdom First Annual Trades Union Directory* of 1861 listed fifty-one in Wales. Most were small, exclusive, 'aristocratic' unions. A variety of trades were included—shoemakers, boiler-makers, carpenters, skinners, shipwrights—but stonemasons (21 societies) were preponderant. There were also 9 branches of the first of the new national unions, the Amalgamated Society of Engineers (founded in 1851), which represented a move away from the old type of local independence in the trade union movement.[4]

Trade union aims in mid century related strictly to labour questions, to improving conditions of work, and, in particular, to the protection and increase of wages. Politics was eschewed as a divisive force; indeed, the rules of many unions forbade political discussions at meetings. Nevertheless, workers' industrial and political interests were often interrelated and in time the unions' concern to advance the well-being of their members led to their assuming the role of political pressure groups. In Wales, as elsewhere, individual unionists and, to some degree, trade societies actively supported the reform demonstrations of 1831-2 and the Chartist agitation, though there was always the apprehension that participation in radical politics would damage the trade union movement. The 1860s saw a marked increase in political involvement, union leaders in the capital, members of the newly formed London Trades Council, providing the major impulse by launching a series of reform organizations early in the decade and taking a stance on Italian unity, Polish nationalism and the American Civil War. They also participated fully in the campaign for extension of the franchise, especially through the activities of the R.L. In the provinces, too, trade union bodies and individual members were often prominent in the agitation. R.L. branches at Merthyr and Cardiff

[3] J. H. Morris and L. J. Williams, *The South Wales Coal Industry, 1841-75*, pp. 269-72.
[4] D. Lleufer Thomas, *Labour Unions in Wales* (Swansea, 1901), p. 20; *United Kingdom First Annual Trades Union Directory* (1861).

were initiated by trades organizations. Merthyr shoemakers formed a reform society in January 1867 while, in Cardiff, the Trades Council, comprising one member from more than a dozen trades and the first such body in Wales, provided the organizational framework for activity and in 1868, in a campaign notable for the degree of working-class participation, exerted its influence behind the successful local Liberal candidate, Colonel J. F. D. Crichton Stuart.[5]

In the late sixties and early seventies trade unionists were to be found in a variety of radical causes and organizations. On their own front, they established in 1868 a permanent focus for debate, the Trades Union Congress (T.U.C.), which from 1871 had a Parliament Committee to promote labour legislation. These years also saw significant trade union developments in the provinces. In south Wales, unionization affected the iron and tinplate industries, while the most rapid and widespread growth occurred in coal-mining, with the Lancashire-controlled Amalgamated Association of Miners (A.A.M.), founded in 1869, attracting strong support.[6] At its peak in March 1874 the A.A.M. had branches in seven Welsh counties and a membership of over 48,000 in south Wales alone. Thereafter, its membership plummeted dramatically and the union collapsed in 1875. An effort to organize the Miners' National Union in the Principality in its stead failed, and the south Wales miners now reverted to district unions, linked only by a sliding scale which for twenty years after 1875 regulated wages according to the selling price of coal. All the district unions were numerically weak and were often not even constituted on orthodox trade union lines. The Cambrian Miners' Association, for example, had 'no lodges, branches or local organisations of any kind' in the seventies and eighties.[7]

Meanwhile, other workers, often on the impulse of English unionists, were also capturing the organizing spirit. Branches of the large amalgamated English unions—carpenters, iron moulders, tailors, stonemasons, plasterers, engineers, blacksmiths, railwaymen, shipwrights—existed in a large number of Welsh

---

[5] HC, L.B. 2, p. 449; *Cardiff Chronicle*, 20 Nov. 1866; *Cardiff Times*, 16, 23 Nov. 1866, 31 Oct., 7, 14 Nov. 1868; *Cardiff and Merthyr Guardian*, 28 Oct., 7 Nov. 1868.

[6] See Aled Jones, 'Trade unions and the press: journalism and the Red Dragon Revolt of 1874', *Welsh History Review*, 12, No. 2 (Dec. 1984), pp. 198–201.

[7] Webb Trade Union Collection, Section A, Vol. XXVI, Wales, pp. 3–16.

towns in the 1870s.[8] Moreover, in Caernarfonshire and Merioneth, in the isolated north-west, the quarrymen, after several abortive attempts in earlier decades, succeeded in 1874 in establishing
a lasting combination, the North Wales Quarrymen's Union
(N.W.Q.U.). At the same time, national unions of unskilled workers
were appearing in Britain. In 1872 the builders' labourers were
organized into the General Amalgamated Labourers' Union,
which operated until the early eighties and was represented in
Wales by the West of England and South Wales Amalgamated
Labourers' Union.[9] Joseph Arch's N.A.L.U., however, made little
impression in the Principality at this time.

While trade unionism slowly made its mark in Wales in the
period before 1886, it nevertheless presents a confused picture.
There were some strongholds and certainly an extensive variety
of trades was affected. Yet its influence was limited and, in general,
unionism in Wales was ill-organized, ephemeral and weak. Those
unions in existence were inevitably preoccupied with local labour
problems and wider activity received only intermittent attention.
Labour legislation was obviously one such concern. Thus, for
example, delegates to the annual meeting of the South Wales
Council of the Miners' National Union at Aberdare in April 1876
were urged by their president 'to do their utmost in favour of
McDonald's Bill [for workmen's compensation on industrial
injury]; it was not possible for them to press the Bill without a
deal of pressure'.[10] Miners, in particular, also campaigned for
further parliamentary reform in the 1870s and 1880s. But generally Victorian trade unions did not undertake a wide political
role.

The growth of local Liberal associations afforded one avenue
for unionists to do so as individuals. A few played prominent
parts, notably W. J. Parry, the quarrymen's leader, who was
secretary of the Caernarfonshire Liberal Association. More
usually, unionists joined the rank and file of the caucus, as they
did in large numbers at Bethesda and in the Rhondda in the
early eighties.[11] The presence of Liberal Working Men's

---

[8] Ibid., Vol. XXXII, p. 225, pp. 286–93; *Industrial Review* (formerly *Beehive*), 2 June–18
Aug. 1877; *Workman's Advocate*, 29 Nov., 6 Dec. 1873.
[9] *Workman's Advocate*, 14 Feb. 1874.
[10] *Merthyr Telegraph*, 21 Apr. 1876; *Beehive*, 22 Apr. 1876.
[11] C. Parry, *The Radical Tradition in Welsh Politics: A Study of Gwynedd Politics 1900–1920*
(Hull, 1970), p. 32; *Cardiff Times*, 23 July 1883.

Associations, as at Newport and Caernarfon, made participation more probable. Often, however, working men were suspicious of the Liberal caucus.

A more likely source of political involvement was the appearance of trades councils. Wales's first such organization, in Cardiff in the mid 1860s, seems to have languished by the end of the decade, to be re-formed in 1884. Trades councils were, however, set up at Swansea (1873), Merthyr (1874), and Aberdare (1875). They were local bodies drawing together the different skilled trades in the towns and, as such, represented an important new platform for the organized working class. On formation, the Aberdare Trades Council, for example, comprised representatives of the local unions of tailors, joiners, carpenters and plasterers.[12] The Merthyr and Dowlais Trades Council was similarly constituted.[13] The function of trades councils was to debate and take a common stand on local problems, primarily of an industrial nature. These normally related to conditions of employment, sometimes involving assistance in strike action. Thus, in the coal stoppage of 1875 the Merthyr Trades Council was active in the workers' cause, attempting to whip up moral and pecuniary support and to promote some sort of conciliation.[14]

In south Wales in these years, the formation of trades councils for political purposes was strongly urged by the Merthyr-published trade union organ, the *Workman's Advocate*. One motive behind the foundation of the Merthyr Trades Council was apparently a desire to return a 'labour' parliamentary representative.[15] J. T. Morgan, radical journalist and Trades Council secretary,[16] stood at the Merthyr School Board election in 1876, while at Aberdare, a Trades Council member, Isaac Thomas, had been returned for the Board of Health the previous year. Trades councils also sometimes acted as political pressure groups. Thus, Aberdare Trades Council in April 1876 requested its member societies to petition in favour of McDonald's Compensation Bill and pressurize local MPs to support it.[17] At times, industrial and political

---

[12] *Merthyr Telegraph*, 3 Sept. 1875; *Aberdare Times*, 15 Apr. 1876.
[13] *Workman's Advocate*, 28 Feb., 23 May 1874.
[14] Ibid., 1, 8 Jan., 26 Feb., 12 Mar., 3 Apr. 1875.
[15] Ibid., 28 Feb. 1874.
[16] For J. T. Morgan, see Aled Jones, op. cit., pp. 218–20.
[17] *Aberdare Times*, 15 Apr. 1876.

affairs mingled, as during the 1875 stoppage when, after the colliers had been forced to accept poor relief, the voters amongst them were disfranchised by the Merthyr Board of Guardians. Both the Merthyr and Aberdare Trades Councils were prominent in the public condemnation of this action, convening protest meetings and appointing special subcommittees to lead the agitation.[18] But the political role of trades councils remained limited.

Some members strongly opposed political involvement. Even in the 1890s, Sidney Webb noted that the skilled trades at Swansea 'manifested considerable opposition to the Trades Council's embarkation into politics'.[19] Moreover, the Welsh trades councils of the seventies and eighties rarely flourished for long. Those at Aberdare and Merthyr lapsed in the industrial recession of the late seventies. That at Swansea continued, but between 1878 and 1889 fell into decline: 'it might as well have been dead, for it was reduced to a very small size and did absolutely nothing at all'.[20] In Newport, an unsuccessful attempt was made to form an organization in 1880, while the re-establishment of a Cardiff Trades Council in 1884 aroused only limited initial response.[21]

For the individual trade unions the early 1880s saw increased political activity, most strikingly with the agitation for further parliamentary reform. In Wales, the colliers were most prominent, particularly after the Lords' rejection of the Franchise Bill in July 1884. The disfranchisement of certain miners, simply because they lived outside borough boundaries, was glaringly anomalous. At their annual demonstration in July 1883 Rhondda miners called for franchise extension and a redistribution of seats.[22] A year later they held protest meetings against the recent Lords' action, while one of their delegates at that year's T.U.C. wished 'the congress would convince the House of Lords the voice of the people was the voice of God, and the people were stronger than Lords'.[23] In the Rhondda the franchise agitation came from the Miners' Association, not the local Liberal Association which was inactive. Miners also held demonstrations elsewhere in support of the

[18] Ibid., 6 Nov. 1875; *Workman's Advocate*, 22 Oct. 1875; *Beehive*, 25 Oct., 6 Nov. 1875.
[19] Webb T. U. Collection, Section A, Vol. IV, pp. 476–8.
[20] Ibid., p. 475.
[21] Ibid., pp. 161, 401.
[22] *Cardiff Times*, 21 July, 1883.
[23] *Cambrian*, 5 Sept. 1884; *The Times*, 10 Sept. 1884.

reform agitation, as at Pontypool and Ystalyfera.[24] In west Wales, the South Wales Anthracite Miners' Association spearheaded the campaign, the culmination of the agitation in that part of the country being a massive demonstration of miners, tinplate workers, agricultural labourers, and other groups at Carmarthen in late August 1884.[25]

As ever, obtaining the franchise was the object in itself but it was also the key to something more. At their annual demonstration in July 1884 Rhondda miners were told that the abolition of 'long pays' (the payment of wages normally on a monthly basis) could not be achieved 'without the Franchise Bill which the Lords were denying them'.[26] Colliers in the Aberdare valley emphasized the need for changes in the Mines Regulation Act and the Laws of Conspiracy.[27] To others the franchise was the passport to labour representation in Parliament. Meetings were generally content to support Gladstone's proposals, though more radical demands were voiced. In December 1884, for example, the Aberdare, Merthyr and Dowlais District Miners' Association called for the extension of the franchise to women and instructed its agent 'to do all that he can to get up meetings for Miss Jeanette G. Wilkinson to advocate her claims on behalf of women's suffrage'.[28]

Participation in the parliamentary reform agitation was one aspect of increased political activity by working men in the early 1880s. The revival of Socialism was another. Socialist ideas had been widely diffused in Britain in the 1830s and 1840s. Chartists and Socialists had much in common and some individuals belonged to both camps. More usually, however, differences of emphasis, ideas and methods led to rivalry. Fundamentally, Chartists held that the solution to misery and distress lay in political reform, while Socialists placed the emphasis on such measures as currency and land reforms, and the nationalization of transport and public works. In the 1830s, it was the mid-Walian Robert Owen who attempted to put such ideas into practice and the Owenite attention to propaganda inevitably meant that some parts

[24] Cardiff Times, 9 Aug. 1884; Tarian y Gweithiwr, 23 Oct. 1884.
[25] The Times, 26 Aug. 1884; Tarian y Gweithiwr, 28 Aug. 1884; Baner ac Amserau Cymru, 3 Sept. 1884; D. V. Evans, 'Some aspects of politics in Eastern Carmarthenshire, 1868–85', pp. 89–91.
[26] Cardiff Times, 26 July 1884.
[27] Aberdare Times, 28 Feb. 1885.
[28] Women's Suffrage Journal, 1 Jan. 1885.

of Wales were affected by the movement. During the 1850s Chartism, as we have seen, took on a more Socialist aspect and Wales made some response to this departure. After Owenism, however, Socialism did not exist as a popular movement until the end of the century, although it was represented by a series of organizations. The most enduring of these was the National Reform League, founded in 1849 by Bronterre O'Brien and continuing until the early 1870s. In the mid sixties it also found expression in the International Working Men's Association. Both were predominantly metropolitan bodies, having little contact with the outlying regions.[29]

In 1879 the foundation of the Manhood Suffrage League testified to the increase in Socialism. Distinctly Socialist in character, it was the successor of the National Reform League. Again, it did not generate national appeal although it reached a wider audience after the launch of the *Labour Standard* in May 1881, which by July had agents in Aberdare, Cardiff, Llanelli and Pontypridd.[30] More significant in the revival of Socialism were the Social Democratic Federation (S.D.F.), originating in 1881, the Fabian Society in 1884, and the Socialist League, a secession from the S.D.F. in 1885. In their early years, only the S.D.F., combining radical political principles with the Marxist demand for the nationalization of all the 'means of production, distribution and exchange', made any noticeable impression in Wales. The second issue of *Justice*, the movement's mouthpiece founded in January 1884, reported a lecture on behalf of the Federation at Cardiff delivered by Henry George, long active as an agricultural radical.[31] At the end of the year the first S.D.F. branch was formed in Wales, at Waun Afon, a small industrial community on the mountain-top between Brynmawr and Blaenafon. The inspiration was one John Price of Waun Afon and, indeed, the branch was dissolved on his death in mid 1885. During the branch's short existence, its handful of members, and Price in particular, attempted to carry out an 'active propaganda' in the area, the S.D.F. executive in London supplying large quantities of Socialist literature and

[29] The ubiquitous Alfred A. Walton of Brecon was active in the League from its inception, became its president in 1867 and also served on the General Council of the International (1867–70), being a delegate to the Lausanne Congress in 1867.
[30] *Labour Standard*, 30 July 1881.
[31] *Justice*, 26 Jan. 1884.

old copies of Chartist newspapers. At a time of local distress and unemployment, some impression was evidently made in the Clydach valley below Brynmawr, from which the executive received correspondence during these months.[32]

There were also communications from north Wales in October 1885 and in the following year, H. M. Hyndman, the S.D.F. President, visited the Dinorwic quarries near Llanberis, where the management, seeking more stringent regulations, had imposed a lockout; his subsequent articles induced charges of libel from the employer, George William Duff Assheton-Smith, and his manager. Hyndman enthusiastically reported that north Wales was ripe for the principles of social democracy: 'The people are much quicker to grasp revolutionary ideas than our own rural population, and seem to turn naturally towards Socialism ...' The major obstacle, he asserted, was the 'nationalism of the people' and therefore recommended 'our short literature [be] translated into Welsh and distributed in the Principality'. The 'revival of the old Nationalist and clannish spirit' currently affecting Wales needed to be rechannelled into Socialist zeal: 'in such circumstances [economic depression and injustice] it is natural that working men should mix up the causes of their misery with a want of direct control over their own immediate business ...'[33]

Some further S.D.F. advance was made in Wales in 1887 when its lecturer, John Fielding, addressed meetings at Swansea, Landore and Cardiff. A society was set up at the last-named but again this proved transient.[34] Essentially, the Federation made no effort to campaign systematically in the Principality in these years and indeed its influence remained insignificant throughout the 1890s too.[35]

Besides influences emanating from London-based organizations, there was also some indigenous inspiration for Socialism in rural Wales in the 1880s. The most striking figure in this respect was Revd Evan Pan Jones, Independent minister at Mostyn, Flintshire, from 1870 until his death in 1922. On the public platform and in print—he edited *Y Celt* (1881–4) and *Cwrs y Byd* (1891–

[32] Ibid., 10 Jan., 7 Mar., 16 May, 25 July, 8 Aug. 1885.
[33] Ibid., 24 Oct. 1885, 2, 23 Jan. 1886. For the Dinorwic lock-out of 1885–6, see R. Merfyn Jones, op. cit., pp. 142–162.
[34] *Justice*, 7 Aug. 1886.
[35] See Jon Parry, 'Trade unionists and early Socialism in south Wales, 1890–1908', *Llafur*, 4, No. 3 (1986), pp. 43–54.

1905)—he was the indefatigable champion of land reform, advocating the taxation of unearned income on land values and even nationalization.[36] Dr Jones's views certainly had an influence on Welsh opinion, even on the young David Lloyd George, but more popular was the less radical programme given tangible expression in the Welsh Land League of 1886.[37]

Socialism made only a small impression on Wales until the closing years of the century. By the mid eighties, a minority only of Welsh people had come into contact with Socialist ideas through the propaganda of the S.D.F. or through the early native roots set down by publicists like Pan Jones. In general, geographical remoteness and linguistic and cultural differences as yet kept the Principality almost immune from the doctrines of the Socialist societies of England. The new movement also faced the entrenched Nonconformist Liberalism of late-nineteenth-century Wales and the tenacity of local, community loyalty, which impeded the development of class-conscious political attitudes. As the S.D.F. executive pointed out, trade unions, still essentially moderate in outlook in the eighties, sometimes adversely exercised their influence too, only the more radical among their ranks being attracted to the various Socialist organizations. Certainly in Wales, unions were firmly Lib–Lab in sentiment and it was not until the 1890s that Socialists formed even a small minority therein.

At the close of our period, in 1886, Wales was fundamentally a non-unionized country and remained so until the following decade. The weak Welsh trade union movement also had a limited concept of its function, relating largely to wages and working conditions. Trade unions in Wales did not become genuinely political instruments until the Socialists introduced a militant spirit in the early part of the twentieth century.

II LABOUR REPRESENTATION

'To the miners of Wales, collectively, we say: "Combine! combine! to have your own representatives in Parliament, and then goodbye

---

[36] See Peris Jones-Evans, 'Pan Jones—Land Reformer', *Welsh History Review*, 4, No. 2 (Dec. 1968), pp. 143–60.
[37] See above, p. 184.

to coal-king tyranny for ever".[38] Working-class radicals had long contended that the remedy for their grievances was labour representation, and Chartism in particular had engendered a large number of candidatures, though most, including those of south Wales Chartist leaders Morgan Williams and William Edwards in 1841, were essentially token efforts. The enfranchisement of urban householders in 1867 meant that such aspirations could more realistically be promoted. Nevertheless, the few working men's representatives who stood in the 1868 general election were heavily defeated in the polls; others suffered the same fate as Alfred Walton at Brecon, withdrawing from contests under local Liberal pressure.

Two new organizations entered the field in the following year. The more radical was the short-lived Land and Labour League, which urged the creation of a third political party. Much more significant was the Labour Representation League (L.R.L.), which, with moderate trade union leaders in the ascendancy, embarked on a conciliatory policy of constituency agreements with the Liberal Party (much as the R.L. had sought in 1868[39]), although frustration later induced its executive to declare for independent action.[40] But, while the League operated for some nine years and generated a number of provincial branches, it failed effectively to mobilize working-class opinion in the country and remained substantially a metropolitan organization. Incursions into outlying areas were largely confined to limited assistance to candidacies, the promotion of which lay essentially in the hands of individual trade unions.

At the 1874 general election the League gave support to fourteen candidates, nine opposing official Liberal nominees. Two miners' representatives were successful, Alexander McDonald at Stafford and Thomas Burt at Morpeth. At Stoke-on-Trent, Alfred Walton, still resident at Brecon, was the 'trade union and working-class candidate'. It proved to be an intervention which split the Liberal vote and enabled the Tory to remove one of the two

[38] *People's Paper*, 24 Mar. 1855.
[39] For the R.L. and the 1868 general election, see R. Harrison, *Before the Socialists*, pp. 147–53.
[40] Henry Broadhurst Collection (BC), L.R.L. Minute Book, 15 Feb. 1873, General Council; see also, 'The Labour Representation League: An Association of Working Men and those Friendly to their Political and Social Advancement' (manifesto issued on the formation of the L.R.L., Sept. 1869).

Liberal incumbents.[41] Within Wales, Merthyr Tydfil was the only constituency in which the League was involved during its existence, supporting the candidature of Thomas Halliday, President of the A.A.M.[42] Like working men's representatives elsewhere, Halliday stood as a Liberal. His election address combined the Gladstonian emphasis on the abolition of income tax, retrenchment and arbitration in international disputes with more radical demands for various pieces of labour legislation, franchise assimilation and compulsory education. His candidature clearly benefited from certain advantages. Most obviously, the Merthyr constituency was propitious to a 'labour' challenge. Not only did the area have a distinguished tradition of working-class radicalism but the 1867 Reform Act had also made it one of the most democratic constituencies in Britain, flooding the electorate with ironworkers and colliers. 'In no borough in the Kingdom do working men possess a greater power than in Merthyr,' wrote Henry Broadhurst, the L.R.L. secretary: 'if they will meet it, a man of their own order is beyond defeat ...'[43] The election also came at the height of the A.A.M.'s strength and prestige, particularly in south Wales. Here, membership rose from 18,581 in September 1872 to 43,344 a year later, to almost 48,000 in March 1874, when the national zenith of 106,368 was reached. South Wales was now its dominant region, with Merthyr and Aberdare among the largest districts, supplying around fifteen per cent of members.[44] In other industries, too, the general election coincided with the high point of trade union organization in south Wales in this period. As we have noted, amalgamated unions penetrated ironworkers, tinplate workers and other groups and this was likely to benefit Halliday's candidature, even though there were often disagreements between district leaders and national executives.[45]

[41] In a paper delivered to the second T.U.C. at Birmingham in 1869, Walton had strongly advocated independent workers' action if the Liberal Party proved intransigent. A. A. Walton, *The Necessity for, and the Best Means of Obtaining, a Direct Representation in Parliament* (1869).

[42] For Halliday, see J. M. Bellamy and J. Saville (eds.), *Dictionary of Labour Biography*, III (1976), pp. 91–4.

[43] BC, L.R.L. Minute Book, cutting from *Reynolds's Newspaper*, letter dated 8 June 1875.

[44] *The Times*, 9 Oct. 1873, 8 Apr. 1874; *Workman's Advocate*, 9 Oct. 1873; Aled Jones, op. cit., pp. 200–1.

[45] See above, pp. 214–15; Aled Jones, op. cit., pp. 198–203.

Related to the growth of the A.A.M. were two strikes over wages conducted by the union in south Wales in 1871 and 1873, both of which were essentially victories for the men.[46] Circumstances were conducive to success, but Halliday's leadership also won respect, Henry Richard testifying to the 'great judgement, temper, and moderation' evident in his handling of the 1873 stoppage.[47] Indeed, the degree of influence he attained in the south Wales valleys in the early seventies was quite remarkable, being an English speaker among a primarily Welsh-speaking population. Finally and vitally, Halliday's candidature of course had the financial support of the A.A.M. which defrayed his election expense bill of £967.[48] Finance was a perennial problem of the working men's candidates in these years. The impoverished L.R.L. was able to contribute nothing in this respect but was available as a useful source of information, advice and literature.

Yet, at the same time, Halliday faced great obstacles in Merthyr. In the first place, there were divisions within the 'labour' camp, many preferring a local candidate. E. M. Elderton, the London barrister, had faced the same objection when challenging H. A. Bruce in 1859, while in 1900 a similar aversion to Keir Hardie was manifested. At the 1874 election the *South Wales Daily News* expressed a popular sentiment: 'Surely there are many working men in the Merthyr Boroughs ... who by character, education, and ability might worthily represent the Merthyr constituency. By nationality, by training, and by habit and sympathy Mr Halliday is out of harmony with the people of Merthyr.'[49] Indeed, the original decision by the A.A.M. to run Halliday was immediately challenged by Aberdare miners' leaders, who preferred one of their own men, Henry Thomas, and Halliday was forced to defend his position against Thomas at the union's conference in Bristol in October 1873.[50] Cries of 'Why not have a Welshman?' were of course particularly apposite in a largely Welsh-speaking constituency. During the election Welsh versions of Halliday's speeches were often given by the Revd T. D. Matthias, Merthyr Baptist minister and a leading figure in the Committee of Working Men

---

[46] See E. W. Evans, *The Miners of South Wales* (Cardiff, 1961), pp. 104–8; J. H. Morris and L. J. Williams, op. cit., pp. 278–83.

[47] *Workman's Advocate*, 31 Jan. 1874; *Aberdare Times*, 31 Jan. 1874.

[48] *The Times*, 8 Apr. 1874.

[49] *South Wales Daily News*, 29 Jan. 1874; see also *Y Gwladgarwr*, 31 Jan. 1874.

[50] *Cardiff and Merthyr Guardian*, 5 July 1873; *Merthyr Express*, 18 Oct. 1873.

which directed the campaign, while it was frequently given out that the candidate was learning the language 'and would soon be able to speak to them in their mother tongue'.[51]

The suddenness of the election found Halliday and his supporters ill-prepared. It also coincided with personal difficulties for the A.A.M. leader who at the time was on bail, facing trial at Manchester Assizes on conspiracy charges. Arriving in Merthyr less than a week before the poll, Halliday clearly had insufficient time in the constituency and was unable to visit some places. Press antipathy was another of the labour representative's problems. Of the newspapers published in Merthyr itself, only J. T. Morgan's *Workman's Advocate* gave support. The *Merthyr Telegraph*, the *Merthyr Express*, *Y Fellten* and *Y Tyst a'r Dydd* were hostile, as were the *Aberdare Times* and *Y Gwladgarwr* in the western valley of the constituency. All expressed satisfaction with the incumbent members and emphasized the balance they provided, Richard Fothergill representing 'commercial interests' and Henry Richard 'the general ideas of the constituency on social, educational and kindred subjects'.[52] Most excitable was the *Aberdare Times*; its editorial following the election result declared:

> To reject either of the present members, especially to accept Mr Halliday, would be one of the most contemptible incidents in the history of electioneering. It is a great misfortune that the candidate who found himself at the bottom of the poll, his proper place, should have had the hardihood to disturb the peace of the borough by his unwelcome presence and presumptuous action. For him to have succeeded in his audacious endeavours would have been a calamity to the Principality.[53]

Other journals, too, spoke of the 'perfect madness' and 'great folly' of changing the representatives.[54] A number of editors, notably of the Nonconformist *Tyst a'r Dydd* and *Y Fellten*, interpreted Halliday's intervention as essentially a threat to Henry Richard, who had long laid claim to be 'a working-class candidate'. Thus, the Nonconformist press uniformly condemned the labour challenge.[55]

---

[51] *South Wales Daily News*, 29 Jan. 1874; *Cardiff Times*, 31 Jan. 1874.
[52] *Aberdare Times*, 31 Jan. 1874.
[53] Ibid., 7 Feb. 1874.
[54] *Y Gwladgarwr*, 31 Jan. 1874; *Seren Cymru*, 30 Jan. 1874.
[55] For the relationship between organized labour and the press in south Wales at this time, see Aled Jones, op. cit.

With the exception of the *Workman's Advocate*, the staunchest newspaper in Halliday's support was the Tory *Western Mail*, an unlikely alliance which created considerable distrust amongst working men. Its arch-rival, the Liberal *South Wales Daily News*, argued that Halliday had discredited his candidature by investing it 'with a suspicious and factitious significance as the chosen protégé of the Bute print'.[56] Others were equally critical. To *Y Tyst a'r Dydd*, the miners' leader was a tool in the *Western Mail*'s hands to oust Henry Richard.[57] And indeed, the *Mail*'s stance was essentially an anti-Richard, anti-Liberal one, its relationship with Halliday being based on 'a mutually acknowledged opportunism'.[58]

Most of all, the A.A.M. President was up against two formidable Liberal incumbents at a time when it was widely held that the Liberal Party and labour should act in partnership. Halliday's action was thus condemned as factious opposition, mere personal ambition.[59] Richard Fothergill's power emanated from his tremendous personal influence in the constituency as one of the largest employers of labour. As in 1868, he also used a subtle form of pressure with references to the sinking of new pits, the construction of a railway and other schemes, thereby suggesting more employment.[60] Henry Richard, in contrast, had an eminence in the country at large. As one local commentator acknowledged: 'He has been MP for the Liberation Society, MP for the Education League, MP for the Peace Society; but withal and beyond MP for all Welshmen and all Wales.'[61] His great strength, though, was the assurance of the religious vote in an overwhelmingly Nonconformist constituency. And here, perhaps, Halliday was most disadvantaged. A handful of Nonconformist ministers gave him backing but most came out in opposition. The patronage of the *Western Mail* with its vehement attacks on 'chapel ascendancy' inevitably roused Dissenting suspicions and rumours circulated that he was a papist and an anti-Liberationist. Halliday's published election address also made no mention of disestablishment or Nonconformist grievances, something he subsequently sought to rectify

[56] *South Wales Daily News*, 5 Feb. 1874.
[57] *Y Tyst a'r Dydd*, 6, 13 Feb. 1874.
[58] Aled Jones, op. cit., p. 212.
[59] *South Wales Daily News*, 29 Jan., 5 Feb. 1874.
[60] *Cardiff Times*, 7 Feb. 1874. For the strengths of Fothergill and Henry Richard, see I. G. Jones, *Explorations and Explanations*, Ch. 5.
[61] *South Wales Daily News*, 3 Feb. 1874.

by emphasizing that he was a Wesleyan, a supporter of religious
equality and one who would vote for such measures in Parliament.[62]

Nor was Halliday by any means assured of a large percentage
of the working-class vote. In the first place, relations between
national organizations like the A.A.M. and local leaders in south
Wales had always had their underlying tensions, which, indeed,
were to intensify and manifest themselves in the secessionist
unionism, the so-called 'Red Dragon Revolt', of miners and
ironworkers in the summer of 1874.[63] Moreover, in 1868 Henry
Richard had presented himself as the working-class candidate and
to many his subsequent conduct had confirmed this. Thus, efforts
to depict him as 'an indifferent observer' to the men's cause in
the 1873 strike were condemned even in local A.A.M. circles.[64]
Further, during the election campaign, Richard, under some pressure from Halliday's supporters, gave firm pledges on various
pieces of 'labour' legislation, thereby incorporating much of his
rival's manifesto. As a large and by no means unbenevolent
employer in the community, Fothergill also attracted working-class
support. He, too, claimed sympathy with workers' grievances
though his commitments were of the vaguest nature.

In view of the strength of the sitting members and other difficulties facing Halliday, his 4,912 votes, 25.3 per cent of the total
poll, as against Richard's 7,606 and Fothergill's 6,908, were re-
markably high. The total poll of 19,426 represented a turn-out
of 5,462 less than in 1868. Richard apparently suffered most here,
losing over 4,000 votes. Fothergill's vote fell by just over 500,
while Halliday received only 864 votes less than H.A. Bruce in
1868, a considerable achievement in view of the difference in
the total poll. In the final analysis, the forces of political Dissent
and economic paternalism ensured the failure of the labour challenge. Yet the election was an indication of the latent power of
the labour vote.

In the summer of 1875 it seemed that Halliday would have
a second opportunity to contest a Merthyr seat when the resignation of Fothergill, now suffering serious financial difficulties,
appeared imminent and there was considerable speculation on

[62] *Workman's Advocate*, 7 Feb. 1874.
[63] See Aled Jones, op. cit.
[64] *Cardiff Times*, 31 Jan. 1874; *Aberdare Times*, 31 Jan. 1874.

possible candidates. On the labour side, Halliday publicly declared his intention to stand, while alternatives were the two London radicals, Lloyd Jones and George Odger. The name of the former had lately become known in the area through articles in the *Beehive*, translated in *Amddiffynydd y Gweithiwr*, in support of the colliers' strike in south Wales, while Odger had lectured in the town in April.[65] Of the three, the republican Odger was apparently the most favoured among local labour leaders and was urged to come forward.[66] He had already been a parliamentary candidate on five occasions and, as such, had been much abused by the middle-class press; 'he has not', observed the *Brecon County Times* in 1868, 'derived much benefit from the repeal of the duty on soap'.[67] Such insult was the everyday hazard of the labour candidate. In 1873, Halliday had been bluntly told by the *Merthyr Telegraph* to 'shower his honours on some constituency more obscure than Merthyr, and harder up for a representative'.[68]

The by-election conjecture took place against a background of industrial tension in south Wales. In the summer of 1874 an economic slump, wage reductions, and distress brought existing discontents with the A.A.M. and the National Amalgamated Association of Ironworkers to the surface and led to a wave of breakaway unionism. The situation deteriorated further amidst widespread dissatisfaction with the A.A.M.'s handling of the 1875 strike, at the end of which the union found itself bankrupt and facing dissolution.[69] The attendant loss of confidence in its president rendered his prospects of parliamentary election in Merthyr now negligible. To Philip Harries, local ironworkers' agent, Halliday's candidature would be 'an act of madness', for in the present climate he did not stand 'a shadow of a chance'.[70] In the event, all the lively by-election debate proved redundant. Another labour initiative, as urged by the L.R.L., was not possible since Fothergill did not relinquish his seat. Yet the activity was not without significance, for the recent industrial struggle had intensified the miners'

[65] *Amddiffynydd y Gweithiwr*, 6 Mar., 17 Apr., 9 June 1875; *Workman's Advocate*, 23 Apr. 1875.
[66] BC, L.R.L. Minute Book, cutting from *Reynolds's Newspaper*, letter dated 8 June 1875.
[67] *Brecon County Times*, 31 Oct. 1868, quoted in R. Harrison, op. cit., p. 174.
[68] *Merthyr Telegraph*, 18 Apr. 1873.
[69] See É. W. Evans, op. cit., pp. 110–14.
[70] BC, L.R.L. Minute Book, Philip Harries to Henry Broadhurst, 12 July 1875.

enthusiasm to elect 'a representative whose opinions and sympathies run in parallel grooves to their own',[71] though that representative was clearly not to be Thomas Halliday. During 1875, the
League had kept a close eye on political developments in the
constituency and had helped to raise funds for the strike, and
its executive meetings were reported in the *Workman's Advocate*
and its sister paper, *Amddiffynydd y Gweithiwr*, founded in August
1874. In reality, though, the League had fallen into decline following the 1874 general election, thereafter participating in only a
few by-elections and ceasing operations in 1878.[72] It had never
been able to surmount difficulties of finance, personal animosity,
the narrow and class character implied in its name, nor indeed
to certify its relationship with the Liberal Party.

Within Wales, efforts to obtain labour representation in Parliament in the 1870s were confined to the Merthyr area. Elsewhere,
enthusiasm sometimes brought public advocacy, as, for instance,
at a meeting of the General Amalgamated Labourers' Union in
Cardiff in January 1874, but did not develop into independent
action.[73] Trade unions, where electorally active, gave their support
to Liberal candidates, as at Newport in the 1874 election.[74] It
was in the Merthyr area, too, that the earliest entry of labour
into local elections occurred. Here working men held meetings
to select candidates for School Board and Board of Guardian
elections though, despite their voting strength, success was far
from assured. At the first Merthyr School Board election in March
1871 all three of their candidates were defeated; 'working men
seem to have no confidence in their own class,' regretted the
Merthyr Telegraph.[75] Three years later, however, the same newspaper
was far from enthusiastic about the return of 'the working man's
candidate', Revd T. D. Matthias, a committed supporter of trade
unionism and of the workers' cause generally; his success illustrated

[71] Ibid., cutting from *Reynolds's Newspaper*, letter dated 8 June 1875; *Amddiffynydd y Gweithiwr*,
9 June 1875.
[72] One such by-election again involved Alfred Walton at Stoke, where in January 1875
he was the official nominee. His ambitions of 'entering as a member the House he had
as a workman assisted to build' were thwarted by the dramatic intervention of a maverick
candidate, Dr Kenealy, and such were the passions aroused by the Tichborne case that
he triumphed by over 2,000 votes. In 1880 Henry Broadhurst came forward as a working-
class candidate, winning with official Liberal backing.
[73] *South Wales Daily News*, 9 Jan. 1874.
[74] *South Wales Weekly Telegram*, 31 Jan. 1874.
[75] *Merthyr Telegraph*, 24 Mar. 1871.

the ignorance of the electorate for 'in no sense—intellectually—are his qualifications equal to the duties of the important office...'[76]

This was not an isolated 'intrusion' into the local politics of the area at this time. The veteran Chartist, William Gould, ex-miner, now a grocer, sat on the Merthyr Board of Guardians, while in Aberdare a committee of working men secured the election of Isaac Thomas, who had similarly 'elevated himself from the working classes' and was soon to become prominent on the Aber-dare Trades Council, to the Board of Health in April 1875. 'Aber-dare', commented a local newspaper, 'is just passing through a most excitable social phase ...'[77] But generally the advance of direct labour representation in Wales, in terms of candidatures and successes, was slow and fitful. On Matthias's removal to north Staffordshire (where he edited the labour *Potteries' Examiner*), the attempt of J. T. Morgan, the newspaper editor-proprietor and trade unionist, to retain the Merthyr School Board seat in the workers' interest in March 1876 failed.[78] John Beynon, a collier, was similarly unsuccessful a year later.[79] The efforts of two colliers to win seats on the Mountain Ash Board of Health in April 1876 fared no better.[80] The first successful working-class candidature for the Aberdare School Board was not until 1886 when David Morgan, the Aberdare miners' agent, topped the poll, having first attempted to win a seat on the Board's inception in 1871.[81] Local elections were frequently dominated by religious rather than politi-cal issues, while independent working-class action, at local and parliamentary level, was enfeebled by a lack of solidarity and by the absence of an effective unifying body, like the A.A.M., through which political aspiration could be directed.

Even in the industrial south, labour remained a largely dormant political force in the late seventies and eighties. This was the period of the ascendancy among Welsh miners of William Abraham ('Mabon'), secretary of the Cambrian Miners' Association, of industrial co-operation between workers and employers, and of

---

[76] Ibid., 6 Mar. 1874. For Matthias, see J. M. Bellamy and J. Saville (eds.), op. cit., Vol. VII (1984), pp. 178–82.

[77] *Aberdare Times*, 20 Mar., 3, 10, 24 Apr. 1875; *Y Gwladgarwr*, 23 Apr. 1875.

[78] *Merthyr Telegraph*, 3, 10 Mar. 1876.

[79] Ibid., 2, 16 Mar. 1877.

[80] *Aberdare Times*, 1, 15 Apr. 1876; *Y Gwladgarwr*, 14 Apr. 1876; *Beehive*, 8 Apr. 1876.

[81] Jon Parry, 'Labour leaders and local politics: the example of Aberdare', *Welsh History Review*, 14, No. 3 (June, 1989), p. 404.

Lib-Labism—firm attachment to the Liberal Party—in politics. The militancy of the early 1870s, embodied in the sudden wave of unionism, industrial conflict, and Thomas Halliday's parliamentary candidature, faded away. Thereafter, there were only fleeting instances of significant numbers of workers rebuffing the middle-class and Nonconformist-dominated local Liberal associations and taking independent action. One occasion was the 1880 general election in Merthyr, when there was substantial collier backing for the coal-owner W. T. Lewis (later Baron Merthyr of Senghenydd) partly in protest against the presumption of Liberal Nonconformity with the candidatures of Henry Richard and his colleague C. H. James, the Unitarian solicitor. One of the members, it was argued, should represent the local economy in the tradition of Richard Fothergill. As one collier explained:

> ... 100,000 workers don't want to be dictated to by the Peace Society on the one hand and Unitarianism on the other. There is something else in these boroughs besides the pulpit. There are iron and tinworks employing 6,000 people; there are many thousands of colliers, and all these naturally demand adequate representation, and will not consent to be walked over by Messrs Richard and James.[82]

Political Dissent ultimately carried the day, though most of those who voted for Lewis were apparently colliers. In Carmarthen District, too, at the same election, a large section of the workers rejected the leadership of the borough Liberal Association and supported a Swansea industrialist, the tinplate owner, John Jones Jenkins. Active in the campaign was the local tinplaters' union led by William Lewis ('Lewys Afan'), who argued that a commercial man was better fitted to represent working men than a London barrister. 'Mabon', on the other hand, exerted his influence among the colliers behind the sitting member and B. T. Williams narrowly retained the seat.[83] Workers did not always exercise their political muscle in unison.

As committed as the miners of the industrial south to the principles of industrial harmony and Lib-Labism were the quarrymen of the north-west. The prominent figure here, the middle-class Nonconformist radical W. J. Parry, was, like William Abraham,

[82] *Western Mail*, 24 Mar. 1880.
[83] D. V. Evans, op. cit., pp. 63–9.

the embodiment of those sentiments. In the late nineteenth century the quarrymen contributed significantly to a number of Liberal electoral triumphs, though there were manifestations of dissatisfaction from time to time. Unhappy with the county Liberal Association's nomination of the wealthy Liverpool merchant William Rathbone for the Caernarfonshire by-election of 1880, W. J. Parry asked, 'Why should the quarrymen give way to a class of tradespeople in their claim to contest the seat? Were they united enough', he went on, 'they could send their President to Westminster.'[84] Similarly, in 1884, he emphasized that the quarrymen's organization, the N.W.Q.U., 'should make sure that representatives are in complete sympathy with its aims'.[85] At the 1885 general election there was talk of a labour candidate in the Caernarfon Boroughs,[86] while in Merioneth, Ffestiniog quarrymen repudiated the local Liberal Party and ran their own Independent Liberal candidate, Morgan Lloyd.[87] Basically though, the corporate body, the N.W.Q.U., preoccupied with industrial troubles, was neither powerful enough, nor indeed sufficiently inclined, to sponsor an independent labour candidature.

By contrast, in the newly created Rhondda constituency the unity and the sheer numerical strength of the miners forced the representation scales in labour's favour at the 1885 general election. In preceding years the Cambrian Miners' Association had joined in the campaign for further parliamentary reform, condemning the House of Lords for obstructing the Franchise Bill and strongly pressing their district's claims for separate parliamentary status. Direct miners' representation was also a theme at its gatherings. In 1885 the miners rejected the coal-owner F. L. Davis, the choice of the 'Three Hundred', the official Liberal organization, in favour of 'Mabon', who in a straight fight triumphed by 867 votes.[88] He was thus the first working man's candidate elected for a Welsh seat, though his political stance

---

[84] *Baner ac Amserau Cymru*, 17 Nov. 1880.

[85] W. J. Parry, *Chwareli a Chwarelwyr* (Caernarfon, 1897), pp. 66–7, quoted by C. Parry, op. cit., p. 29.

[86] *South Wales Daily News*, 6 July 1885.

[87] See Merfyn Jones, op. cit., pp. 65–7; R. Emyr Price, 'Lloyd George and Merioneth politics, 1885–86. A failure to effect a breakthrough', *Journal of the Merioneth Historical and Record Society*, VII (1973–6), pp. 292–307.

[88] See L. J. Williams, 'The first Welsh "Labour" MP', *Morgannwg*, VI (1962); E. W. Evans, *Mabon: A Study in Trade Union Leadership* (Cardiff, 1959).

was typically Liberal. Thereafter, the miners' leader was unchallenged, unopposed at all future elections by a Liberal and rarely by a Conservative. In 1886, reflecting the reality of local political power, the 'Liberal Three Hundred' were replaced by a 'Liberal and Labour Association', the first such organization in the Principality.

Nevertheless, throughout Wales, largely middle-class local Liberal associations, controlled by Nonconformist ministers, shopkeepers and solicitors, were very reluctant to accept working men as candidates, and were indeed to remain so over subsequent decades. Some associations, Caernarfonshire for example, had from the first no working-class representation. Others had a token few, insufficient to play an influential role. Those which began with democratic intentions rarely remained so because of dependence on a few rich contributors. By the mid 1880s working men were becoming less acquiescent, not in terms of repudiation of the Liberal Party—for years yet, labour leaders in Wales remained staunchly loyal to the traditional community values of Nonconformist Liberalism—but insofar as they wanted due emphasis on the labour side of the Lib-Lab alliance. In the Rhondda, they sought and secured their own man. Elsewhere they pressed the claims of their own choice but in most cases could but despairingly object to the nominee of the Liberal caucus.

The period 1868–86 witnessed undramatic but perceptible advance for the cause of labour representation in Wales. Discussion of the theme became more widespread and, with some success, local and parliamentary candidatures occurred in parts of the industrial south. These initiatives were political manifestations of an increasing working-class consciousness, though popular aspirations, immersed in Nonconformity and Liberalism, remained as yet firmly Lib-Lab. In particular, the trade union movement was wedded to radical Liberalism. In Britain the number of Lib-Lab MPs increased from three in 1880 to eleven in 1885 (including, of course, William Abraham for the Rhondda constituency), slipping to ten the following year. Dissatisfied with this position, the T.U.C. formed an Electoral Labour Committee in 1886 to promote the return to Parliament of working men or 'candidates favourable to the interests of labour', but the principle that labour's interests could be secured through co-operation with the Liberal Party remained very much intact. Though Keir Hardie's fierce attack on the respected Henry Broadhurst at the 1887 T.U.C. in Swansea dramatically signalled the beginning of a new, militant, socialist challenge to the 'old guard' leadership, the conversion of trade unionism to the concept of an independent labour party proved a difficult task.

XIV
CONCLUSION

The period 1840–86 was one of transformation and upheaval in much of Welsh life. Economic and social change was accompanied by decisive political developments; the election results of the 1880s confirmed the passing away of the traditional political order while, in the country at large, Welsh popular radicalism was a powerful force. Both cause and effect of the growing political consciousness were the extra-parliamentary agitations affecting Wales decade after decade in the Victorian era.

Agitational techniques were taught, political principles and attitudes ingrained, and popular influence over government extended. Reform activity centred essentially on propaganda and pressure. National societies invariably published their own newspapers and journals to act as organs for their particular movement; but much, of course, depended on winning the sympathy of the popular press. The distribution of tracts and other literature and the employment of travelling agents were central to the educating process too. The convening of public meetings and the raising of petitions as demonstrations of popular support were long-established means of pressure, while electoral action at municipal and parliamentary level presented excellent opportunities for pressing candidates on their views and, as the franchise broadened, for playing a more deliberate role. In the period covered by this study reform societies pursued their objectives in a fundamentally constitutional manner, though frustration inevitably led to the consideration, or even exercise, of illegitimate action. Chartists most obviously went down this road but even the A.C.L.L., traditionally the epitome of rational pressure, had its desperate aspects. In 1841, for example, thwarted by frequent disruption of public meetings, it determined to fight might with might and promoted working-class associations in part 'to provide the free traders with strong-arm men capable of dealing with Chartist attacks'.[1] Similarly, physical clashes occurred between Liberationists and Church

---

[1] N. McCord, *The Anti-Corn Law League*, p. 98.

defenders and between opponents and supporters of the Contagious Diseases Acts. The A.C.L.L. also seriously considered the
non-payment of taxes as a plan of campaign, while the 'fiscal
strike' became official C.S.U. policy in the early months of 1844.
Local Nonconformists most frequently contravened the law by
refusing to pay Church rates; 'all honour to the Pontypool Dissenters', ran a typical response from the *Nonconformist* newspaper
during such action in 1846.[2]

Nineteenth-century reform movements invariably conducted
their agitations with great energy, commitment and purpose. But
success, of course, required much more than these characteristics,
especially when combating powerful vested interests in the
country. Significantly, victorious campaigns like those against slavery, the Corn Laws, and the Contagious Diseases Acts achieved
their aims in favourable political conditions. Others like parliamentary reform, political Nonconformity, and temperance had their
gains, but certainly by the mid 1880s had failed to attain their
ultimate goals. The advance of democracy had not yet reached
manhood suffrage, a number of Nonconformist grievances had
been removed but the Church was not yet disestablished, Sunday
Closing Acts had been passed for Wales, Scotland and Ireland
but local option was not yet achieved, elementary education was
not amended to meet the principles of the N.E.L., while labour
politics and the women's rights movement were still in their
infancy.

If legislative achievements were limited there were, however,
significant by-products. The operations of national reform organizations served to develop political consciousness by bringing national issues to 'the dark corners of the land', thereby considerably
broadening the sphere of Victorian political life. While local societies may not have been tremendously effective in terms of popular
pressure, for those involved in, or even affected by, their activities
a political and social education was provided. The links established
between outlying areas and large English cities, and the pen-
etrations of radical English newspapers carrying news and correspondence from the localities, helped to break down insularity
and parochialism, serious impediments to political development.

---

[2] *Nonconformist*, 28 Jan. 1846.

Participation in reform society activity offered other benefits too. Any activist capable of undertaking arduous and often tedious organizational work, and willing to do so, invariably found himself or herself in office, thereby enabling the acquisition and exercise of political skills, and maybe the gaining of a measure of personal prestige.

Obtaining information on the operation of local reform societies in nineteenth-century Wales can be an elusive experience. Although some reform agitations in the localities no doubt had but a brief effervescence, much activity for various reasons went unrecorded in the provincial press. Occasional references suggest more indigenous societies than can be discerned. Thus, for example, Revd William Rees ('Gwilym Hiraethog'), speaking in support of the Liberation Society at Caernarfon in 1878, recalled the earliest disestablishment society founded in the region, in the Vale of Edeirnion, Merioneth, over forty years previously: 'That society had its headquarters at Llandrillo, and branches in the different neighbourhoods, with an annual meeting, where notes were prepared, and a sermon on the subject presented.'[3] But such local enterprise and commitment are often obscure and inaccessible.

At the same time, it was in the interests of national pressure organizations to claim as many affiliated societies as possible and clearly some local branches were no more than names on official lists. While useful in creating the impression of wide influence and in maintaining the optimism and enthusiasm of activists, this could be a source of exasperation too. As the surviving Llanidloes Chartists pronounced in 1858: '... all Political Reform Associations or branches of such which exist in name, are highly injurious to the progress of Reform generally, as by their mere existence they hold forth the delusive hope of speedy and beneficial changes, which their inactivity fails to produce'.[4] In the same way, unrealistic expectations were raised by exaggerated claims of the impact of reform movements on public opinion, where winning a majority of the country's population was always unlikely, given the considerable indifference and conservatism as well as the opposition. Nevertheless, there can be no doubting the powerful attachment of some people to the promotion of various causes, indeed to

[3] Ibid., 27 Nov. 1878.
[4] *People's Paper*, 24 July 1858.

the extent that those causes dominated their lives. The commitment of some Corn Law repealers, Chartists, disestablishment
campaigners and others, often in the face of fierce personal attacks
and frequent disappointments, was unremitting, even though there
were inevitably times when impatience, frustration and internal
divisions surfaced over such issues as policy and tactics, relations
with central executives or maybe local frictions, as revealed for
instance at a Caernarfon Liberationist meeting in 1883 where
one disgruntled speaker observed:

> Some have laboured diligently more than 50 years to teach to the Welsh
> the principles of religious and civil liberty, etc. They have been discouraged
> and condemned, especially by the leading men among the Welsh Meth-
> odists. We well recollect how they were persecuted and called rebels, for
> pleading against the 'Corporation and Test Act' and 'Catholic emancipa-
> tion' ... The Methodists have now come over to the old advocates of
> liberty, and they are exceedingly thankful to them, but they have no claim
> to sit always on the front benches of the platform, and hide those who
> have suffered the heat of the day in the struggle.[5]

Indeed, this politicization of the Calvinistic Methodist denomination and of Dissent as a whole was of crucial importance, for,
in Wales especially, Victorian politics is incomprehensible without
due recognition of religio-political activity. Certainly the reform
organizations which made most impression in nineteenth-century
Wales were those directly associated with political Nonconformity,
that is, the Liberation Society, the United Kingdom Alliance and
the N.E.L., while others, like the A.C.L.L., which took a strong
religious and moral line struck responsive chords. Time and again
it was the leaders of religious Dissent within communities who
gave the impetus to local reform agitations.

The period upon which this study concentrates, the half century
or so up to 1886, marked the florescence of extra-parliamentary
agitation in Britain. In the early decades of the century, prior
to the reform crisis of 1831–2, this form of popular politics was
undeveloped in terms of organization, strategy and public support,
while in late century political parties commanded the terrain, possessing nation-wide constituency bodies of broad appeal. Women
were included in these political organizations, notably in the Primrose League, founded to promote Disraelian Conservatism in

---

[5] *Y Cronicl*, Jan. 1884, pp. 35–6.

1883, and in the Women's Liberal Federation of 1887. Thereby, a new relationship between the political parties and the people was forged, which worked to the detriment of pressure from without. Developments within the Liberal Party were central here for, while reform movements made efforts to convince and pressurize politicians of all persuasions and accordingly professed independence of party, in reality they naturally inclined towards the Liberals as the most likely vehicle for gaining their legislative demands. By the mid 1880s the spread of local Liberal associations, including Working Men's Associations, and the influence of the N.L.F. afforded opportunities for advancing principles inside the party's organizational structure. This tended to subsume the pressure groups and signalled the passing of their heyday. In Wales specifically, the creation in 1886–7 of Liberal Federations for north and south Wales, brought together in a Welsh National Liberal Council, did much to shift the focus of organized pressure to within official Liberalism, while Welsh Liberal MPs also emerged as an effective parliamentary pressure group for the first time in the years after 1886, advancing in particular the national causes of disestablishment, land and educational reform, and home rule. The identification of Wales with the Liberal Party became complete, embracing not only Nonconformity but evoking deep working-class loyalty and drawing middle-class women into its orbit. The operation of the array of extra-parliamentary reform agitations during the Victorian era was at the heart of that process.

BIBLIOGRAPHY

1. MANUSCRIPTS
2. OFFICIAL PAPERS
3. NEWSPAPERS AND PERIODICALS
4. PAMPHLETS
5. REPORTS
6. WORKS OF REFERENCE
7. OTHER BOOKS
8. ARTICLES
9. THESES

Place of publication is London, unless otherwise stated.

1. MANUSCRIPTS
Birmingham Public Library
Lovett Collection, The London Working Men's Association: newspaper cuttings and correspondence.
National Complete Suffrage Union, Minute Book of the Committee for General Purposes.

Birmingham University Library
Chamberlain Papers
National Education League, Miscellaneous Papers

Bishopsgate Institute, London (Howell Collection)
Cash Book of the Reform League, 1865–9
George Howell's Draft Autobiography
Letter Books of the Secretary of the R.L., 1865–9
Letters and Articles by George Howell, 1867–75
Letters to George Howell, 1864–1910
Minute Books of the General and Executive Councils of the R.L., 1865–9
R.L. Election Reports, 1868
R.L. Miscellany (including George Mantle's Letter Book)

British Library
Cobden Papers (Add. MSS 43, 647–78)
Place Papers (Add. MSS 27, 810)
Place Newspaper Collection, Sets 7, 8, 9 (Corn Laws) and 56 (Reform)
Sturge Papers (Add. MSS 43, 722)

British Library of Political and Economic Science, London School of Economics
Broadhurst Collection, Minute Books of the Labour Representation League
Webb Trade Union Collection (Section A)

Cardiff Central Library
Bute Papers, Boxes XX, XXI and XXII
Cardiff Election Papers, 1866–8 (MS 4813)

Fawcett Library, City of London Polytechnic
Josephine Butler Papers
H. J. Wilson Papers

Minute Books of the National Association for the Repeal of the Contagious Diseases Acts, 1871–86
Letter Book of the National Association, 1883–6
Minute Book 6the Ladies' National Association for the Repeal of the Contagious Diseases Acts, 1875–84

Greater London Record Office
Minutes of the Anti-State-Church Association
Minute Books of the Liberation Society

Gwent Record Office, Cwmbrân
Miscellaneous MSS

Labour Party Library, Walworth Road, London
Vincent Collection, Miniken-Vincent MSS

Manchester Public Library
Letter Books of the Anti-Corn Law League
J. B. Smith Papers
George Wilson Papers

National Library of Wales, Aberystwyth
(a) *General Manuscripts*
787B, Minute Book of the Merioneth Reform Association
1025C (Ieuan Gwynedd 1), Essay on the Elevation of the Working Classes, *c.* 1850
3317B, Electoral Address of Dr T. Price, Baptist Minister, Aberdare, to the Electors of Brecknock Boroughs, 1866
5418E, Account of Thomas Thomas, Baptist College, Pontypool, by his son T. H. Thomas
5503–5B, Henry Richard MSS
8305–11D, 8319E, Thomas Gee MSS
8321C, Letters of John Matthews
8823–4C, 8835–8C, W. J. Parry MSS
10327E, Information on John Jenkins
12780C (D. E. Jenkins 50), Essay on 'Chartism in Wales'
12888E, E. R. Horsfall-Turner, 'Chartism in Montgomeryshire'
13568C (G. E. Evans 350), Information on John Jenkins
14199C (Rees Jenkin Jones), Unitarianism in South Wales
14205B (Rees Jenkin Jones), A Reply to 'Chartism Unmasked' (1841)
14984A, Diary of Clarkson's Tour on Behalf of the Anti-Slavery Association, 1824
15404C, Revd William Williams, 'Caledfryn', A Scrapbook
15405A, Letters of Revd William Williams, 'Caledfryn'
15439–54 2B, Minutes of the Cardiff Nonconformist Ministerial Union, 1867–94
21171D, Minute Book of the North Wales Liberal Federation, 1886–91

(b) *Deposited Collections*
Aston Hall Correspondence, no. 4879
Cwrt Mawr MSS, 818–9E (Spinther I and II)
Glansevern Collection (papers of A. C. Humphreys-Owen)
Llangibby Castle Collection
Maybery Papers
Minor Deposits, 684B, 725A, 1207B
Olive Mary Jones Collection
Rendel Papers

Tredegar Park MSS

Public Record Office
Home Office Letters and Papers, 40/30; 40/57; 40/59; 45/54; 45/265B; 45/453; 45/OS
    253; 45/OS 347A (material relating to Chartism in Wales)
Privy Council I, Political Societies

West Sussex Record Office, Chichester
Cobden Papers

2. OFFICIAL PAPERS
Hansard's Parliamentary Debates, Third Series
Censuses of England and Wales, 1801–1901
Parliamentary Papers (PP), 1840, XL, *Report on the State of Elementary Education in the Mining
    Districts of South Wales*
PP 1847, XXVII, *Report of the Commissioners of Inquiry into the State of Education in Wales*
PP, 1850, XXIII, 1851, XXIII, *Reports of H. Seymour Tremenheere on the State of Population
    in the Mining Districts*
PP, 1851, XXVII, *Report from the Select Committee on Newspaper Stamps*
PP, 1866, LVII, *Electoral Returns relating to the Counties of England and Wales, 1865–66*
PP, 1868–9, VIII, *Report from the Select Committee on Parliamentary and Municipal Elections*
PP, 1868–9, L, *Return of the Number of Electors on the Register in each of the Parliamentary Cities
    and Boroughs . . .*
PP, 1894, XXXVI, XXXVII; 1895, XL, XLI; 1896, XXXIII–XXXV, *Evidence, Report
    and Appendices of the Royal Commission on Land in Wales and Monmouthshire*
PP, 1911, LXII, *Return showing with regard to each Parliamentary Constituency in the United Kingdom
    the Total Number, and, as far as possible, the number in each class, of Electors on the Register
    for the year 1911*

3. NEWSPAPERS AND PERIODICALS

Aberdare Times	*County Observer*
Aberystwyth Observer	*Y Cronicl*
Advocate and Merthyr Free Press	*Cylchgrawn Rhyddid*
Amddiffynydd y Gweithiwr	*Democratic Review*
Annual Register	*Denbighshire and Flintshire Telegraph*
Anti-Bread Tax Circular	*Y Diwygiwr*
Anti-Corn Law Circular	*Y Drysorfa*
Baner ac Amserau Cymru	*Y Dysgedydd*
Beehive	*English Chartist Circular*
Birmingham Journal	*Englishman*
Brecon County Times	*Englishwoman's Journal*
Brecon Journal	*Englishwoman's Review*
Brecon Reporter	*Y Fellten*
Carnarvon and Denbigh Herald	*Flintshire Observer*
Cambrian	*Free Trader*
Cambrian News	*Freeholder*
Cardiff Chronicle	*Glamorgan, Monmouth and Brecon Gazette and*
Cardiff and Merthyr Guardian	* Merthyr Guardian*
Cardiff Times	*Y Gweithiwr / The Workman*
Carmarthen Journal	*Y Gwladgarwr*
Charter	*Yr Haul*
Chester Courant	*Yr Herald Cymraeg*
Colliery Guardian	*Hereford Journal*
Commonwealth	*Justice*

Labour Standard
Labourer
The League
Liberator
Liverpool Mercury
Llandudno Register and Herald
Llanidloes and Newtown Telegraph
London News
Manchester Examiner and Times
Manchester Guardian
Merthyr and Aberdare Times
Merthyr Express
Merthyr Star
Merthyr Telegraph
Monmouthshire Advertiser
Monmouthshire Beacon
Monmouthshire Merlin
Montgomeryshire Express
Morgan Llewelyn's Journal
National Education League Monthly Paper
National League Journal
National Reformer
National Union
National Vindicator
Newport Gazette
Newtown and Welshpool Express
Nonconformist
North Wales Chronicle
North Wales Express
Northern Star
Notes from the People
Pembrokeshire Herald
Penarth Observer
People's Paper
Poor Man's Guardian
Potteries Examiner
Principality
Protest

Radical
Red Republican
Reform Gazette and Manchester Critic
Reformer and South Wales Times
Republican Herald
Reynolds's Newspaper
Salopian Journal and Courier of Wales
School Board Chronicle
Seren Cymru
Seren Gomer
Shield
Shrewsbury Chronicle
Shrewsbury Free Press
Shrewsbury News
Shropshire and Montgomeryshire Times
Silurian
Staffordshire Sentinel
Star of Gwent
South Wales Daily News
South Wales Echo
South Wales Evening Telegram
South Wales Weekly Telegram
Swansea and Glamorgan Herald
Swansea Journal
Tarian y Gweithiwr
Ten Towns Messenger and Birmingham Times
Tichborne News and Anti-Oppression Journal
The Times
Y Tyst a'r Dydd
Udgorn Cymru
Welshman
Western Mail
Western Vindicator
Women's Suffrage Journal
Women's Trade Union Journal
Working Man
Workman's Advocate
Wrexham Weekly Advertiser

4. PAMPHLETS

Address and Rules of Newport Working Men's Association for benefiting politically, socially and morally, the useful classes (Newport, n.d., c. 1838)
Bruce, H. A., The Present and Future Prospects of the Working Classes in the Manufacturing District of South Wales (Cardiff, 1851)
Idem, Merthyr in 1852 (Cardiff, 1852)
Essays on Reform (1867)
Hanham, H. J., The Reformed Electoral System in Great Britain, 1832–1914 (Historical Association, 1968)
James, C. H., What I remember about Myself and Old Merthyr (Merthyr Tydfil, 1894)
Jenkins, E., Chartism Unmask'd (Merthyr Tydfil, 1840)
Jenkins, J., The Ballot and Ministerial Reform: What Ought to be Done? (1852)
Jones, I. G., Communities: The Observers and the Observed (Cardiff, 1985)

Idem, Henry Richard, Apostle of Peace, 1812–1888 (Llangollen, 1988)

Lowndes, F. W., *The Extension of the Contagious Diseases Acts to Liverpool and Other Seaports Practically Considered* (1876)

Morgan, K.O., *Freedom or Sacrilege? A History of the Campaign for Welsh Disestablishment* (Penarth, 1965)

Morgan, T., *The Life and Work of the Reverend Thomas Thomas, D.D.* (Carmarthen, 1925)

National Complete Suffrage Union, Tracts (Birmingham, 1843)

National Education League, Instructions to Agents (Birmingham, 1875)

National Reform League, Only Authorised Programme of the National Reform League Demonstration, 11th February 1867 (1867)

Parry, W. J., *Cymru a Datgysylltiad: Cymdeithas Rhyddhad Crefydd* (Caernarfon, 1885)

Rees, T., *Miscellaneous Papers on Subjects relating to Wales* (1867)

Reform League, Official List of Branches (1867)

Reform Meetings: The Real Facts (1866)

The Reformers' Almanack and Political Year Book (1850)

Ritchie, J. E., *Freehold Land Societies—History, Present Position and Claims* (1853)

Roberts, O. O., *Facts for Farmers: or, Agriculture and the Corn Laws* (1841)

Roberts, S., *Farmer Careful of Cil-Haul Uchaf* (Conwy, 1881)

Idem, Pleadings for Reform, Published Fifty Years Ago (Conway, n.d., *c.* 1881)

Thomas, D. J., *The Temperance Movement in Newport, Mon., 1837–1937* (Newport, 1937)

Thomas, T., *The Civil Duties of Christians. A Sermon occasioned by the Late Outrages at Newport, Monmouthshire* (n.d., *c.* 1839)

Idem, A Proper Consideration of the Cause of the Poor (Pontypool, 1841)

Idem, A Course of Lectures on the Present Duties devolving on Christian Professors as members of a Civil Community, Lectures 1–6 (1847)

Walton, A.A., *The Necessity for, and the Best Means of Obtaining, a Direct Representation in Parliament* (1869)

Welsh Nonconformity and Welsh Representation (Liberation Society, 1866)

5. REPORTS

Complete Suffrage Almanack for 1844

Cynhadledd o Weinidogion y Gwahanol Enwadau Cristionogol yn Manchester (n.d., *c.* 1841)

Ladies' National Association for the Repeal of the Contagious Diseases Acts, *Annual Reports*, 1870–86

Liberation Society, *Annual Reports*, 1845–86

Liberation Society, *Reports of the Triennial Conferences*, 1847–86

Manchester National Society for Women's Suffrage, *Annual Reports*, 1867–80

National Association for the Repeal of the Contagious Diseases Acts, *Annual Reports*, 1870–5, 1880–6

National Complete Suffrage Union. *Report of the Proceedings of the Conference of Delegates, held at Birmingham, 5 April 1842, and three following days* (Birmingham, 1842)

National Complete Suffrage Union, *Annual Reports*, 1843–5

National Education League, *Annual Reports*, 1869–75

National Liberal Federation, *Annual Reports*, 1879–87

National Reform Union, *Report of the Proceedings at the National Reform Conference, March 1865* (1865)

National Society for Women's Suffrage, *Annual Reports*, 1871–92

Proceedings of the First Anti-State-Church Conference (1844)

Proceedings attending the Formation of the National Federation of Liberal Associations; with Report of the Conference at Birmingham, 31 May 1877 (Birmingham, 1877)

6. WORKS OF REFERENCE

Banks, O., *The Biographical Dictionary of British Feminists, Vol. I, 1800–1930* (1985)

Bellamy, J. M., and Saville, J. (eds.), *Dictionary of Labour Biography*, 7 vols. (1972–84)

Berrow, M., *Women 1870–1928: Select Guide to Printed and Archival Sources in the United Kingdom* (1981)
Dictionary of National Biography
Dictionary of Welsh Biography down to 1940 (1959)
Dod's Parliamentary Companion
Harrison, R., Woolren, G. B., and Duncan, R., *The Warwick Guide to British Labour Periodicals* (1977)
James, A. J., and Thomas, J. E., *Wales at Westminster, A History of the Parliamentary Representation of Wales, 1800–1979* (Llandysul, 1981)
Jenkins, R. T., and Rees, W., *A Bibliography of the History of Wales* (Cardiff, 2nd edn., 1962)
Jones, P. H., (ed.), *A Bibliography of the History of Wales* (Cardiff, 1989, microfiche edn.)
Kelley's Directory of Monmouthshire and the Principal Towns and Places in South Wales (1884)
McCalmont, F. H., *Parliamentary Poll Books* (Nottingham, 1910)
Pigot's Directory (1835)
Post Office Directory of Monmouthshire and the Principal Towns and Places in South Wales (1871)
Slater's Royal National Commercial Directory of Monmouthshire, North and South Wales (1868)
United Kingdom First Annual Trades Union Directory (1861)
Williams, W. R., *Parliamentary History of Wales, 1541–1895* (Brecknock, 1895)

7. OTHER BOOKS
Aberdare, Lord, *Letters of the Rt. Hon. Henry Austin Bruce*, 2 vols. (Oxford, 1902)
Adams, F., *History of the Elementary School Contest* (1882)
Adams, W. E., *Memoirs of a Social Atom*, 2 vols. (1903)
Addis, J. P., *The Crawshay Dynasty* (Cardiff, 1957)
Arnot, R. P., *The South Wales Miners, 1898–1914* (1967)
Awbery, S., *Labour's Early Struggles in Swansea* (Swansea, 1949)
Baber, C. and Williams, L. J., (eds.), *Modern South Wales: Essays in Economic History* (Cardiff, 1986)
Barker, M., *Gladstone and Radicalism: The Reconstruction of the Liberal Party 1885–94* (1975)
Barnes, D. G., *History of the English Corn Laws, 1660–1846* (1930)
Bassett, T. M., *The Welsh Baptists* (Swansea, 1977)
Beddoe, D., *Discovering Women's History: A Practical Manual* (1983)
Bell, P. M. H., *Irish and Welsh Disestablishment* (1969)
Bessborough, Earl of, *Lady Charlotte Guest: Extracts from her Journal, 1832–52* (1950)
Best, G., *Mid-Victorian Britain, 1851–75* (1971)
Blackburn, H., *Women's Suffrage: A Record of the Women's Suffrage Movement in the British Isles* (1902)
Blake, R., *Disraeli* (1966)
Briggs, A., *Victorian People: A Reassessment of Persons and Themes, 1851–67* (1954)
Idem, (ed.), *Chartist Studies* (1958)
Idem, The Age of Improvement (1959)
Idem, and Saville J. (eds.), *Essays in Labour History* (1960)
Briggs, J. and Sellers, I. (eds.), *Victorian Nonconformity* (1973)
Broadhurst, H., *The Story of his Life from a Stonemason's Bench to the Treasury Bench* (1901)
Butler, J., *Personal Reminiscences of a Great Crusade* (1898)
Carter, H., *The Towns of Wales* (Cardiff, 1966)
Cole, G. D. H., *A Short History of the British Working-Class Movement* (1927)
Idem, Chartist Portraits (1940)
Idem, British Working-Class Politics (1941)
Conacher, J. B., *The Aberdeen Coalition 1852–55: A Study of Mid-Nineteenth Century Party Politics* (1969)
Coupland, R., *Welsh and Scottish Nationalism* (1954)
Cowherd, R., *The Politics of English Dissent* (1959)

Cowling, M., *Disraeli, Gladstone and Revolution. The Passing of the Second Reform Bill* (1967)
Daunton, M. J., *Coal Metropolis: Cardiff, 1870–1914* (Leicester, 1977)
Davies, E. T., *Religion in the Industrial Revolution in South Wales* (Cardiff, 1965)
Idem, *Religion and Society in the Nineteenth Century* (Llandybïe, 1981)
Davis, W. J., *British T.U.C.: History and Recollections*, Vol.I (1910)
Dodd, A. H., *The Industrial Revolution in North Wales* (Cardiff, 2nd edn., 1951)
Drake, B., *Women in Trade Unions* (1920)
Dunbabin, J. P. D., *Rural Discontent in Nineteenth-Century Britain* (1974)
Elsas, M. (ed.), *Iron in the Making: Dowlais Iron Company Letters, 1782–1860* (1969)
Epstein, J. H., *The Lion of Freedom: Feargus O'Connor and the Chartist Movement 1832–1842* (1982)
Evans, B., *Cofiant y diweddar Barchedig T. Price, MA, Ph.D., Aberdâr* (Aberdare, 1891)
Evans, E. W., *Mabon: A Study in Trade Union Leadership* (Cardiff, 1959)
Idem, *The Miners of South Wales* (Cardiff, 1961)
Evans, T., *The Background of Modern Welsh Politics, 1789–1846* (Cardiff, 1936)
Foster, J., *Class Struggle and the Industrial Revolution* (1974)
Fraser, W. H., *Trade Unions and Society* (1974)
Frost, B., *The Tactics of Pressure* (1975)
Frost, T., *Forty Years' Recollections* (1880)
Fulford, R., *Votes for Women* (1957)
Gammage, R. G., *History of the Chartist Movement* (1854, rep. 1969)
Gash, N., *Politics in the Age of Peel* (1953)
Idem, *Reaction and Reconstruction in English Politics, 1832–52* (1965)
Gillespie, F. E., *Labour and Politics in England, 1850–67* (Durham, North Carolina, 1927)
Gosden, P. H. J. H., *Friendly Societies in England, 1815–71* (1961)
Griffiths, R., *Cofiant y Gohebydd* (Denbigh, 1905)
Hadfield, A. M., *The Chartist Land Company* (Newton Abbot, 1970)
Halévy, E., *A History of the English People in the Nineteenth Century*, 6 vols. (1949–52)
Hamer, D. A., *Liberal Politics in the Age of Gladstone and Rosebery* (Oxford, 1972)
Idem, *The Politics of Electoral Pressure: A Study in the History of Victorian Reform Agitations* (1977)
Hamer, F. E., (ed.), *The Personal Papers of Lord Rendel* (1931)
Hanham, H. J., *Elections and Party Management: Politics in the Time of Disraeli and Gladstone* (1959)
Harrison, B., *Drink and the Victorians: The Temperance Question in England, 1815–72* (1971)
Idem, *Separate Spheres: The Opposition to Women's Suffrage in Britain* (1978)
Harrison, J. F. C., *The Early Victorians, 1832–51* (1971)
Harrison, R., *Before the Socialists* (1965)
Heckter, M., *Internal Colonialism: The Celtic Fringe in British National Development* (1975)
Hennock, E. P., *Fit and Proper Persons: Ideal and Reality in Nineteenth-Century Urban Government* (1973)
Herbert, T. and Jones, G.E. (eds.), *People and Protest: Wales 1815–1880* (Cardiff, 1988)
Himbury, D.M., *The South Wales Baptist College* (Llandysul, 1957)
Hobhouse, S., *Joseph Sturge, his Life and Work* (1919)
Hobsbawn, E. J., *Primitive Rebels* (1959)
Idem, *Labouring Men: Studies in the History of Labour* (1964)
Hollis, P., *The Pauper Press: A Study in Working-Class Radicalism of the 1830s* (1970)
Idem, *Class and Class Conflict in Nineteenth-Century England, 1815–50* (1973)
Idem (ed.), *Pressure from Without in Early Victorian England* (1974)
Idem, *Women in Public: The Women's Movement 1850–1900* (1979)
Idem, *Ladies Elect* (1987)
Howell, D. W., *Land and People in Nineteenth-Century Wales* (1978)
Hughes, G. A. (ed.), *Men of No Property: Historical Studies of Welsh Trade Unions* (1971)
Humphrey, A. W., *History of Labour Representation* (1912)

Humphrys, G., *Industrial Britain: South Wales* (Newton Abbot, 1972)

Inglis, K. S., *Churches and the Working Classes in Victorian England* (1963)

Jeffreys, J. B., *Labour's Formative Years* (1948)

Jenkins, D., *The Agricultural Community in South-West Wales at the Turn of the Twentieth Century* (Cardiff, 1971)

Jenkins, G. H. and Smith, J. B. (eds.), *Politics and Society in Wales, 1840–1922. Essays in Honour of Ieuan Gwynedd Jones* (Cardiff, 1988)

Jennings, L. J. (ed.), *The Croker Papers: The Correspondence and Diaries of the Late Rt. Hon. John Wilson Croker*, 3 vols. (1885)

John, A. H., *The Industrial Development of South Wales, 1750–1850* (Cardiff, 1950)

Idem, and Williams, G., *Industrial Glamorgan from 1700 to 1900* (Cardiff, 1980)

Jones, A., *The Politics of Reform 1884* (Cardiff, 1980)

Jones, D. J. V., *Before Rebecca: Popular Protests in Wales, 1793–1835* (1973)

Idem, Chartism and the Chartists (1975)

Idem, The Last Rising: The Newport Insurrection of 1839 (1985)

Jones, G. J., *Wales and the Quest for Peace* (1969)

Jones, I., *David Rees, Y Cynhyrfwr* (Swansea, 1971)

Jones, I. G., *Health, Wealth and Politics in Victorian Wales* (Swansea, 1979)

Idem, Explorations and Explanations: Essays in the Social History of Victorian Wales (Llandysul, 1981)

Idem, Communities: Essays in the Social History of Victorian Wales (Llandysul, 1987)

Jones, J. I., *A History of Printing and Printers in Wales and Monmouthshire* (Cardiff, 1925)

Jones, J. O., *The History of the Caernarvonshire Constabulary, 1856–1950* (Caernarfon, 1963)

Jones, R. J., *The Unitarian Students at the Presbyterian College, Carmarthen, in the Nineteenth Century* (Aberdare, 1901).

Jones, R. M., *The North Wales Quarrymen 1874–1922)* (Cardiff, 1982)

Jones, T. G., *Cofiant Thomas Gee* (Denbigh, 1913)

Koss, S., *Nonconformity in Modern British Politics* (1975)

Lambert, W. R., *Drink and Sobriety in Victorian Wales, c. 1820–c. 1895* (Cardiff, 1983)

Leno, J. B., *The Aftermath* (1892)

Leventhal, F. M., *Respectable Radical: George Howell and Victorian Working-Class Politics* (1971)

Lewenhak, S., *Women and Trade Unions* (1977)

Lewis, E. D., *The Rhondda Valleys* (1959)

Liddington, J. and Norris, J., *One Hand Tied Behind Us: The Rise of the Women's Suffrage Movement* (1978)

Lindsay, J., *A History of the North Wales Slate Industry* (Newton Abbot, 1974)

Longmate, N., *The Breadstealers* (1984)

Ludlow, J. M. and Jones, L., *The Progress of the Working Classes, 1832–1867* (1867)

Maccoby, S., *English Radicalism, 1832–52* (1938)

Idem, English Radicalism, 1852–86 (1938)

Maltby, S. E., *Manchester and the Movement for National Elementary Education* (1918)

Martin, Sir T., *Queen Victoria as I Knew Her* (1908)

Masheder, R., *Dissent and Democracy* (1864)

Mather, F. C., *Chartism and Society* (1980)

May, T. C., *Trade Unions and Pressure Group Politics* (Farnborough, 1975)

McCord, N., *The Anti-Corn Law League, 1838–46* (1958)

McHugh, P., *Prostitution and Victorian Social Reform* (1980)

Miall, A., *Life of Edward Miall* (1884)

Miall, C. S., *Life of Henry Richard, MP* (1889)

Miall, E., *The British Churches in relation to the British People* (1849)

Minchinton, W. E. (ed.), *Industrial South Wales, 1750–1914* (1969)

Morgan, D., *Suffragists and Liberals: The Politics of Women's Suffrage in England* (Oxford, 1975)

Morgan, E., *Valuable Letters, Essays and other Papers of the Late Reverend John Elias of Anglesey* (Caernarfon, 1847)

Morgan, J. V., (ed.), *Welsh Religious Leaders in the Victorian Era* (1905)

Idem (ed.), *Welsh Political and Educational Leaders in the Victorian Era* (1908)

Morgan, K. O., *Wales in British Politics 1868–1922* (Cardiff, 3rd. edn., 1980)

Idem, Rebirth of a Nation: Wales, 1880–1980 (Oxford and Cardiff, 1981)

Morley, J., *The Struggle for National Education* (1873)

Idem, Life of Richard Cobden (1903)

Morris, J. H. and Williams, L. J., *The South Wales Coal Industry, 1841–75* (Cardiff, 1958)

Musson, A. E., *British Trade Unions, 1800–75* (1972)

Neale, R. S., *Class and Ideology in the Nineteenth Century* (1972)

Oakley, A. and Mitchell, J. (eds.), *The Rights and Wrongs of Women* (1976)

O'Leary, C. C., *The Elimination of Corrupt Practices in British Elections, 1868–1911* (Oxford, 1962)

O'Leary, J. G. (ed.), *The Autobiography of Joseph Arch* (1966)

Parry, C., *The Radical Tradition in Welsh Politics: A Study of Liberal and Labour Politics in Gwynedd 1900–20* (Hull, 1970)

Pelling, H., *The Origins of the Labour Party, 1880–1900* (1954)

Idem, A History of British Trade Unionism (1963)

Idem, Social Geography of British Elections, 1885–1910 (1967)

Idem, Popular Politics and Society in Late Victorian Britain (rev. edn. 1979)

Perkin, H. J., *The Origins of Modern English Society, 1780–1880* (1969)

Plummer, A., *Bronterre: a Political Biography of Bronterre O'Brien, 1804–64* (1971)

Poirier, P., *The Advent of the Labour Party* (1958)

Prentice, A., *History of the Anti-Corn Law League*, 2 vols. (Manchester, 1853)

Price, G. V., *A History of the Baptists of Cefn Mawr and District, Denbighshire: The Ministers, People and Times* (1964)

Read, D., *The English Provinces, c. 1760–1960* (1964)

Idem, Cobden and Bright: A Victorian Political Partnership (1967)

Idem, England 1868–1914 (1979)

Rees, A. D., *Life in a Welsh Countryside* (Cardiff, 1950)

Rees, J. F., *The Problem of Wales and other Essays* (Cardiff, 1963)

Richard, H., *Memoirs of Joseph Sturge* (1864)

Idem, Letters on the Social and Political Position of Wales (1867)

Idem, Letters and Essays on Wales (1884)

Richards, T. (ed.), *Er Clod: Saith Bennod ar Hanes Methodistiaeth yng Nghymru* (Wrexham, 1934)

Robb, J., *The Primrose League, 1883–1906* (1942)

Robson, R. (ed.), *Ideas and Institutions of Victorian Britain* (1967)

Roderick, A. J. (ed.), *Wales through the Ages*, Vol. 2 (Llandybïe, 1960)

Rogers, J. E. T. (ed.), *Speeches of John Bright, MP*, 2 vols. (1869)

Rose, J. H., *The Rise of Democracy* (1897)

Rothstein, T., *From Chartism to Labourism* (1929)

Rover, C., *Women's Suffrage and Party Politics in Britain, 1866–1914* (1967)

Rudé, G., *The Crowd in History: A Study of Popular Disturbances in France and Britain, 1730–1848* (1964)

Russell, B. and P. (eds.), *The Amberley Papers: The Letters and Diaries of Lord and Lady Amberley*, 2 vols. (1937)

Saville, J., *Ernest Jones, Chartist* (1952)

Schoyen, A. R., *The Chartist Challenge: A Portrait of George Julian Harney* (1958)

Scorpion (William Williams), *Cofiant Caledfryn* (Bala, 1877)

Seymour, C., *Electoral Reform in England and Wales, 1832–85* (1915)

Shannon, R. T., *Gladstone and the Bulgarian Agitation* (1963)

Smith, D. (ed.), *A People and a Proletariat: Essays in the History of Wales, 1780–1880* (1980)

Smith, F. B., *The Making of the Second Reform Bill* (1966)

Solden, N. C., *Women in British Trade Unions, 1874–1976* (1978)

Somerville, A., *Whistler at the Plough* (Manchester, 1852)
Idem, Free Trade and the League (1853)
Southall, J. E., *The Welsh Language Census of 1891* (Cardiff, 1894)
Southgate, D., *The Passing of the Whigs, 1832–86* (1962)
Taylor, M. S., *The Crawshays of Cyfarthfa Castle* (1967)
Thomas, D. Ll., *Labour Unions in South Wales* (Swansea, 1901)
Thomis, M. I. and Grimmett, J., *Women in Protest, 1800–50* (1982)
Thompson, D. (ed.), *The Early Chartists* (1971)
Idem, The Chartists (1984)
Thompson, E. P., *The Making of the English Working Class* (1963)
Vicinus, M. (ed.), *Suffer and Be Still* (1972)
Idem, (ed.), *The Widening Sphere: Changing roles of Victorian Women* (1977)
Vincent, J. E., *Letters from Wales* (1889)
Vincent, J. R., *The Formation of the British Liberal Party, 1857–68* (1966)
Idem, Pollbooks: How Victorians Voted (1967)
Wallas, G., *Life of Francis Place* (1898)
Walpole, S., *Lord John Russell*, 2 vols. (1889)
Ward, J. T. (ed.), *Popular Movements, c. 1830–50* (1970)
Idem, Chartism (1973)
Watson, R. S., *The National Liberal Federation from its Commencement to the General Election of 1906* (1907)
Wearmouth, R. F., *Some Working-Class Movements in the Nineteenth Century* (1948)
Webb, S. and B., *History of Trade Unionism* (1894)
Whorlow, H., *The Provincial Newspaper Society, 1836–86* (1886)
Wilks, I., *South Wales and the Rising of 1839* (1984)
Wilkins, C., *The History of Merthyr Tydfil* (Merthyr Tydfil, 1867)
Wilson, A., *The Chartist Movement in Scotland* (Manchester, 1970)
Wootton, G., *Pressure Groups, 1720–1970* (1975)
Williams, D., *John Frost: A Study in Chartism* (Cardiff, 1939)
Idem, The Rebecca Riots: A Study in Agrarian Discontent (Cardiff, 1955)
Williams, G., *Samuel Roberts, Llanbrynmair* (Cardiff, 1950)
Idem, (ed.), *David Rees, Llanelli: Detholion o'i Waith* (Cardiff, 1950)
Idem, (ed.), *Merthyr Politics: The Making of a Working-Class Tradition* (Cardiff, 1966)
Idem, Religion, Language and Nationality in Wales (Cardiff, 1979)
Williams G. A., *Artisans and Sans-Culottes* (1968)
Idem, The Merthyr Rising of 1831 (1978)
Idem, The Welsh in Their History (1982)
Idem, When Was Wales? (1985)
Williams, J. R., *Quarrymen's Champion: The Life and Activities of William John Parry of Coetmor* (Denbigh, 1978)
Williams, R., *Montgomeryshire Worthies* (1894)
Wright, D. G., *Democracy and Reform, 1815–85* (1970)

8. ARTICLES
Armytage, W. H. G., 'The Chartist land colonies, 1846–48', *Agricultural History*, 32 (1958)
Ashton, O. R., 'Chartism in Mid-Wales', *Montgomeryshire Collections*, 62, Part 1 (1972)
Blewett, N., 'The franchise in the United Kingdom, 1885–1918', *Past and Present*, 32 (1965)
Clark, A., 'Monmouthshire Chartists', *Presenting Monmouthshire*, 39 (1975)
Croker, J. W., 'The anti-Corn Law agitation', *Quarterly Review*, LXXI (Dec. 1842)
Fraser, D., 'Birmingham and the Corn Laws', *Transactions of the Birmingham Archaeological Society*, LXXXII (1967)

Idem, 'Nottingham and the Corn Laws', *Transactions of the Thoroton Society of Nottingham*, LXX (1966)

Gossman, R. J., 'Republicanism and nineteenth-century England', *International Review of Social History*, 7 (1962)

Griffiths, P., 'Pressure groups and parties in late Victorian England', *Midland History*, III, No.3 (1976)

Hanham, H. J., 'Liberal organisations for working men, 1860–1914', *Bulletin of the Society for the Study of Labour History*, No. 7 (1963)

Hargest, L., 'The Welsh Educational Alliance and the 1870 Elementary Education Act', *WHR*, 10, No. 2 (1980)

Harrison, B. and Hollis, P., 'Chartism, Liberalism and the life of Robert Lowery', *English Historical Review*, LXXXII (1967)

Herrick, F. H., 'The origins of the National Liberal Federation', *Journal of Modern History*, XVII (1945)

Himmelfarb, G., 'The politics of democracy: the English Reform Act of 1867', *Journal of British Studies*, VI, No.1 (1966)

Idem, 'Commitment and ideology: the case of the Second Reform Act', *Journal of British Studies*, IX, No.1 (1969)

Howell, D. W., 'The agricultural labourer in nineteenth-century Wales', *WHR*, 6, No. 3 (1973)

Humphries, I., 'Cardiff politics, 1850–74', *Glamorgan Historian*, 8 (1972)

Ingham, S. M., 'The disestablishment movement in England, 1868–74', *Journal of Religious History*, 3 (1964)

John, A. V., 'The Chartist endurance: industrial south Wales, 1840–68', *Morgannwg*, XV (1971)

Jones, A., 'Trade unions and the press: journalism and the Red Dragon Revolt of 1874', *WHR*, 12, No. 2 (1984)

Jones, D., 'Self-help in nineteenth-century Wales: the rise and fall of the female friendly societies', *Llafur*, 4, No. 1 (1984)

Idem, 'Did friendly societies matter? A study of friendly societies in Glamorgan, 1794–1910', *WHR*, 12, No. 3 (1985)

Jones, D. J. V., 'Chartism at Merthyr: a commentary on the meetings of 1842'. *Bulletin of the Board of Celtic Studies*, XXIV, Part 2 (1971)

Idem, 'Welsh Chartism', *Bulletin of the Society for the Study of Labour History*, No. 23 (1971)

Idem, 'Chartism in Welsh communities', *WHR*, 6, No. 3 (1973)

Idem, 'Women and Chartism', *History*, 68, No. 222 (1983)

Idem, and Bainbridge, A., 'The "Conquering of China": crime in an industrial community, 1842–64', *Llafur*, 2, No. 4 (1979)

Jones, G. A., 'Further thoughts on the franchise, 1885–1914', *Past and Present*, 34 (1966)

Jones, I. G., 'Franchise reform and Glamorgan politics in the mid-nineteenth century', *Morgannwg*, II (1958)

Idem, 'The elections of 1865 and 1868 in Wales with special reference to Cardiganshire and Merthyr Tydfil', *Transactions of the Honourable Society of Cymmrodorion* (1964)

Idem, 'The anti-Corn Law letters of Walter Griffith', *Bulletin of the Board of Celtic Studies*, XXVIII, Part 1 (1978)

Jones, R. M., 'The North Wales Quarrymen's Union, 1874–1900', *Transactions of the Caernarvonshire Historical Society*, XXXV (1974)

Jones, R. T., 'The origins of the Nonconformist disestablishment campaign', *Journal of the Historical Society of the Church in Wales*, 20, No. 25 (1970)

Jones-Evans, P., 'Evan Pan Jones—land reformer', *WHR*, 4, No. 2 (1968)

Judge, K., 'Early Chartist organisations and the Convention of 1839', *International Review of Social History*, 20, Part 3 (1975)

Kemp, B., 'Reflections on the repeal of the Corn Laws', *Victorian Studies*, V (1962)

Kitson-Clark, G., 'The electorate and the repeal of the Corn Laws', *Transactions of the Royal Historical Society* (1951)

Lambert, W. R., 'The Welsh Sunday Closing Act, 1881', *WHR*, 6, No. 2 (1972)

Idem, 'Thomas Williams, JP, Gwaelod-y-Garth (1823–1903): a study in Nonconformist attitudes and actions', *Glamorgan Historian*, 11 (1975)

Idem, 'Some working-class attitudes to organised religion in nineteenth-century Wales', *Llafur*, 2, No. 1 (1976)

Lawson-Tancred, M., 'The Anti-League and the crisis of 1846', *Historical Journal*, III (1960)

Leys C., 'Petitioning in the nineteenth and twentieth centuries', *Political Studies*, 3, No. 1 (1955)

Machin, G. I. T., 'The Maynooth Grant, the Dissenters and Disestablishment, 1845–47', *English Historical Review*, LXXXII (1967)

Idem, 'A Welsh Church rate fracas, Aberystwyth 1832–33: the making of a political Dissenter', *WHR*, 6, No. 4 (1973)

Maehl, W. H., 'The north-eastern miners' struggle for the franchise, 1872–74', *International Review of Social History*, 20, Part 2 (1975)

Morgan, J., 'Denbighshire's "annus mirabilis": the borough and county elections of 1868', *WHR*, 7, No. 2 (1974)

Morgan, K. O., 'Gladstone and Wales', *WHR*, 1, No. 1 (1960)

Idem, 'Liberals, Nationalists and Mr Gladstone', *Transactions of the Honourable Society of the Cymmrodorion* (1960)

Idem, 'Democratic politics in Glamorgan, 1884–1914', *Morgannwg*, IV (1960)

Idem, 'Cardiganshire politics: the Liberal ascendancy, 1885–1923', *Ceredigion*, V (1967)

Idem, 'Peace movements in Wales, 1899–1945', *WHR*, 10, No. 3 (1981)

Morgan, W. T., 'Chartism and industrial unrest in south Wales in 1842', *National Library of Wales Journal*, X, No. 1 (1959)

Mosse, G. L., 'The Anti-League, 1844–46', *Economic Historical Review*, XVII (1947)

Neale, R. S., 'Class and class-consciousness in early nineteenth-century England: three classes or five', *Victorian Studies*, XII (1968)

Nelmes, G. V., 'Stuart Rendel and Welsh Liberal political organisations in the late-nineteenth century', *WHR*, 9, No. 4 (1979)

Nossiter, T. J., 'Voting behaviour, 1832–72', *Political Studies*, XVIII (1970.

Parry, C., 'Gwynedd politics: the rise of a Labour Party', *WHR*, 6, No. 3 (1973)

Parry, J., 'Trade unionists and early socialism in south Wales, 1890–1908', *Llafur*, 4, No. 3 (1986)

Idem, 'Labour leaders and local politics, 1888–1902: the example of Aberdare', *WHR*, 14, No. 3 (1989)

Parry, R. I., 'Yr Annibynwyr Cymraeg a Threth yr Ŷd, 1828–45', *Y Cofiadur*, No. 19 (1949)

Pretty, D. A., 'Richard Davies and Nonconformist radicalism in Anglesey, 1837–68: a study of sectarian and middle-class politics', *WHR*, 9, No. 4 (1979)

Ravenstein, E. G., 'On the Celtic languages in the British Isles; a statistical survey', *Journal of the Royal Statistical Society*, 42 (1879)

Rees, R. D., 'Glamorgan newspapers under the Stamp Acts', *Morgannwg*, III, (1959)

Idem, 'South Wales newspapers under the Stamp Acts', *WHR*, I, No. 3 (1962)

Rogers, E., 'The history of Trade Unionism in the coal-mining industry of north Wales to 1914', *Transactions of the Denbighshire Historical Society*, XII–XXII (1963–74)

Rowe, D. J., 'The Chartist Convention and the regions', *Economic History Review*, XXII (1969)

Salter, F. R., 'Political Nonconformity in the 1830s', *Transactions of the Royal Historical Society* (1953)

Saville, J., 'The background to the revival of Socialism in England', *Bulletin of the Society for the Study of Labour History*, No. 11 (1965)

Smith, F. B., 'The "dependence of license upon faith"; Miss Gertrude Himmelfarb on the Second Reform Act', *Journal of British Studies*, IX, No. 1 (1969)

Strange, K., 'In search of the Celestial Empire: crime in Merthyr, 1830–60', *Llafur*, 3, No. 1 (1980)

Tholfsen, T. R., 'The origins of the Birmingham Caucus', *Historical Journal*, II, No. 2 (1959)

Thompson, D., 'Notes on aspects of Chartist leadership', *Bulletin of the Society for the Study of Labour History*, No. 15 (1967)

Wager, D.A., 'Welsh politics and parliamentary reform, 1780–1832', *WHR*, 7, No. 4 (1975)

Williams, G., 'Chartists, "Rebecca" and the Swansea Police', *Gower*, 12 (1959)

Williams, G. A., 'Friendly societies in Glamorgan, 1795–1832', *Bulletin of the Board of Celtic Studies*, XVIII (1959)

Idem, 'The making of radical Merthyr, 1800–36', *WHR*, 1, No. 2 (1961)

Idem, 'South Wales radicalism', *Glamorgan Historian*, 2 (1965)

Idem, 'Merthyr 1831: Lord Melbourne and the Trade Unions', *Llafur*, 1, No. 1 (1972)

Williams, H. G., 'The Forster Education Act and Welsh politics, 1870–74', *WHR*, 14, No. 2 (1988)

Williams, L. J., 'The first Welsh "Labour" MP', *Morgannwg*, VI (1962)

Idem, 'The new unionism in Wales', *WHR*, 1, No. 4 (1963)

Wills, W. D., 'The Established Church in the diocese of Llandaff, 1850–70: a study of the Evangelical Movement in the south Wales coalfield', *WHR*, 4, No. 3 (1969)

9. THESES

Ashton, O. R., 'Chartism in mid-Wales' (University of Wales MA thesis, 1971)

Bell, A. D., 'The Reform League from its origins to the Reform Act of 1867' (University of Oxford Ph.D. thesis, 1961)

Crowley, D. W., 'The origins of the revolt of the British Labour Movement from Liberalism, 1875–1906' (University of London Ph.D. thesis, 1952)

David, I. W. R., 'Political and electioneering activity in south-east Wales, 1820–51' (University of Wales MA thesis, 1959)

Davies, J. M., 'A study of the effect of the Reform Act of 1884 and the Redistribution Act of 1885 upon the political structure of Glamorgan' (University of Wales MA thesis, 1979)

Dunsmore, M. R., 'The working classes, the Reform League and the reform movement in Lancashire and Yorkshire' (University of Sheffield MA thesis, 1961)

Evans, D. V., 'Some aspects of politics in east Carmarthenshire, 1868–85' (University of Wales MA thesis, 1972)

Evans, T., 'Political thought in Wales, 1789–1846' (University of Wales MA thesis, 1924)

Fox, K. O., 'The emergence of the political Labour Movement in the eastern section of the south Wales coalfield, 1894–1910' (University of Wales MA thesis, 1965)

Hughes, G. R., 'Bywyd Caledfryn a'i weithgarwch fel gŵr cyhoeddus' (University of Wales MA thesis, 1958)

Humphreys, I., 'Cardiff politics, 1850–75' (University of Wales MA thesis, 1970)

John, A. V., 'The Chartists of industrial south Wales 1840–68' (University of Wales MA thesis, 1970)

Keeler, J., 'The Denbighshire elections of 1868' (University of Wales MA thesis, 1972)

Lamb, W. K., 'British Labour and Parliament, 1865–93' (University of London Ph.D. thesis, 1933)

Martin, C. E., 'Female Chartism: a study in politics' (University of Wales MA thesis, 1974)

Owen, G. E., 'Welsh anti-slavery sentiment, 1795–1865: a survey of public opinion' (University of Wales MA thesis, 1964)

Parry, A. J., 'The Church Defence Institution, 1859–96, with special reference to Wales' (University of Wales MA thesis, 1982)

Parry, O., 'The parliamentary representation of Wales and Monmouthshire during the nineteenth century—but mainly until 1870' (University of Wales MA thesis, 1924)

Parry, R. I., 'The attitude of the Welsh Independents towards working-class movements, 1815–70' (University of Wales MA thesis, 1931)

Price, R. E., 'Lloyd George's pre-Parliamentary career' (University of Wales MA thesis, 1974)

Strange, K., 'The condition of the working classes in Merthyr Tydfil, *circa* 1840–50' (University of Wales Ph.D. thesis, 1983)

Thomas, K., 'Chartism in Monmouthshire and the Newport Insurrection, 1837–39' (University of Wales MA thesis, 1981)

Thomas, R. G., 'Politics in Anglesey and Caernarvonshire 1826–52 with special reference to the Caernarvon Boroughs' (University of Wales MA thesis, 1970)

Wager, D. A., 'Welsh politics and parliamentary reform, 1780–1835' (University of Wales Ph.D. thesis, 1972)

Williams, L., 'Movements towards social reform in south Wales, 1832–50' (University of Wales MA thesis, 1933)

Williams, T. H., 'Wales and the Corn Laws, 1815–46' (University of Wales MA thesis, 1952)

INDEX